"Take and Eat": From Fall to Feast

A Biblical Theology

TK Dunn

Endorsements

"T.K. Dunn's *"Take and Eat": From Fall to Feast* stands out among the many biblical theologies published in recent years. Taking his cue from a motif Scripture itself highlights at key junctures, Dunn creatively and compellingly traces eating as a paradigm for understanding redemptive history. And, as only a true scholar-pastor can, Dunn insightfully shows how understanding Scripture in light of this paradigm fruitfully applies to our lives today. The reader will find much to savor—as I myself did—in this satisfying biblical-theological feast!"

Benjamin J. Noonan
Professor of Old Testament & Hebrew
Columbia International University

"Dunn shows an ordinary phrase is indicative of an important theme in biblical theology and traces it through the biblical storyline. Written in a popular and engaging style, many will find this a helpful lens for putting the story of the Bible together with many new insights. I am hopeful this will be a blessing to the church and to non-Christians as well."

Peter J. Gentry
Senior Professor, The Southern Baptist Theological Seminary
Distinguished Visiting Professor of Old Testament & Sr. Research Fellow of the Text & Canon Institute at Phoenix Seminary

-----

Take and Eat": From Fall to Feast is a fresh resource for new and mature believers to trace the Bible's story. I can easily envision it used for small groups sharing a meal and discussing scripture together for evangelism and discipleship. It provides a rich theological foundation while remaining accessible. Dunn encourages scriptural conversations in an approachable way as he guides us through the Bible's narrative using a common human experience: a shared meal.

Ben Ward, D.Min.
Theological Education Strategist
International Mission Board

"TK Dunn has provided us with a munificent feast, serving the key courses of the Christian story from Genesis to Revelation, from Creation to New Creation, linking them together in a creative and productive way through studying the command to 'Take and Eat'. His lively exposition, story-telling and practical application will provide his readers with a very helpful guide for understanding the scope of biblical theology and living a life of true discipleship."

John Gillespie
Professor of French Language and Literature (Emeritus),
Ulster University
Senior Teaching Fellow, C.S. Lewis Institute, Belfast
Clerk of Session, Portrush Presbyterian Church

"In *"Take and Eat": From Fall to Feast,* Dunn masterfully navigates through the theme of taking and eating to reveal the biblical storyline of redemption. He stays focused on this innovative approach to enlighten us about God and His love for His people. This is an important topic that will edify all those who will "take and eat" of the contents of this book."

David Croteau
Dean, Seminary and School of Counseling
Columbia International University

"From the pangs of hunger to the building anticipation of a family feast, we understand the importance of food in life. Spiritual life is no different. TK Dunn presents a work crafted with a balance of depth and accessibility that is a helpful addition to biblical theology. Anchored in fidelity to Scriptural truth, *"Take and Eat": From Fall to Feast* explores the relevance and relatability to humanity of the story of redemption that spans eternity."

Bryan Pittman, D.Min.
Associational Mission Strategist/DOM
Union County Baptist Association, SBC

"Take and Eat": From Fall to Feast

A Biblical Theology

TK Dunn

Energion Publications
Cantonment, Florida
2024

Copyright © 2024, TK Dunn. All rights reserved

Unless otherwise marked Scripture quotations are from The ESV® Bible (The Holy Bible, English Standard Version®), © 2001 by Crossway, a publishing ministry of Good News Publishers. Used by permission. All rights reserved.

Scripture quotations marked (NIV) are taken from the Holy Bible, New International Version®, NIV®. Copyright © 1973, 1978, 1984, 2011 by Biblica, Inc.™ Used by permission of Zondervan (www.zondervan.com). All rights reserved worldwide. The "NIV" and "New International Version" are trademarks registered in the United States Patent and Trademark Office by Biblica, Inc.™

ISBN: 978-1-63199-919-2
eISBN: 978-1-63199-920-8

Energion Publications
1241 Conference Rd
Cantonment, FL 32533

pubs@energion.com
energion.com

Leigh.
The Fall has separated us.
The Feast will reunite us.
I hope there will be fajitas.

Table of Contents

Acknowledgements vii
Invocation ix
Foreword xi

Introduction 1

First Course: Starters 15

1   Made In His Image..15
2   "Take and Eat": Garden Party...39
3   "Take and Eat": Be Like God..63

Second Course: Seafood Soup 112

5   "Take and Eat": Food For You..113
6   "Take and Eat": Covenantal Diet..129

Third Course: The Main Course.. 162

7   "Take and Eat": The Tempter Strikes Again 163
8   "Take and Eat": Passover in the Upper Room 183
9   "Take and Eat": A New Creation Mandate 213

Last Course: Dessert 252

10   "Take and Eat": A Wedding Feast.....................................253

Tea and Coffee: A Biblical Theological Conclusion................ 280

Bibliography..287

Acknowledgements

I wish to express my personal gratitude to Henry Neufeld and *Energion* for working with me on this project and bringing it to publication. His enthusiasm and support were instructive and clarifying. I'm deeply indebted to the many mentors who have sharpened my thinking and theological perspectives: Peter J. Gentry, Stephen Wellum, Thomas R. Schreiner, and Michael Haykin, from SBTS; Christopher Ash and Mike Gilbart-Smith, from the Proclamation Trust; Tom Greggs, from the University of Aberdeen; David Croteau, David DeWitt, and Benjamin Noonan, from CIU, to name but a few. The fruits of their advice, teaching, and writing are (I hope) evidenced in this book. I am especially grateful to Professor Schreiner for his encouragement and for providing the foreword to this book, and to Professor Gentry's supportive critique. This book has been made better because of the input of these men.

Thank you to my family at Tabernacle for your love, kindness, and enthusiasm for the Word. You have willingly sat through rough editions of what is found within these pages. Your engagement with the theology has served to refine and enhance the concepts I endeavor to convey.

My family continues to be a support and encouragement to me. To Yesenia, I'm thankful for our happy home with peace that allows me to set aside time where I can read, write, and talk through my ideas. To my parents, brothers, and in-laws, I'm grateful for your prayer support and penetrating questions that have helped shape the theological presentation below.

Finally, I acknowledge the many others who have helped mold me. Authors, preachers, professors, teachers, and friends have left an indelible mark on me as a man and as a Christian. This project is a work of love for the grand narrative of redemption in and through the Lord Jesus Christ, which itself is a fulfilment of the glorious will of the eternal and Triune God who reveals himself in Scripture. My prayer is that you will find it a helpful and edifying resource for your faith in Christ.

Any errors herein belong to me alone.

Invocation

Sovereign and eternal Lord, this book is a retelling of your vast, grand, great, and more glorious actions in and throughout history. To hear and believe your story of redemption is the joy and privilege of every person that you have called to be your own in and through the work of Jesus. Your eternal Son took upon himself the flesh of the First Adam to become the obedient Final Adam. Through his fulfilment of your purposes, he has not only provided forgiveness to those who repent, but has unwound the curse of death, and is even now preparing the New Creation.

For myself, I acknowledge my sinfulness. But for your grace and forgiveness, this book would be impossible. Thank you for the forgiveness of my sins, for I know they are many. Hide me behind the cross. Let the object of this book not be me, nor my reflections or ideas, but you in your majesty, holiness, power, grace, and love.

I pray that readers will taste and see that you are good, trustworthy, and welcoming. Let it be that, through this book, your Spirit will show us our sinfulness, help us rest in the salvation offered through Jesus, and conform us into the likeness and image of Jesus. Use this project to enlarge your kingdom so that many more will sit together at the wedding feast of the Lamb with rejoicing in our hearts that the work you have begun in us has been completed.

Until then, may any and all who read these pages be encouraged to return to the source of truth and "take and eat" the bread of life.

Soli Deo Gloria.

Foreword

The generation in which we are living has seen a revival of biblical theology, especially in evangelical circles. This revival attests to the evangelical belief in the final and full authority of scripture, to the conviction that there is always more light to be gained from the word of God. As Adolf Schlatter said, the first task in reading the Bible is observation, and we haven't seen everything there is to see. As evangelicals we are not surprised by this state of affairs because we confess that the scriptures come from the mind of God who is infinite in his wisdom. Thus, the more we linger over the scriptures the more we see the beauty and wonder of God's plan, purpose, ways, and character.

The interest in biblical theology reflects a conviction that the story line in the scriptures is discernible and instructive. God intended for his people to comprehend and see the overarching plan of redemption. Such a conviction is not a new insight. The importance of God's plan was discerned from the beginning of church history, and we see this clearly in the writings of Irenaeus in the second and third centuries. In the canon of scripture we do not have a random collection of books with no organizing structure. Instead the Bible has a narrative, a story, a rehearsal of God's promises to save a people for the glory and honor of his name. Understanding the story is not more important than knowing and loving God himself, but these two should not be set in opposition to one another. As we understand God's unfolding purposes we praise the God whose ways are unsearchable and whose judgments inscrutable (Romans 11:33).

As we do biblical theology, we should not make the mistake of privileging biblical theology over systematic theology. Most recognize today that biblical and systematic theology are not enemies but allies. The best biblical theologies are informed by systematic theology, and the best systematic theologies are rooted in biblical theology. Indeed, biblical and systematic theology are not in hermetically sealed compartments. Anyone who has read deeply in systematic theology throughout the history of the Christian Church realizes the biblical foundation of systematic theology. Good systematic theology can correct defective biblical theologies, and good biblical theology can refine systematic theology that has strayed from the biblical witness.

One of the joys of biblical theology is that the story line in the Bible can be rehearsed from a number of different angles. The whole story of the Bible can be told in terms of God's Kingdom, God's promise, the covenants, the promise of the land, the presence of the Lord, the grace of God, etc. The different angles and approaches cast fresh light and a new perspective on God's revelation. It is like a jewel with many facets that can be viewed from different standpoints. In other words, there is not only one way to do biblical theology! An infinite God can and should be studied from a variety of perspectives. Of course, these perspectives are not contradictory but complementary since there is no contradiction in biblical revelation from a God who always speaks the truth.

All of this brings us to this book by Tim Dunn. Dunn has approached the storyline of the Bible from the perspective of eating. I was struck by the creativity of such an inroad into the scriptural witness. We find a fresh and insightful aperture through which the biblical narrative can be viewed. It is also striking that eating plays such a central role at key junctures in the story. Thus Dunn tells the story from creation to new creation, from Passover to the Lord's Supper, from the old covenant to the new.

New windows are opened for readers as we read the scriptures from the perspective of partaking of food. I was reminded that Jesus himself is the living bread as we read in John 6, and that we must eat his flesh and drink his blood to have eternal life. Dunn reminds us that every time we eat the flesh of animals we eat something that has died. So too, we live through the death of the Savior. As Augustine said about the bread of life discourse: "believe and you have eaten." I hope as readers you partake joyfully of the rich feast that Dunn sets before us.

Thomas R. Schreiner
James Buchanan Harrison Professor of
New Testament Interpretation
Southern Baptist Theological Seminary
June, 2024

Introduction

The biblical storyline of redemption is punctuated by several critical moments that serve as signposts to grab our attention and tell us that God is directly impacting the world. At many of those key events, we encounter the idea of taking and eating. This biblical truth is very similar to our own experience as we live our lives. Many of the most important events in our lives tend to be marked by meals. Shortly after we bring a child home, pot pies arrive to help the exhausted new parents. Birthday parties are marked by ever more (and then ever less) extravagant meals, cakes, candles, presents, and parties. We celebrate graduating by dressing up in a long robe and silly hat before enjoying a fancy meal at a nice restaurant. First dates often include inquisitive small talk over cappuccinos and cookies. Engagement dinners give way to wedding receptions, which, in time, lead to anniversary dinners at favorite restaurants. Pizza and soda are bought for the lads who help move furniture into our new house. Thanksgiving and/or Christmas dinners around the table with friends and family are the source of many fond memories. And, eventually, the cycle restarts all over again with the next generation.

Many of our best moments often include getting dressed up, feeling pretty or handsome, and celebrating with good food. There's a ritual to the act of observing these very common milestones. In fact, those moments are often the foundation for some of our most precious memories: Graduating from college with our best friends and going to *that* restaurant together; the stress-relieving joy of the beautiful reception hall on our wedding day tells us *all* the effort was worth it; tearfully sharing stories at the wake of a beloved friend. Every culture has some form of these memorable meals. When we "take and eat" together, we're making memories that are powerful because we can draw upon them during different seasons of life. This is because we enjoy eating *together*.

An invitation to "take and eat" is therefore something that is commonly understood. Whether we reside in the West today or in East Asia in the 5th Century or in ancient Babylon, this is a strand of symbolic communion that pervades human civilization. Because of the pervasiveness of this symbolism, it's not surprising that we find the imagery of food used by the author of time itself. In the grand narrative of God's interaction with the human story, we consistently encounter dramatic milestones that reveal the next critical plot point, and very often these milestones involve food. Just as meals mark the stories of our own lives, the storyline of redemption has moments where our spiritual forefathers were forced to "take and eat" in bizarre, even frightening, contexts. Yet, through those culinary courses, God was leaving remarkable theological reflections that still resonate today. It's by dwelling on these extraordinarily important theological events that we can craft a unique biblical theology of how God was intimately involved in the minute details of his creation. Studying the storyline of scripture through these signposts can help us mature in our understanding of Christ's glorious work of salvation and teach us more about the heart, mind, and purposes of our Triune God. The symbols that we will consider in this book remind us that God continues to be involved in the life of his people.

The Premise: "Take and Eat"

The premise of this book is that one can present the gospel in all its redemptive glory by tracing this singular theme. When we consider the command to "take and eat," we can see the trajectory of history from the Fall in Genesis to the Feast in Revelation. These moments when the supernatural penetrates the natural world move the biblical storyline forward. From the utopia of Eden, we see the tantalizing glimmer of the New Jerusalem; but to get there we must pass through the hazy, smoke-filled ruins of the Fall, wander through the wilderness, and gaze in horrified shame at the cross. At each of these crucial moments in the human story, we find either a promise associated with "taking and eating," a direct command to "take and eat," or a temptation to "take and eat." These moments will form the skeleton of our own journey. We won't cover every moment where food is consumed in scripture, or even where important moments are conveyed in similar terms, because the idea is to present the overarching metanarrative, the bigger picture, of God's story of redemption through Jesus.

Through this symbolic imagery, we will encounter the major figures in the narrative of salvation, from Adam and Eve, to the serpent, to the Savior. We will also explore many of the glorious themes of scripture such as creation, redemption, restoration, and how to live as a believer in the kingdom of God. But most significantly, we will hopefully gain a better grasp of the nature of God, his love for humanity, and the work of God the Son becoming our redemption in the cross and resurrection. The end point of a healthy theology ought always to be to turn our eyes away from ourselves and towards our Triune God. Even as we "take and eat" (and read), we are entirely dependent on God's ongoing compassionate grace.

Biblical Theology: What is it?

The means of presenting this theme will be through a form of theological interpretation called *biblical theology*. Biblical theology is something of a nebulous term. For many, the idea of *doing* theology requires us to *use the Bible* so how can it be a complicated conception to do *biblical* theology? The problem arises because of the underlying methods of reading the Bible. If you have read even a single book before, you know that the best way to read is to start at the beginning and traverse the scenic route until the end. For any new believer, then, it's reasonable to assume that when you come to the Bible the best thing to do is to start in Genesis and read through to the end. But, of course, by the time Numbers and Leviticus come along, the new believer is bamboozled. What on earth is this about? Is this important? Why do I need to know all this stuff? In other words, if our friend considers the passages in Leviticus about eating restrictions for Israel, she is forced to enquire if they're relevant today or not? If so, why do so many Christians enjoy crab legs wrapped in bacon? If these restrictions do not apply today, why not? And, importantly, if they *don't* apply today, do we still need to read and understand Leviticus? How is she to *understand* how to worship God and ascertain how God wants her to live when she is reading the Bible?

The problem is one of interpretation. How do we read the Bible to get correct theology from it? There have been many proposals to answer this question, and biblical theology is one such proposal. Alongside *biblical* theology sits the (arguably) older tradition of *systematic* theology. In this method, the idea is to construct a theological system from scripture that seeks to comprehensively tie the various doctrines of the faith together into a cohesive, logical framework. Think of a house: Creation is the door (for our material realm begins at creation), and as you enter the systematic theological "house" of Christianity you see various rooms that make up the structure. Each "room" is a doctrine that is linked to the rest but can be explained and enjoyed in isolation (though always understood to be part of the whole). For systematic theologians, whilst creation may be the *door*, the *primary* theology resides *outside* the house. This is *theology proper*, the doctrine of God and (often linked) the doctrine of scripture. God is the architect of the "house." Systematic theology must always begin with God because he is the source of all things. As the source of life, no *thing* that does exist can exist without God. Therefore, before one approaches the Bible to study, one must first understand the voice *behind* scripture; but, of course, one can only do this by *knowing* scripture. Thus, the systematicians have provided "guardrails" to help keep us on track. These can include the ancient creeds, catechisms, and theologies that (can) shape how we approach the text of scripture. In systematic theology, the architect (God) explains how to move about the house (doctrine) through scripture, but, importantly, the house *is explained by the system of theology that the interpreter is using.*

In contrast, biblical theology tends towards a redemptive historical framework of history; God is acting within time for the purposes of redemption in, by, and through, Jesus. In other words, biblical theology moves through the storyline of scripture (and therefore human history) as God progressively revealed it, with the pinnacle of that story being the incarnation, life, death, resurrection, and ascension of Jesus Christ. Biblical theologies can trace ideas or themes from Genesis to Revelation (though not necessarily always stopping at every book or author); it's the journey to, or from, Jesus, that is in view, rather than the construction of a neat and tidy logical system of stacked and interrelated doctrines. In essence, biblical theology is moving from the start to the finish. The storyline of scripture (the metanarrative or narratival arc) is moving in one direction: From creation to consummation, Genesis to Revelation, the Fall to the Feast. That is a *horizontal* movement. But scripture's ultimate purpose is worship (doxology); we're not only moving *forward* in a linear line, but we are simultaneously moving *upward* in our understanding of God and his purposes for creation through Christ, culminating in worship.

Endeavoring to make this book flow more simply, I have opted to use the biblical theological method, though I will not be neglecting systematic theology; rather, I'm going to be using the tools of theological studies in general to hew from the marble of scripture a sculpture of the gospel that reveals not only the storyline of redemption in Christ but aspects of systematic theology and pastoral application. Neither the systematic or biblical theological method is superior; both have limitations and weaknesses. Generally speaking, most preachers will tend to *practice* biblical theology in sermons, whereas theologians tend to prioritize systematic structures. Rather than seeing the two disciplines as being in competition, we would be better served to see them as complementary, each serving the other as they engage in dialogue with one another. The best systematic theologians are able to appreciate the progressive revelation of scripture's storyline, literary facets, historical events, and pronouncements of God, whilst the best biblical theologians understand how the narrative of the Bible is the trellis upon which the vine of systematic theology rests. To remove either discipline would be to either make scripture little more than a series of doctrinal propositions (in systematics) or a moral story that runs the risk of losing its doctrinal anchoring (in biblical theology). Vitally, scripture itself is composed of both elements. Indeed, the two most *theological* books in the New Testament are arguably Romans and Hebrews; Paul's letter to the Romans builds a system of theology and the author of Hebrews is doing biblical theology.

A core aspect of biblical theology is *typology*. This basically means that, throughout the storyline of scripture, there are signposts that point us in the direction of Jesus. These signposts can be large or small, bright or dim, clear or unclear. They can be people (such as Adam), places (such as Israel or Jerusalem), things (such as the temple), or events (such as the Sabbath). The New Testament typically illuminates these signposts because Jesus is in some way their fulfilment. Thus, as we move through the storyline of scripture we're introduced to these signs and then, in the New Testament, those signs are identified and explained through Christ's fulfilment. This means that not only are we moving *forward*, and not only is our comprehension driven *upward* towards God in worship, but we are also witnessing *escalation*. For example, the ark in which Noah and his kin sheltered is a *type* of baptism (1 Peter 3:20). We call this fulfilment the *antitype*: Baptism is the antitype of Noah's ark. Baptism corresponds to Noah's ark in the deluge because to be baptised is to take refuge in the ark of the New Covenant and to die to self in the water and arrive safely through it in our symbolic resurrection with Christ as we emerge from those waters (1 Peter 3:21).

The principle of escalation is that "later is greater" because fulfilment is greater than the signpost, just as marriage is greater than dating. There is, however, another side to typology that must be understood. Jesus the Christ is *human* from the incarnation; but prior to the incarnation he was, and still remains, God the

Son. Thus, the greater reality that is appreciated through the escalation of the type/antitype dichotomy is that *all* the types find their complete expression in Jesus, who is the *archetype*. For example, the sacrificial lamb of Passover is a *type* of the sacrificial Lamb who died to take away the sins of the world (John 1:29). Jesus is the fulfilment of the sacrificial system because he was *a* sacrifice, but his fulfilment of that type was *escalated* with the fact that his was the *once-for-all sacrifice* (Hebrews 10:12). He is the archetype of the entire sacrificial system, first introduced in Genesis 3:21 and carried through the entire canonical witness.

Underlying both systematic and biblical theology sits *exegesis*. This is the point of departure for biblical interpretation. It basically means "to draw out from" the text. To do this, we approach a text in the Bible with an understanding that we cannot simply rip a verse or passage out of its location in scripture. Comprehending the verse in its textual and redemptive historical location is called the *context*. Sentences flow together to form paragraphs, which, in turn, form arguments, or stories, or narratives that eventually create a principle or idea. Thus, we need to read Genesis 3 in light of the preceding and following chapter to understand how the studied chapter fits into the larger context.

Methodology

In this book, I'm proposing a method of "mountain climbing" interpretation. By this, I mean that we will follow the horizontal progression of scripture as we climb the mountain of the historical storyline. At various peaks in the mountain we will stop and consider where we are in our journey to ask pastoral questions about how this applies to us, why it matters, and how it can fit into a system of theological interpretation. But, as any mountaineer will tell you, climbing is more than going *forward*, it's also going *upward*. Thus, at each horizon (in this book, our horizons will be the symbolic moments where we encounter "take and eat") we will be enabled to return to our theology proper, to God, and worship. As we move forward in the storyline of scripture, we will better grasp our understanding and knowledge of God himself because of how he is acting *inside* our world through his creation, his covenants, his covenant community, and, eventually, through his Christ.

In this regard, however, we're going to consider the metanar-

Figure 1: Redemptive History's Peaks

rative of the Bible not *only* as mountain climbing, but as a sandwich. Just as any good sandwich maker will tell you, you need to have two ends and a center; the best sandwiches are mirror images. There will be bread, mayonnaise, cheese, and your choice of meat, followed by the same in reverse order. In theological terms we call this a *chiasm*. It's like a triangle that moves ever inward to the center before moving back out again. In this book, we're going to see that the two slices of bread are creation and the new creation. The next layer will be the Fall on the front end, paralleled with the unwinding of the curse on the other side. As we move progressively inward, towards the center, we will see the covenant communities formed in both Old and New Testaments, and the regulations and expectations for those, before centering everything on Jesus, who is the center of all. Of course, as mentioned above, all are intrinsically linked together; we are moving forwards and upwards, but this sandwich illustration captures what is called *recapitulation*. This idea means that Jesus not only *saves us from sin* but reverses the consequences of sin itself. This reversal and renewal is understood to be the blessings of the kingdom of God which are present in part and promised to come in full. Therefore, the structure of this book will be threefold. We're climbing the mountain as we move *forward* in the progressively revealed narrative of the Bible, *upward* with the ultimate peak of the mountain being the Christ-event; this leads to doxology. But, in a sense, as we *descend* the mountain, we will see how the Bible is a single, cohesive, *horizontal* narrative that moves us beyond the Christ-event to the end of all ends, the *new creation*, in a mirroring image.

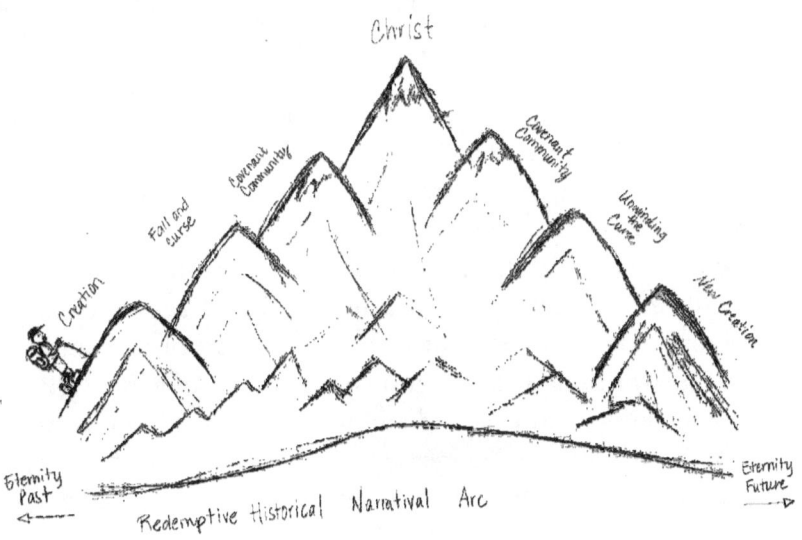

Figure 2: Redemptive Historical Narratival Arc Mirror Image

Outline

Purely to satisfy my own quirkiness, I have broken down the outline of this book to reflect the various courses of a meal (it is, after all, called *"Take and Eat"*). Our first course will begin with chapter one where we will engage the idea of what it means to be human beings made in the likeness and image of God, and as male and female. This chapter will explore the beauty of creation through the lens of humankind's overseership as regents under God, as displayed in the Creation Mandate. Situated within the Creation Mandate, however, it will be argued that Adam and Eve's *first* and most fundamental purpose is worship. In Eden, that expression of worship will be demonstrated through obedience.

Chapter two will consider God's plentiful provision in the garden. They are commanded to "take and eat" of any vegetative produce in Eden for their sustenance and pleasure. We are left with a vision of utopic idyllic paradise. And yet, as the chapter will explore, there is a single command that will provide the evidence of their obedience: Do not "take and eat" from a single tree. This command comes with a warning that disobedience to God leads to death. With that piercing cymbal echoing across creation, we move into chapter three.

When Satan tempts the unsuspecting regents with the forbidden fruit, he invites them to "take and eat" not only of fruit, but of disobedience. He is inviting Adam and Eve to switch allegiances, to join in an ongoing rebellion. We will watch as the entire creation order is upended when sin slithers into the garden. Utopia turns to dystopia. Peace turns to pain. Harmony turns to disharmony. Life turns to death. An exploration of the implications of sin will follow as the human plaintiffs and their seductive serpent-lord stand trial and are prosecuted by God who then pronounces his righteous judgements on all three. But in the very midst of his judgement hides a single promise upon which the entire storyline of the Bible rests.

The second course, *Seafood Soup*, covers the deluge in the day of Noah and the Exodus. Whilst there is a re-creation event when Noah steps off the ark, we are nevertheless forced to realize that, although the earth has been washed, sin remains because it also found safe passage in the inhabitants of the ark. God makes a new covenant with Noah and provides new food for Noah to "take and eat": Meat. But a consequence of this new permission is a further rupturing of the original creation order.

Chapter five will explore the covenant with Israel through the lens of the covenantal diet. This will begin with the deeply symbolic meal of the Exodus: Passover. Israel is told to "take and eat" a certain diet and cuisine, forsaking numerous types of foods as a way of setting up a distinguishing distinction between those who are in the covenant community and those who are outside of it. Of course, there are numerous laws given to Israel that separates the people from the Gentiles who remain in rebellion; that being said, despite the holy instruction of God to Israel, it is clear sin slithers throughout the covenant community.

The Main Course will begin in the wilderness with Jesus facing Satan. As the Second Adam, Jesus will face the same temptation as Adam (and, indeed, more temptations than Adam, and in a weaker state that Adam). When engaging with the serpent, Jesus and Satan will both trade barbs using the Bible, and it will be clear that, for the very first time, Satan will meet his match.

Leaving the wilderness, Jesus begins his ministry attacking the sinful rebellion. In chapter seven, we will explore the effects of his ministry before we return to the Passover meal in the Upper Room. Through his command to "take and eat" of his body and "take and drink" of his blood, Jesus introduces a New Covenant that both abrogates and supersedes the covenant given through Moses. Something different and new is coming. But it comes through the most horrific event of all time.

Chapter eight will consider life after Jesus' resurrection. The New Covenant community will be comprised of a new creation humanity preparing for the new creation world. This chapter will explore how Jesus adopts, and adapts, the original Creation Mandate given to Adam. To do this, we will consider the vision God gives Peter in Acts 10 where he commands Peter to "take and eat" food that had been considered unclean under the law of Moses. This dramatic vision teaches Peter, and subsequently the church, that the gospel of Christ is establishing a kingdom that crosses all earthly borders, lineages, and divisions.

Our final course, *Dessert*, will consider the great meal when all believers will "take and eat" at the wedding feast of the Lamb. Thus, chapter nine will ground our eternal hope in the work of Christ in the past and the reign of God over all things. Theology doesn't end at the cross but is given light and life by the Christ-event. Scripture is pregnant with the hope of a future when the scars of the old world are removed, and the new creation arrives in all its fullness. This chapter will explore these promises for the future as a parallel with the creation in Eden.

Finally, our theological banquet will conclude with *Tea and Coffee*. This conclusion will be a summation of the redemptive arc of scripture and try to produce a biblical theological application that draws the various strands of our theme together. It will consider how we have seen humanity fall into sin and be restored into holiness through Jesus. By his majestic work we are restored in our worship, our purpose, and our humanity so that we can reside forevermore in the presence of our God. We will work and eat and worship throughout eternity in diligent service to God.

The ultimate purpose of this book is to bring glory to God for his work of redemption within time. This book is not designed to be a definitive theology, but perhaps a launching point into the gospel's beautiful multifacetedness. By taking the singular theme of "take and eat," we will cover the entire narrative of Christ's redemptive work in broad brushstrokes. I hope that you will see some of the beauty that is hidden in full view in the opening sections of the Bible. Through our exploration of the Old and New Testament's usage of "take and eat," we will see that even within Genesis there is the hope and promise of redemption and restoration. It's my prayer that by reading this book you see both how God has orchestrated history to make the work of Jesus the center of all things and to bend your knee in joyous worship of the God who is, and the God who saves.

First Course: Starters

1

Made In His Image

Then God said, "Let us make man in our image, after our likeness. And let them have dominion over the fish of the sea and over the birds of the heavens and over the livestock and over all the earth and over every creeping thing that creeps on the earth." So God created man in his own image, in the image of God he created him; male and female he created them. And God blessed them. And God said to them, "Be fruitful and multiply and fill the earth and subdue it and have dominion over the fish of the sea and over the birds of the heavens and over every living thing that moves on the earth." (Genesis 1:26-28)

The LORD God took the man and put him in the garden of Eden to work it and keep it. (Genesis 2:15)

Introduction

Everyone loves an origin story. Our world is replete with such stories. Every TV show or movie we watch must have an inception point, a story of beginning. There are certain stories, however, that attempt to tell the biggest narrative of all: Ours. Every worldview must find answers for four fundamental questions of life: Where did we come from, where are we going, why is there suffering, and is there is a greater power out there? Further questions will develop depending on how we answer the previous one: If there *is* a greater power that exists out there, can we know him/her/it, and, perhaps more importantly still, are we and that power "friends"?

In the book of Genesis, we're introduced to the creation of all things. We read that God is the creator and originator of all life and matter. Nothing that exists in this realm could exist without God. This is a fundamental truth that every Christian must accept. God is the creator. But, beyond simply creating, we see God is a personal God. He reveals himself within creation and *to* creation. The great opening of Genesis is not so much an origin story about the creation of all things so much as it provides a glimpse into the mind of God himself; he reveals to us some of the mechanics of creation as well as some of his motivation for creation. We also learn about the creation of humanity as well as the purpose for humanity. In describing this for us, God is also revealing much about his own nature. This is because humans are uniquely made to display the communicable attributes of God.

Creating Humanity

Before the dawn of creation, Moses tells us that the world was without form. There was darkness and there were waters over which the Spirit of God was hovering. The implied idea is that the Spirit is sustaining the void and preparing for the coming of life. Moses then tells us that God created the heavens and the earth. Whilst the earth was without form, and the waters moved, there was darkness within the created realm. But over the next six days the Triune God created all things that were created.

God created lights that would brighten up the days and guide the evening. There was to be land that would separate the waters, and the waters were to be restricted by boundaries so that vegetation could sprout on the dry earth. These plants would yield fruit and seeds, each according to their kind. In the waters there would be sea creatures of every kind, swimming in shoals throughout the oceans. Their heavenly counterparts would soar into the skies, catching the winds. To these animals a command was given: Be fruitful and multiply. As in the waters and the air, God then created living creatures for the land: Livestock, creepy crawlies, and beasts of the earth. All were created according to their own kinds. From the majestic galaxies that light up the night sky, down to the least important single-celled organism, and everything in between, God created them all. God looked at his creation with delight and declared that "it was good."

But when we get to the end of the first chapter, although the earth has all kinds of wonderful animals and birds and aquatic beings, there is something missing: Us. Everything else has been lovingly, carefully, and attentively created, without doubt. The architecture and structure of the universe which employs the massive gravitational force of the sun over the earth and the quantum mechanics that appear to hold things together all display the handiwork of a master designer who has been intimately involved in every aspect of creating. But despite the care given in the creation of all the previously created beings, nothing else will have the dignity, the value, or the purpose which is reserved exclusively for the climax of creation: Humanity. In verse 26, therefore, God begins to create his masterpiece.

Created In the Image of God

In verse 26 God decided to make man "in his image," and "after his likeness." The decision to create humanity was followed by a brief summation of the purpose of humanity. It's clear from the outset that human beings were to *reflect* God in some way. Historically, there have been many attempts to explain what it means to be an image bearer. The three most common interpretations highlight three unique characteristics of human beings.

In the first view, the *substantive* view, the idea is that we reflect God because we have higher critical reasoning skills. We can think in conceptual ways. We can reason and rationalize. This is perhaps most ironically summarized by Aristotle's definition of humanity as the "rational animal." Humans can think about the future, and the past, in ways that demonstrate our uniqueness in the animal kingdom. No other creature develops society or civilization. There are animals with hierarchies and social experiences, of course, but none that comes close to the human imagination or creative power that develops organized communities with infrastructure like ours. We, alone, construct monuments to past achievements of the species. It is humanity that values history and artistic talent and beauty. We revel in music and movie and theatre and culture. We have all experienced moments of being amazed at the sheer impressiveness of the architecture of a cathedral or the power of a song or the delicate brushstrokes of a painting. To be an image bearer, according to this view, is to reflect God's evident intelligence, creativity, and expression.[1]

The second view, the *relational* view, suggests that to be made in the image of God is to be relational like God. After all, God is, within himself, Triune. He is Father, Son, and Spirit, in perfect unity and holiness, never separate, but nevertheless distinct in his personhood. Just as he is, in himself, a relational God, he makes humans with whom he seeks and desires communion. This does not mean that he *needs* us; but it does suggest that he *wants* us. Just as humans crave community, God himself enjoys community and desires to share with us the munificence of his glory, the depth of his love, the breadth of his grace, and the intimacy of his presence. Like God, we too desire love, community, and relationships. The very idea of "love" is not the modern adaptation of butterflies in the tummy, sweaty palms, and an embarrassing red face (surely I wasn't the only one!?); rather, to love in this relational sense means to *know* someone deeply and truly. In this view, there are two horizons to relationality: The horizontal communities in which we find meaning, value, and purpose, but also the vertical relationship between God and man, which corresponds to covenantal community characterized by our worship of God.

The third view is, generally speaking, the dominant view in current thought. This is the *functional* view and argues that

---

[1] There is a fascinating antithesis of this view that actually takes the reverse position. For some, the fact that humans can willfully be *irrational* is a determining factor of human uniqueness. This is summarized by the idea that it is our *emotions* that make us human. Consider the dystopian movie, *The Matrix*, where it's boldly stated that "to deny our impulses is to deny the very thing that makes us human." The *impulse* rather than the *logical action* is what matters. I'm indebted to my colleague Jonathan Reibsamen for drawing my attention to this contrarian perspective.

humans are given an authority to *rule* over creation that mirrors God's rule over the cosmos. Just as God is Lord of the universe, humans are given priority over creation as his divinely appointed regents. Thus, the argument goes, after God determined to make humans in his image and likeness, he then continued to lay out what their duties would be: "Let them have dominion over the fish of the sea and over the birds of the heavens and over the livestock and over all the earth and over every creeping thing that creeps on the earth." In other words, humanity reflects God by the fact that humans exhibit authority over creation.[2] The image that we bear is an earthly, material, and limited representation of God's cosmic, universal, transcendent, being: "To be made in the 'image of God' is to be given regal status."[3] Gregory of Nyssa explains it this way:

> *[Man's] creation in the image of the nature that governs all demonstrates precisely that he has from the beginning a royal nature... This human nature, created to rule the world because of his resemblance to the universal King, has been made like a living image that participates in the archetype by dignity and by name.*[4]

Recent scholarship suggests, however, that the divine image may in fact not be any of these options, but rather these three aspects are *consequences* of image bearing. We are created with attributes that are meant to look, and sound, and feel, something like God. Now, obviously, we *aren't* God, that is all too clear. But we do have rationality that reflects God: We *can* think and reason. However, Peter Gentry rightly notes that our image bearing is not founded on our intellectual reasoning.[5] And, yes, we are relational

---

2 J. R. Middleton, *The Liberating Image: The Imago Dei in Genesis 1* (Grand Rapids, IL: Brazos, 2005), p. 26.

3 T. Desmond Alexander, *From Eden to the New Jerusalem: An Introduction to Biblical Theology* (Grand Rapids, MI: Kregal Academic, 2008), p. 77.

4 P. Schaff et al., eds. *A Select Library of the Nicene and Post-Nicene Fathers of the Christian Church*. 2 series (14 vols. each). Buffalo, N.Y.: Christian Literature, 1887-1894; Reprint, Grand Rapids, Mich.: Eerdmans, 1952-1956; Reprint, Peabody, Mass.: Hendrickson, 1994., 2 5:391.

5 Peter J. Gentry, "Humanity as the Divine Image in Genesis 1:26-28," *Eikon: A Journal for Biblical Anthropology*, 2 (1), 2020 and Peter J.

in a way that reflects God: We *can* know and love people, even strangers and outsiders, and we are able to enjoy covenant community with God. Yet, this too, is not the foundation or essence of image bearing.[6] And it's true that we have authority like God: We *can* bring order to our world, for good or ill. However, this too is not the source of our being an image bearer.[7]

Perhaps a fourth view is needed to provide a clearer definition of what it means to be made in the image of God. In this view, Adam was created *as* the image of God. Flowing from what he *is* (a reflection of God) are the aspects of what he *does*: Applying intellect rationally, enjoying covenantal relationships, and exercising regal authority. This is because, as the image of God, Adam is a *representation* of God. Indeed, such a fourth view makes the most sense of the incarnate Son, Jesus, who, though being God, came to be flesh, and is the exact imprint of God (Hebrews 1:3) and the visible image of the invisible God (Colossians 1:15). It's this view that I will be using to make the argument of this recapitulating

---

Gentry, "Sexuality: On Being Human and Promoting Social Justice," *Eikon: A Journal for Biblical Anthropology*, 2 (2), 2020. It should further be noted, as Gentry does, that nowhere in the Old Testament does any author speak of the *head* or the *mind* as being the source of our will; rather, scripture consistently speaks of the *heart* being the seat of a person's emotions, desires, and faculties. He states: "The biblical language differs markedly from our own in the Western world. For us, the heart is associated with emotions, feelings, love…for the Bible, the heart is the centre [sic] of our being where we reason and think and make decisions and plans" (Gentry, "Sexuality: On Being Human and Promoting Social Justice," p. 115). This means that for the Hebrews the heart was the "key term…for identifying personhood" and it is striking that it is never used of the animal kingdom: Only human beings" (Ibid). That being acknowledged, for simplicity, I will speak of *intellect* and *will* as being a component of the divine image (not the source or essence), even though scripture locates the will in the heart not the head.

6   See Gentry's arguments in *Kingdom through Covenant*, Gentry, "Sexuality: On Being Human and Promoting Social Justice," and Gentry, "Humanity as the Divine Image in Genesis 1:26-28".

7   Gentry, "Sexuality: On Being Human and Promoting Social Justice," p. 116: "A merely functional definition of the divine image falls short…"

theme of redemption because Christ will be the greater Adam. It ought to be clarified, therefore, that the three aforementioned *consequences* of image bearing aren't the *nature* or *essence* of the divine image. Humanity *is* the image of God and *therefore* reflects these aspects of God.[8] In other words, we *can* rule *because* we are the image of God.[9] This clarification is important; it means that human beings can portray, in our limited way, reflections of God's rule, relationality, and creative wisdom because we are made *in* or *as* the image of God.[10] With that understanding, it's also accurate to say that we've been given a purpose.

It is most likely the case, therefore, that to be an image bearer is to *reflect* God's cosmic rule as regents over creation *through* the utilization of the unique attributes we as a race exhibit, and, by concerted effort through our relational unity and union, being *enabled* to undertake the *task* of ruling as regents. Image bearers are to reflect God, enjoy communion (both with God vertically and others horizontally), and rule over his creation.[11] Matthew Barrett explains it like this: "The image of God is created as a viceregent, one meant to live in covenant with the Lord of the covenant and

---

8   Gentry, "Humanity as the Divine Image in Genesis 1:26-28," p. 69. Gentry states: "The exposition in *Kingdom through Covenant* argues that ruling is the result of the divine image and not the image itself."

9   Peter J. Gentry, "Sexuality: On Being Human and Promoting Social Justice," *Eikon: A Journal for Biblical Anthropology*, 2 (2), 2020, p. 116.

10 See T. Desmond Alexander, *From Eden to the New Jerusalem: An Introduction to Biblical Theology* (Grand Rapids, MI: Kregal Academic, 2008), Peter J. Gentry and Stephen J. Wellum, *Kingdom Through Covenant: A Biblical-Theological Understanding of the Covenants* (Wheaton, IL: Crossway, 2012), Matthew Levering, *Engaging the Doctrine of Creation: Cosmos, Creatures, and the Wise and Good Creator*, (Grand Rapids, MI: Baker Academic, 2017), and Anthony A. Hoekema, *Created in God's Image* (Grand Rapids, MI: William B. Eerdmans Publishing Company, 1994), for various interpretations of how we understand "image" and "likeness."

11 Although we haven't come to the events of Genesis 3, yet, it should be noted that the created intention of humanity is being addressed in this chapter; subsequent events change humanity's position and role within creation, as will be discussed in chapter 3.

in his name exercise dominion over the creation (Genesis 1:28). Adam is but a little king in the kingdom of the great King, the lord of the covenant."[12] This fourth option allows for each human being to uniquely *be* the image of God and *consequently* display reason, relationship, and royal authority whilst preserving a communal aspect of our purpose at the same time.

Humans are also made in the likeness of God. The idea encapsulated here is that Adam was a son of God: "The word "likeness" in Genesis is closely associated with the creation of the human race, human genealogy, and sonship."[13] Together, being made in both the likeness of God and the image of God, Adam was a "servant king and son of God [who] will mediate God's rule to the creation in the context of a covenant relationship with God on the one hand and the earth on the other."[14] By being *made in the likeness* of God we can say that Adam was the *son* of God and in covenant relationship *with God*, but also made to be *dependent on God*; he was similar to God, but distinct because of his creaturely attributes. By *bearing the image* of God, Adam stood in covenant relationship over *creation* as a servant, and serving, king.[15] To *be* an image bearer *is* to both *represent* and *reflect* God "in terms of royal rule"[16] whilst to be made in the likeness of God is to acknowledge that we *are similar* to God in the "action of creating human life, *but not in the same way*."[17]

The implication from this discussion concerning humanity's bearing the divine image and being made in the likeness of God is that human beings "are hardwired for covenant relationships

---

12 Matthew Barrett, *Canon, Covenant and Christology Rethinking Jesus and the Scriptures of Israel*, edited by D.A. Carson (Downers Grove, IL: InterVarsity Press, 2020), pp. 48-49.
13 Gentry and Wellum, *Kingdom Through Covenant*, p. 199.
14 Gentry and Wellum, *Kingdom Through Covenant*, p. 201.
15 Gentry and Wellum, *Kingdom Through Covenant*, p. 200.
16 Peter J. Gentry, "Humanity as the Divine Image in Genesis 1:26-28," *Eikon: A Journal for Biblical Anthropology*, 2 (1), 2020, p. 64.
17 Gentry, "Humanity as the Divine Image in Genesis 1:26-28," p. 64, emphasis in original.

with our creator and with the creation."[18] The foundation for our authority over creation rests in both the divine image and the likeness of God, not in any supposed biological superiority.[19] This means that a critical distinction between humans and the animal kingdom is that human beings "are endowed with personhood, while animals are not" and that humans are made as the divine image.[20] In other words, humans are unique *because* of the divine image, not because we are more rational, relational, or regal than our animal neighbors. The divine image is something that *God* has given to every human being; therefore, our uniqueness is grounded in what he has said about us, not how we perceive ourselves as a species.

Adam, as the *image* of God, reflects God and exercises regal authority through covenant community. But in God's *likeness* he is a son of God, bound up in and to God for God's good pleasure. Just as parents give birth to miniatures of mom and dad, with characteristics of both gene pools, in a way we're blessed by God to be made in his likeness and can legitimately be called his children. He is our father. We share his likeness. And Adam reflected God without sin in his nature or his heart. But he wasn't to be alone.

A Woman Fit for Adam

In verse 27 we see that there is more to this origin story than simply Adam being a king and a son. For our current purposes, we note that God is at pains to highlight that human beings bear God's image. It's repeated in the first two lines of this stanza alongside the reminder that God created humanity. The fact that both our creation by God and his bestowing upon us his image is so intricately entwined in this stanza is not accidental: Human beings

---

18   Gentry, "Sexuality: On Being Human and Promoting Social Justice," p. 117.
19   Gentry, "Sexuality: On Being Human and Promoting Social Justice," p. 117.
20   Gentry, "Sexuality: On Being Human and Promoting Social Justice," p. 116.

are created unique *and* are uniquely created. God creates humans differently in order to make us different. We're not simply another animal. We have a higher dignity, value, and purpose.

In the third line, however, we realize that both sexes were created by God. The fact that both sexes are referenced here, in this specific stanza, where man's creation is carefully linked to this concept of image bearing makes clear that God sees humanity as a *whole* as bearing his image.[21] Thus, *both* sexes bear the image of God. Just as God created ʿ*âdâm* in his own image, and in the image of God he created him, God created humanity to be both male and female: Two pieces of a single puzzle.

This brings us to the creation of woman. Throughout Genesis 1, the drumbeat of creation was that everything God created was "good." After the creation of the image bearer, creation was deemed to be "very good." However, in Genesis 2 God recognized that Adam was alone. And this, like a cymbal crashing on our peaceful reverie, disrupted the repeated rhythm of "and God saw that it was good." Rather, in verse 18, the LORD God said that it "is *not* good that the man should be alone; I will make a helper fit for him."

Consequently, a remarkable scene takes place after God determined to make this helper for Adam. Adam, as the gardener, and in his capacity of authority, was situated in the garden when God brought before him the beasts and birds to name them. I imagine this scene like a modern wedding. Adam, the groom, sitting at the front, looking at these animals as they were brought before him, just as a bride is preceded by her bridesmaids. God walked them "down the aisle," as it were, towards Adam, to be named. He named this one "cow," but it was not fit for him. He named the next one "horse," but it was not fit for him. He named this one "pig," and it *most definitely* was not fit for him. Sheep, goats, pelicans, eagles, ostriches all came before him, but despite the many amazing variations and wonderful types of beasts and birds, Adam remained alone. Many "bridesmaids" came down the

---

21 Gentry, "Humanity as the Divine Image in Genesis 1:26-28," p. 69.

aisle, but each time the groom said, "This isn't the one fit for me." And thus, in the midst of the perfect garden of God, there remains this single, but glaring, proclamation of "not good."

Then Adam felt an unusually strong tiredness descend upon him. Yawning, he closed his eyes and fell into a deep slumber. During this divine anesthesia, God performed an operation where he removed a rib from Adam, and then sewed up the wound. From the material of this rib, God fashioned a helper fit for him. Adam awakened. And, if we return to our wedding ceremony imagery, having been disappointed by the many bridesmaids, now Adam was then informed there's one more being to come down the aisle. As the heavenly orchestras started playing Pachelbel's *Canon in D*, the LORD God presented to Adam his helper: Woman.

It's at this moment that we hear Adam speak for the first time in Scripture. My own personal translation from the Hebrew is that Adam says: "Aw yeah! Now *that's* my boo!" As any groom yearns to see the face of his bride coming to the altar towards him, Adam, likewise, set his eyes on woman for the first time and exclaimed in delight, "This *at last* is bone of my bones / and flesh of my flesh; / she shall be called Woman, / because she was taken out of Man." This was the first wedding. Adam called his bride Woman, and the editorial explanation is that, henceforth, "a man shall leave his father and mother and hold fast to his wife, and they shall become one flesh" (Genesis 2:24). Adam and Eve became one flesh in marriage; together they bore the image of God, and, as we shall see, they needed one another in order to fulfill humanity's God-given purpose.

One final point from this first marriage ought to be considered and that comes at the end of Genesis 2. In verse 25, Moses made the point that both Adam and Eve were "naked and were not ashamed." This speaks of the innocence and perfect vulnerability that this sinless couple enjoyed. Theirs was a relationship of complete unity and shared purpose. Paul speaks of this idea in 1 Corinthians 7 when he explains that, in marriage, spouses give up their bodily autonomy because two have been made one. This lack of shame, this utter vulnerability, is heralded here as a good thing. It's not something to fear nor to reject but is a beautiful portrait of how they were complementary; there was no competition, no resistance, no injuriousness experienced between them. Matthew Henry's oft-quoted exposition of the creation of Eve is well worth repeating: "The woman was made of a rib out of the side of Adam; not made out of his head to rule over him, nor out of his feet to be trampled upon by him, but out of his side to be equal with him, under his arm to be protected, and near his heart to be beloved."[22]

We understand this even further when we consider this word "helper" (*'ezer*). Adam needed a helper who would be fit for him. Woman was to be someone who was equal *to* him and yet different *from* him. He didn't need a clone; he needed a companion. This word 'helper' is often misinterpreted as a position of lesser responsibility and perhaps even of lower importance. To see it in this light is to miss the point entirely. Adam didn't need a secretary; he needed someone to help him do things that he couldn't do on his own. Her task wasn't to serve *Adam*, but, rather, to serve *with* Adam. When God provided Adam with Eve, God gave him someone who could help him by being capable in areas he lacked or in which he was incomplete. Eve was to be a *blessing* for Adam as his helper. It's together, as man *and* woman, that God would call humanity to both flourish in Eden and to extend his image throughout the created realm.

This fact tells us that Adam or Eve alone was not capable of totally fulfilling the responsibilities image bearers are required to undertake. Of course, this does *not* mean that every man or woman must be married otherwise they are only half the image of God.[23] After all, Jesus is the image of the invisible God, and he was not married. Why would Paul wish that all would be like him in

---

[22] Matthew Henry, *Commentary on the Whole Bible: Complete and Unabridged* (Peabody, MA: Hendrickson, 1991), 2nd edition, p. 7.

[23] "Each man and woman bears the image of God apart from his or her counterpart." Bruce K. Waltke, Charles Yu, *An Old Testament Theology: An Exegetical, Canonical, and Thematic Approach* (Grand Rapids, MI: Zondervan, 2007), p. 217.

his singleness if that diminished the image of God in us? And what of those who are too young to marry? Or who were married but are no longer in such estate due to death or divorce? Such erroneous views would not only diminish their image-bearing but would also dehumanize such individuals. Rather, to bear the image of God as a human being is to be as *human* as we can be in our nature as created beings. The point is that, as a race, we need both sexes to reflect God's image through relationship as we, collectively, work towards fulfilling our common and ordained purpose.

A Creation Mandate for Humanity

After the creation of Adam and Eve, God blessed them. This is the climax of our origin story. Humans resided in the garden of Eden, blessed and commissioned by God. In verse 28, God gave Adam and Eve their duties as his regents. Together, as gardeners in this Eden, they were to fulfil two tasks: Be fruitful and multiply, and exercise dominion over creation. These twin tasks are often termed the "Creation Mandate."

A point of context might be helpful here. In the ancient world, powerful men took great pride in their gardens. We need only think of the hanging gardens of Babylon as an example of such an idea. Only wealthy or powerful men had the time and resources to spend their afternoons tending to plants and trees: Horticulture was a status symbol. Adam and Eve, in bearing God's image and reflecting him to the world, were to be the consummate gardeners. Placed in the greatest garden the world has ever seen, and trained by the greatest gardener that has ever existed, they were well situated for the work of the Creation Mandate.

Be Fruitful and Multiply

When God told Adam and Eve to be fruitful and multiply, he meant to create. This was one way in which they could reflect God as his image bearers. God had just created all things from nothing (*ex nihilo*), and Adam and Eve were to create mini-Adams and Eves through their new marital relationship. Creating, therefore, was one aspect of displaying our full humanity as made in the likeness of God. As sons of God, we create more sons of God. All animals procreate, but creating *image bearers* is a unique way humans are differentiated from the animal kingdom: Adam and Eve were to be *creative* creatures. As Adam and Eve procreated, the number of human beings would increase, and they would expand throughout creation. As they spread, they would bring the rest of the world under their dominion.

Subdue the Earth and Have Dominion

The second command given to Adam and Eve is to subdue the earth and have dominion over every living thing that moves. In our modern world, "to subdue" typically means "bring to subjection" and "have dominion" typically means "exert domination." This is not an accurate reflection of God's initial design and desire for humanity's regency. Instead, we might better think in terms of "cultivation." The idea is to explore creation and make it useful to us and yield its service to us. As gardeners in Eden, working and overseeing the handiwork of God, Adam and Eve were to be cultivators rather than dictators.

This point is critical; just as God *created* all things out of the power of his voice, he also *declared* that all his creation was *good*. There was no evil, no sin, no death, no violence, no failure, and no wicked misuse of power. Thus, when we read that Adam and Eve were to have dominion over creation, we're not to envision things such as abuse, or misuse, of authority. Rather, as they watched how God governed both of them, walking with them in the cool of the day, communing with them and teaching, laughing, guiding, and loving them, they would then display that attitude to those under their own care. This is because they understood that they were regents over God's creation *and* made in his likeness to share in the "family traits." It was not *their* world; even under their regency it remains *his* world. They were part of it, even as they also had a delegated responsibility over it.

Their duties of "subduing the earth" had a larger connotation than merely building fences and spreading seed over the land. It speaks of cultivation and care. Their task was to intentionally spread the authority of God, as devolved to them as his regents, across the material world. As they procreated, and as those children moved outward with their own families, the rule of God as displayed in and through his image bearers would extend across and throughout the world. In each new region, they would then subdue the varied created beings and cultivate the local vegetation as God had commanded until the whole world was filled with his image and the glorious rule of his regents.

As such, Adam and Eve were not to be idle or bored. Eden, for them, was certainly a place of idyllic perfection, but it was not a place for laziness. They were gardeners in God's own garden and were to procreate, oversee, guide, maintain, and enjoy his creation. Part of that enjoyment was to be found in completing the task of cultivation. To be in the presence of God is not to sit idly on a cloud stumming a golden harp. Such an idea sounds terribly dull and boring (especially if you can't play the harp!). Humans weren't designed to be lazy; we were made to work. But we were also made to enjoy work. In fact, we were made to reflect God *in the fact that we work*. Incidentally, it's important to note that *both* Adam and Eve were made to work. Within certain circles there's an insistence that a woman's primary task is to bear children while a man provides for the family through productive labor. To be sure, keeping a home is certainly a form of work; but to say that the Creation Mandate excluded women from productive, external work is too far outside the realm of the text.[24]

These two commands were given before the Fall. This reminds us that we're not only creative creatures but also *working* creatures. Both aspects ultimately reflect the God who created all things and, even now, is at work to sustain all things and move us towards the culmination of the end of time. Thus, the twin tasks of humanity

---

24 Rebekah Merkle, *Eve in Exil and the Restoration of Femininity* (Moscow, ID: Canon Press, 2016), p. 110.

were intertwined; to subdue the earth, they must expand. And, to do so, Adam needed Eve and Eve needed Adam. Neither sex could fulfil the duties given to humanity without the other.

The Creation Mandate was given to Adam and Eve because they were made in the image of God. They were enabled to do what God had commanded because they could watch and learn from him in person. He's the master creator and the perfect gardener. He's the mind behind the organization of creation. But they had access to him: They walked with him and talked with him in their innocence and sinlessness. He, in turn, was able to direct, and model, and teach them how to cultivate creation and exercise a loving and gracious leadership over it that wasn't dictatorial. He demonstrated what it meant to image God: To be like, to live like, and to love like God. And, vitally, this is what it means to be *truly* human.

Created to Worship

Being in the presence of God is ultimately to be in a place and posture of worship. This is made clear when we combine Genesis 1:26-28 with Genesis 2:15. God placed Adam and Eve into the garden as his regents and gardeners to reflect him and expand his rule throughout creation. But we see that the language *used* for this work in Eden is the phrase "to work it and keep it." T. Desmond Alexander has made a convincing argument that this language demonstrates that Eden itself is actually a Holy of Holies in the midst of the temple of the world.[25] This argument bears significant weight because the same words are used of the priests for the tabernacle and, later, the temple, where the priests were commanded to "guard all the furnishings of the tent of meeting, and keep guard over the people of Israel as they minister at the tabernacle" (Numbers 3:8). The words for work/serve and keep/watch in the Hebrew are *'ābad* (עָבַד) and *šāmar* (שָׁמַר). Both are used in Numbers 3:7 and 3:8 as well as in Genesis 2:15.[26] This

---

25 Alexander, *Eden to the New Jerusalem*.
26 This implies that Adam is "portrayed as a kind of Levite who fulfills

informs our understanding of the ultimate task given to Adam and Eve in the garden of Eden: They were to be priests of God as well as regents under God. Just as priests in the tabernacle were to mediate the love and grace of God to the people of Israel, we can see that Adam and Eve had a similar responsibility: "The garden of Eden is not viewed by the author of the Genesis account as a piece of Mesopotamian farmland, but as an archetypal sanctuary, that is a place where God dwells and where man should worship him."[27]

Thus, we can argue that Adam was "commissioned to keep or guard the garden so that it would *remain* holy."[28] Serving in this Holy of Holies, Adam and Eve were not only regents ruling on God's behalf, gardeners cultivating God's creation, and priests mediating God's love to the world: They were also worshippers. Fundamental to their purpose was worship. As they were cultivating creation, as they were procreating, and as they were subduing the earth and exercising dominion over it, their actions were to be understood as actions of *worship*: "Genesis 2:8-17 pictures Adam as a kind of king-priest worshipping in a garden sanctuary."[29]

At the very heart of the garden, then, stood the gardeners, the images of God, whose task was to cultivate creation and expand throughout the world in such a way as to bring everything into covenantal relationship with God. When this was accomplished, the entire material realm would be brought into a posture of holy worship. But, as we shall explore below, problems developed due to sin. This provides a secondary implication to the task of worship, which is better understood through Numbers 3:8. There, the priests were expected to "keep guard over the people of Israel as

---

his role or task by maintaining the priority of worship." Gentry and Wellum, *Kingdom Through Covenant*, p. 212.

27 G. J. Wenham, "Sanctuary Symbolism in the Garden of Eden Story', *Proceedings of the World Congress of Jewish Studies* 9 (1986), p. 19.

28 G. K. Beale, *The Temple and the Church's Mission: A Biblical Theology of the Dwelling Place of God*, New Studies in Biblical Theology 17 (Leicester: Apollos, 2004), p. 70, emphasis mine.

29 Gentry and Wellum, *Kingdom Through Covenant*, p. 215.

they minister at the tabernacle." Part of the duty of followers of God is to provide spiritual protection.

In the garden, Adam was to protect Eve, and, together, they were to protect all of creation. But from what? In Genesis 1 and 2, they didn't yet know of dangers and threats to the God-established order. But by the time God was giving commands to the priests of the tabernacle the world was in rebellion. True worship, therefore, is bound up not only in presenting praise, homage, adoration, and reverence to God, but also in ensuring the statutes and words of God are properly protected, preserved, presented, and proclaimed. Just as Adam and Eve were to cultivate creation by their working it and keeping it, so, too, were the priests to order the people of faith around the words and will of God. In doing so, they would be offering to the world a demonstration of how one can live in right relationship to God in the midst of rebellion.

In the very middle of creation, at the very heart of the material world, Adam and Eve got to reside in a Holy of Holies, as the images of God. There they walked with God and communed with him in perfect harmony and humility. They had the purpose of ordering creation, expanding throughout the world, and representing God as his image bearers. They were to rule over creation in a way that reflected God's justice, purity, holiness, and love; they were to relate to one another and their offspring in a way that demonstrated covenantal community, whilst also showing empathy and compassion towards the "lower" life forms; they were to creatively develop, adapt, and mature as their knowledge of the world grew, harnessing the various landscapes, ores, and minerals for their use as regents of God Most High. Theirs was a lofty life indeed!

Application

There are several critical lessons that we can learn from this introduction to the grand narrative of humanity. Firstly, humanity bears the image of God. This gives dignity, value, and worth to both men and women. We should value life from conception through to the moment of death. Every human life has inherent value, dignity, and worth because every human being is made in the image of God. This means that Christians ought to be fiercely involved in speaking out for the unborn, those with disabilities, those in poverty, refugees, those caught up in warzones, those who are in physical, emotional, and mental decline, the elderly, and those who are ill. It's because we recognize the beautiful gift and privilege of bearing the image of God that Christians need to be at the forefront of discussions on these topics, seeking to implement protections for all human life. This also means that we ought to care for *all* life, from the womb to the tomb, not merely our current cultural preferences. Christians must be consistently advocating for the sanctity and value of life against our culture that calls death "choice" and considers value based upon a perceived "usefulness to society." We must value the homeless person as much as the person in the Governor's mansion. We must give dignity to the addict in seeking to help provide a means of escape from their enslavement. We must love the immigrant. We must show God's gracious compassion to our gay neighbors and our atheist friends and our Islamic or Buddhist or Hindu colleagues and peers. It's our duty as protectors of our fellow man that we prioritize the needs of those who may be unable to speak for themselves. Our voice must be loud, clear, and firm that life matters because human life is a unique expression of the majesty and beauty of our creator God.

Secondly, human beings are to reflect God's image in our exercise of authority over creation, in our relationships, and in our intellectual and emotional faculties. Humans are made for community and communion. Isolation is detrimental to our emotional and spiritual wellbeing in many ways. When we love others, we're living examples of God's love towards us. By showing grace and compassion on those around us, both humans and animals, we are reflecting the God who had grace and compassion on us. The kingship that humanity was created to display and accomplish over creation is meant to be a miniature expression of the loving, benevolent, and gracious rule that God has over the entire cosmos.

Such demonstrations are not found merely in the tending of our own gardens, but, on the macro level, as nations seek to exercise a concern for nature and creatures within our borders, as well as economically and societally. We should be concerned about the intentional force-feeding of caged animals whose quality of life is nonexistent. We should engage with our governments about maltreatment of animals as well as abuse towards other human beings because our exercise of headship over creation is meant to be as cultivators rather than dictators.

Relationally, we ought to desire communion and community with various people groups. At the local level, we should seek to be in harmony with our family and friends. Moving beyond our immediate circle, we should seek to cultivate healthy, Godly, worship-oriented relationships with our churches and fellow believers. We should seek to extend the kingship of our God throughout the realm of our lives as we live as image bearers. Whether that be in our homes, our marriages, our sports clubs, our schools, or our places of employment, we're to seek to display the types of relational maturity and faithfulness and integrity that God bestowed upon Adam and Eve. These relationships should be focused on cultivating opportunities to bring honor and worship to our Triune creator who is, in himself, perfect community and who enjoys perfect communion as Father, Son, and Holy Spirit.

Perhaps the most intimate and vulnerable relationship we can think of is the relationship of marriage. Adam and Eve experienced marriage in all its openness, vulnerability, humility, grace, and compassion, without any competition, insecurity, nagging, arguing, or disappointment. They had the opportunity to love one another in a way that, albeit in their limited human experience, could conceivably reflect the love of the Persons of the Godhead: Selfless, undivided, and unconditional. Their marriage was to be the pinnacle and paradigm for all future marriages that would come from their offspring, and each one was to be a portrait of

God's love within himself and towards creation. Yet, although they didn't know it, their marriage was a mystery that pointed towards something more than even this.

But notice; although we bear the image of God, we nevertheless need to be reminded that we are *not* God. The Creator-creature distinction is a division between the infinite and the finite. As human beings, we're made to reflect God as the moon might reflect the sun; but no one could ever confuse the two. God is the absolute, infinite, eternal, perfection of all that he is in his glorious essence and majesty. We get the privilege and responsibility of conveying *something* of his majesty and royal holiness to the world but always with limitations.

The fact that we're not God is most readily visible in the fact that part of our joyous obligations as created beings is to be *worshippers*. As Adam and Eve were to work and keep the garden as priests in a Holy of Holies, we're likewise to be worshippers. It's built into the fabric of our nature. We are worshipers. And there's a healthy humility in being reminded of that. We're not God, but we get to reflect God. And, just as we reflect him to the world, we draw attention to his glory by guiding others towards him. This is part of our creational, priestly, Adamic work as human beings: To bring others to God to worship him. When we're properly fulfilling the Creation Mandate, we advance the knowledge of our God throughout creation so that more of the created order is brought into his presence to worship him.

Worship, therefore, ought to be the foundational attitude that underpins everything we do. As Christians, our worship has been redirected from ourselves to our Savior and our God. Thus, everything that we're called to do ought to be done as if unto God as an act of worship (Colossians 3:23). When Adam named the animals and talked with God and gave the words of God to Eve, he was worshipping. In the garden, he was a worshipper and a priest, mediating the love and kingship of God to the world. Likewise, albeit through the lens of Calvary rather than Eden, we're meant to live our lives as worshippers in the presence of God.

Whether it's in the office or school or home, we're to serve God by attuning our lives to his beauty and goodness. Worship is not something reserved for a fancy building on Sunday mornings; it's part of what it means to be a human made in the image of God. While you have the breath of life flowing through your lungs, you can worship the Lord of life.

Finally, we were made to work. The idea of "work" in the garden of Eden was not one of toil but of privilege. It was a mark of Adam's position over creation that he got to work to cultivate creation. The animals, for all that they go about their chores, didn't have "work" in the same way that he did. Mankind's work is but a small reflection of God's cosmic work. As he oversees the angelic realm and superintends the stars in their orbits and sustains everything that exists, we, too, are to oversee the things under our care and bring order out of the chaos under our control. Whilst our work may be smaller in scope, it is nevertheless important and purposeful. Humans weren't created to live isolated, lazy, and boring lives.

Our cultivation of creation is to excite creativity and curiosity. As Adam and Eve were meant to spread the image of God throughout the world through childbearing, the world was to be brought under humanity's headship and exploration. This means that we were always meant to be inquisitive about the things under the earth and in the skies and oceans. Our task, to be undertaken worshipfully, is to discover and learn about the world God has given us with a sense of wonder so that we would grow in our awe at the intricate care that God has taken in every facet of the world, from the smallest boson to the largest constellation. How could such knowledge lead to anything but an even deeper expression of worship?

Conclusion

This is our origin story. It wasn't the beginning of *everything*. But it was the beginning of our story. Everything began with, and in, paradise. Adam and Eve were placed into the garden of Eden as royal gardeners and children of God. But they were so much more; they were made in the very image of their creator. Although distinct from him, they nevertheless were made in such a way that they would exhibit aspects of God's glory, power, intelligence, relationality, and authority. As the first human beings, they were made with absolute freedom and with no experience of sin or shame, fear or frailty, disease or death. Instead of being separated from God, they enjoyed his presence. They knew what it was to stand in the very presence of God as sinless regents, overseeing his creation in perfect harmony and peace with the animal kingdom. Theirs was absolute freedom to be holy and to be good.

Although they were made free and without sin, as we have seen, Adam and Eve were still human beings with limitations. They would need sustenance. And God would give them everything that they needed in order to live in observance of his expectations. God would tell Adam and Eve, in the heart of the garden, what they were permitted to "take and eat."

2

"Take and Eat": Garden Party

And the LORD God commanded the man, saying, "You may surely eat of every tree of the garden..." (Genesis 2:16)

Introduction

My family love eating. We love food. I especially love eating freshly grilled meat, but that's for another chapter. There is a very real and tangible grace in the fact we are made with an array of tastebuds that can taste millions of different flavors, with nasal receptors that can enjoy millions of different scents, and with a digestive system that can break down a multitude of different food types. In our family dinner-table prayers, I often thank the Lord for this very sweet gift. After all, it would have been so much easier for God to simply have us need a boring paste, or mere grass, or something as bland as kibble to provide our sustenance. Think, perhaps, of a car needing fuel. We could have been designed in a similar way: Plug the hose in, fuel up, and away we go. Instead, from the beautiful aromas of a fine wine sauce to the tart berries in a delicious Christmas dessert dish, we're able to taste it all.

Indeed, our taste buds and nasal receptors work in concert so that eating is not simply about taste. There is a very unusual restaurant in London in which the main dining room is completely dark. The idea is that we *taste* food differently if we can't *see* it. Instead, in the dark, we're forced to rely much more on our senses of smell and taste to identify, understand, and even to enjoy the individual items on our plate. I confess that the main attraction for such a venue (at least for me) is that I can eat my spaghetti pasta any which way I please (those of you with Italian family members will understand!).

But there is something absolutely theological about this concept of food. God created us with the ability to *enjoy* the process of filling our bodies with the requisite nutrients and sustenance. In fact, not merely is it true that we can enjoy our food, but we get to experiment, explore, develop, and create new concoctions. Think of the various types of salads we can order in almost any local eatery. We are indeed blessed.

Of course, it must be noted that, for most human beings throughout the majority of human history, the *choice* in food was limited by region and wealth more than by preference. However, in our age, with supermarkets down the block, we can choose ingredients from almost any continent, create dishes of cuisines from almost any culture, and not only ingest them, but enjoy them. This is a wonderful gift of God that reveals that God designed humanity to enjoy the tangible aspects of our creaturely existence. This is often an overlooked blessing (and, also, often an abused gift): God wants us to reflect him even in the manner in which we enjoy and appreciate our daily bread. This generosity is dramatically visible in the garden.

Food to Eat for All

God gave Adam and Eve the privilege of being in control over the created realm. Theirs was the task of overseeing and administrating creation as his regents because they were image bearers and as his children because they were made in his likeness. But although Adam and Eve were made in the *image* of God, they weren't *actually* God. They were created beings. We called this the Creator-creature distinction. Thus, although God is self-sustaining, Adam and Eve were not. They needed food to sustain themselves, to have energy, and to go about the purposes for which God had brought them into the world.

God's provision for them was that they would satisfy themselves on the vegetation of Eden. He provided food for Adam and Eve and for all creation and said: "Take and eat." Then, as the Edenic paradise expanded throughout the created realm, they would cultivate numerous more types of trees and berries and fruits and vegetables. Their concoctions of vegetarian food would be flavorful, bountiful, and, no doubt, delicious. I suspect part of God's joy was watching Adam and Eve notice and experience everything in much the same way a parent watches their newborn's first steps with avid interest and pride. Something that is, ultimately, so *fundamental* and, in a way, *unremarkable*, is nevertheless a wonderful thing because of the depth of *relational* investment. It isn't simply *any* child taking those steps, it's *my* child. God looked upon Adam and Eve with a fatherly joy at their stuttering confusions and surprises as they meandered throughout Eden with eyes agape at the sheer complexity and intricacy and beauty of everything they saw.

Perhaps, like toddlers, they would enthusiastically taste everything that sprouted from the ground or grew atop a tree. God, their father, might laugh as the lemons caused their face to turn into a pucker at the sour taste and beam as they downed yet another handful of peanuts. The pleasure of our heavenly father at our childlike experiences in his world is something that new parents across the world and across time have experienced. They were able to explore and experience all that he had created *for them.*

The reason for such a free exploration of the vegetation is that God had given Adam and Eve permission to eat any fruit from the vegetation of the land. They were allowed to eat fruits from trees, berries from bushes, and vegetables from the ground. Not only were Adam and Eve encouraged to eat such vegetative produce, but, in fact, God said that all animals would be sustained from such sources. This was how his creation was to exist. And it was a grand chain that encompasses everything. There were equivalents in each of the various domains. The vision we get is one of joyous plenty. The food given to Adam and Eve would not only be nutritious but also delicious. Creation, in all its majesty, was God's masterpiece, created to be *enjoyed* and explored. This is why the words "take and eat" are so delightful. The food provided by the Master Gardener would tantalize the tastebuds and scintillate the senses. It was *good* food. As a skilled chef basks in the aromas and tastes of their creation, and bids the diner to begin, God had provided a veritable platter for his beloved creatures.

What is to be noted, however, is that the food that would sustain creation was to be *vegetation*. This presents a very vital distinction between vegetative life and animal life. Even though both can be said to be "alive" it isn't right to say that such "life" is equal. God had clearly created the world with a hierarchy of value. At the top of the chain of authority were the image bearers, who ruled over everything with a delegated authority that flowed from his absolute sovereignty. Below Adam and his descendants sat the animal kingdom. Animals had the spirit of life within them and thus had a higher value than plant matter; nevertheless, animals weren't given the divine image. This vegetation might be "alive" in the sense that plants and trees and bushes are organisms fulfilling mechanical and biological tasks, but they don't have the same sentience as the animal kingdom. There was a very evident distinction between a plant and an animal. We see this most poignantly when we think of emotions. Plants don't suffer and experience emotions in the way that animals or humans experience pain.[1]

Thus, God said that all animal life was given permission to enjoy all the food produced by vegetative life. No matter wheth-

---

[1] As I was researching this chapter, I was amazed to discover that there is a growing field of botanic studies that suggest plants indeed do have some kind of "intelligence", can respond to stimuli, and can, in fact, *remember* specific events. Nevertheless, it must surely be acknowledged and accepted that such organisms *are* inherently different from animal life: Animals have *agency* in determining what they will do, where they will go, and how they will do whatever they decide to do. Plants lack such agency. Michael Pollan, *The Omnivore's Dilemma, A Natural History of Four Meals* (Penguin, New York: 2006) and Michael Pollan, *The Botany of Desire: A Plant's-Eye View of the World* (Random House Trade Paperbacks, New York: 2001).

er it was a lion or a manatee, God gave them the same type of food to eat. Their diet was to be vegetarian. And yet, despite this restriction, there doesn't appear to have been any negative effect on their physiology. It seems to be the case that, from creation, all animals were created to be able to get their specific nutrients from a plant-based diet. Of course, as we all are aware, this state of affairs didn't last. Nevertheless, there *was* something valuable about the sheer abundance of plant life and the nutritional value of such foodstuffs that meant that Adam and Eve *were* sated, *were* satisfied, and *were* supplied with all that they needed. Whether this means that their food was better suited for them at this stage, or whether it means that they, themselves, changed physiologically due to subsequent events is up for debate. What is incontrovertible, according to the biblical witness, is that humanity and the animal kingdom were given the means of feeding themselves and it was sufficient to their needs. Remember, that it was *this* world that God called "good." It wouldn't have been a "good" creation if the very pinnacle of his creation did not have suitable nutrition to survive and thrive.

Every Tree of the Garden

God gave to Adam and Eve everything that was vegetation. Despite their uniqueness as regents and children of God, they nevertheless didn't get special treatment when it came to what they could eat. The garden was to be their supermarket. As both introductory chapters to the Bible explain, God gave Adam, Eve, and the animal kingdom food from the ground and food from the trees. There was no implicit or explicit conception that the food in the garden wasn't sufficient for all those who would seek to satisfy themselves with what was on offer. Further, though as an aside, there was no suggestion that Adam and Eve were forbidden from eating animal produce, such as, say, eggs or milk. The specific command, however, was that the prominent basis of their diet was to be vegetative.

The point of Genesis 1:30 is not that Adam and Eve and the animals only consumed vegetation (though that is true), but rather that the required sustenance for survival ultimately comes from God. This can be seen in verse 29, where God stated that it was he who had given every plant yielding seed for the sustenance of the animal kingdom. It was *for* this purpose that God provided the vegetation. The plants and trees weren't merely decorative, they were to sustain the animals and image bearers. Thus, the garden was a place of bounteous supply. Adam and Eve weren't ever concerned with the amount of food available. We read in the text that *every* plant and *every* tree and *every* green plant was to be used as a source of good food. In Hebrew literature, repetition captures our attention immediately and we're meant to understand this as a plenteous feast. Adam and Eve and the animals were well supplied and satisfied in all that the Lord had provided for them.

The image we must conjure up in our mind's eye is not one of lazy humans exploiting creation, growing fat on its produce whilst the animals were starving. Rather, we must remind ourselves that Adam was to be a gardener in Eden. His task was to see the territory God had given him as a royal residence in which his duty was to ensure the flowers were in bloom, the plants in good health, and the trees in plentiful stature. Adam was to cultivate creation as a matter of respect to *his* overlord as well as to provide for his own survival within creation.

As mentioned above, to be a gardener was a position of wealth and prestige because you could devote time and energy to something that the majority of the population couldn't afford to participate in. However, for Adam, there was something more. Yes, he was a gardener, but he was, in a sense, also a farmer. Adam's task was to cultivate the bushes and the trees and the plants to ensure that there was enough to go around. This work included his own family; he had to ensure that Eve was fed proportionate to her own needs. In this purpose, we can see that Adam and Eve had a royal and regal task, but also a common task. They were to exercise authority over creation, but that didn't mean that they were to be absent regents, nor greedy landlords. They were to be involved in the life and perspective of creation. At this stage, the animal life in the garden was as dependent on Adam and Eve as the humans themselves were on God. In this vital component of *being* a created being, Adam was reminded of his absolute dependency on God.

It's fair to say that Adam was simultaneously at the mercy of God and at the head of humanity. On the one hand, nothing came to Adam except by the grace of God's provision. It was God who sustained creation, who provides the seasons for growth and seasons for planting. It was God who brought forth the rains and the sun to ensure the gestating vegetation had the nutrients for growth. And yet, at the same time, it was *Adam* who cultivated the garden and exercised direct authority over the animals. In *this* capacity as head gardener, it was Adam who was responsible for all of the human race, and, indeed, the animal kingdom as well.

Adam, therefore, was the head of humanity. This means that Adam bore covenantal headship over all of the future humans that would spring from his marriage to Eve. They would be made in *his* likeness, just as he was made in the likeness of God. And, because Adam was a son of God his children would then bear the image of God as well. This meant that, both biologically and spiritually, Adam's descendants would bear his nature. Humanity would be "in" Adam in the sense that, standing before God, he represents us as our leader, our founder, our forebear, and our spokesman. As a conscientious head gardener, such a leader was a good model. Just as Adam learned from God, he would train up his own children in the way that they should go. In due course, it's reasonable to anticipate that Adam's holy family of image bearers would spread across the whole earth, cultivating creation, subduing it, and bringing it under the righteous and sovereign rule of God. In this case, Adam was unique as humanity's head.

The Rule in the Garden

There are two rules in my house. It has been remarked to me on more than one occasion that my two rules make me a very bad son of Adam. These rules are governed by instinctive fears and bad experiences in my life. The first rule is that if you see a spider indoors, you kill it. When it comes to arachnids, I am positively and unashamedly macabre. Everything about them terrifies me and makes my skin crawl. Yes, I know they kill flies and are almost never going to bite you where I live. (*Almost* is an exceptionally unhelpful word in this context, by the way.) The second rule in my household is even more pathetic. I hate onions and desire that there will never be an onion on my plate. My wife, however, loves onions. This is why this rule had to be updated post-marriage. Initially, I didn't want onions in the house for fear they might sneakily make their way into my lasagna. When we got married, we developed a wonderful compromise whereby she would freely cook with onions, but chop them large enough so that I, the responsible and mature grown-up that I am, can heroically pick them out. I'm very aware that this is childish. I'm equally aware that I don't care. I can eat most things, and will typically try everything at least once, but I draw the line at onions.

My onion "phobia" began in my grandmother's house (she was an amazing woman so it's very unfortunate that these two weird issues of mine developed in her house). One fateful day, I, in my toddler naïveté, decided to copy my beloved grandmother. She was chomping down on what looked like an apple. When she set it down, I grabbed it, took a large bite out of it, and was traumatized ever thereafter. Because what looked like an apple to me, was, you guessed it, an onion. It took a moment or two for my slow brain to react to the unexpected taste. You see, I was *anticipating* the juicy sweet flavor of a granny smith; instead, my taste buds were confused by the bitterness, the weird tanginess, and the acidic grossness of a white onion. Thus, the seeds of the rules of my house were planted in the soil of my scowling soul.

In our culture, we have an attitude towards rules that often borders on the anarchic. It can be the case that we are so distrustful of those above us in work, at home, in government, or in law enforcement, that we treat all rules and regulations with suspicion. It seems to be that our natural disposition is that a rule is bad because, by definition, it impinges upon my freedom. And, in our Western society, personal autonomy and freedom has almost been elevated to the supreme position and highest human right. Therefore, any rule that hinders my autonomy and sense of freedom must be inherently bad, coercive, or oppressive. Of course, this is nonsensical when considered rationally. After all, if *everyone* is absolutely "free" in the absolute sense, then *everyone* is free from all obligations to one another. Such ideas are utterly chaotic. This is why humanity has consistently implemented rules as a communal means to control the wilder and more dangerous of our passions and excesses. Despite this, the prevailing attitude is that rules imposed from outside my own person are oppressive and, at best, unhelpful, but at worst, so horrific as to necessitate rebellion. And it *is* true that some rules *are* morally, ethically, and spiritually bad. But many rules are good and serve to protect us. Nevertheless, our tendency is to buck against the rules, to push back, or to see how far we can go in getting away with breaking them, whether they are for our good or otherwise.

Knowing this, and no doubt having experienced that base tendency for yourself, it might be a surprise to realize that in the Garden of Eden there was only one rule. And Adam didn't think it was bad, unjust, or unfair. He accepted it because it came from God. Remember that Adam and Eve had been personally created by God and given immense dignity by him in being made in God's image. Adam and Eve were given authority over all of creation and were able to cultivate his garden on his behalf, tending to the animals, and generally enjoying his world. What they understood at this point, however, was that it was *his* world. They were *part* of it, even if they were at the pinnacle of it. Thus, if the owner of the garden wanted to impose a rule on everyone in his garden? That was reasonable and acceptable.

I have family members who have house rules that are different to those in my house (though, to be fair, I've not met many who have my house rules). When I'm in their house, to honor them, I follow their rules. Per their wish, I take off my shoes. It's their house, it's their rule, and it's their reasonable expectation that, if I am going to be in their house, I observe their rules. This was Adam's perspective: It was God's garden and God's rule. Adam felt this way about God's rule because he knew God personally and intimately. As such, he knew that God loved him, and therefore trusted God that his rule wouldn't harm him. Thus, when God told Adam that he wanted him to observe a single rule, he didn't push back or buck against it. He agreed to the terms because it was God's garden and Adam had been placed there as God's creation with God's commission. Contrary to *our* natural passions and proclivities towards rules and obligations, *Adam's* natural disposition was one of acquiescence, respect, and honor. He accepted God's rule. In fact, it was Adam's task as image-bearer and regent over creation to not only obey the rule, but to ensure *everyone* obeyed God's rule. He was, in a sense, to be more than merely the Lord's regent and a priest in the Holy of Holies in Eden; he was to be a prophet, declaring the words of God to, in time, Eve, and their offspring.

The Tree of the Knowledge of Good and Evil

After God created Adam, in the Genesis 2 account, he placed him in the garden. This was *before* God subsequently created Eve. Adam was tasked with the priestly task of working it and keeping the garden. In a demonstration of Adam's humility and submission to God he was to observe God's single rule. God had told Adam that every tree in the garden was suitable for the provision of nutritious food for him. Adam was permitted to eat of every tree in the garden except one: The tree of the knowledge of good and evil.

We don't know what type of tree it was and therefore we don't know the type of fruit. Many sermons speak, and pictures present, the fruit as a bright red apple, but we aren't told what fruit it was. More important to the text is the issue of what exactly the fruit from the tree would provide Adam and Eve. It has been suggested that Augustine of Hippo (AD 353-430,) a church father who was instrumental in the formation of the Western Christian tradition, believed that the tree possessed the power to teach Adam and Eve about sex and sexuality.[2] In this view, the vice that gripped Adam and Eve predominantly centered around their innocence in the garden and the tree risked giving them knowledge that they didn't need. This view is very unsatisfactory. It is true that Augustine spoke harshly about sexual sin (specifically in relation to his own experiences and behavior prior to his conversion), but that is stepping beyond the bounds of Genesis.

A second view is that eating from the tree would give Adam and Eve conceptual knowledge of morality. In other words, at this point, Adam *only* knew obedience to God. He has had no opportunity nor temptation to know anything to the contrary. He didn't have any means to, or desire to be, disobedient. Instead, he lived in perfect unity and relationship with God. The command not to eat from the tree did not lead to temptation because Adam's nature was not naturally geared towards desiring illicit pleasures. Rather, he was naturally disposed towards obedience. The fact that God gave Adam this command was to function as a test for Adam to demonstrate his *willingness* to respect God. The fruit of the tree, in this view, would reveal to Adam the nature of rebellion. The tree would give Adam the knowledge of morality, by which he would come to understand not *only* obedience, but *also* disobedience. An awareness of the two sides of obedience would open Adam up to the conception of disobedience and therefore perhaps to innate temptation.

---

[2] See, for example, Elaine Pagels, *Adam, Eve, and the Serpent* (Vintage Books, New York: 1989).

A third view is that the tree would give Adam an *experiential* knowledge of morality. In a sense, this third view is the second view with a vital component added to it: Experience. Rather than mere *knowledge* of the two sides of morality, the tree would give Adam the actual *experience* of disobedience. He would go beyond merely *knowing* wrong to experiencing all the implications that accompany immorality. Thus, if he were to eat of the tree, it would not only be an *action* of disrespect, but also an *attitude* change. It would imply his *nature* had changed and his disposition towards God had changed.

God placed the tree in the midst of the garden to be a test for Adam and, subsequently, Eve. They were to demonstrate their desire and willingness to honor and respect God by refusing to eat of it. Every time they walked by the tree without reaching out to grab the fruit of the knowledge of good and evil, they were consciously declaring their allegiance to God in his garden. And, consequently, they had no actualized knowledge or experience of the moral option of disobedience. It's this third interpretation that is the most plausible explanation about the fruit of the tree, though the text doesn't explicitly define the exact aspect of "good and evil" the tree would provide. What we can say with absolute confidence about the tree of the knowledge of good and evil, therefore, is that it stood in the midst of the garden (Genesis 3:3) and its fruit was strictly not to be consumed by Adam. Beyond that, the text doesn't give any further details and we must be careful reading too much more into it that cannot be reasonably inferred from this passage and Genesis 3.

This teaches us that God expects obedience from his creatures. This rule functions as an intrinsic reminder to Adam that God has exercised *his* authority over Adam just as Adam would exercise the delegated authority over creation. For any human who desires to be in community and communion with God, we must acknowledge this Creator-creature distinction. If we're to approach God, it will be on his terms, because he is God. If we desire to honor God, it must be achieved by doing what God desires. As the creator,

God has every right to exercise his authority in setting boundaries and rules. As the creature, we have every obligation to do as he demands. The demand for obedience is not immoral nor unjust for, if we grasp the doctrine of God correctly, he acts for our good and his glory. The rules he imposes are purposeful and beneficial to us because he, as the creator, knows what is best for us.

A question often asked about this passage is whether it was "fair" for God to place this tree of temptation in the garden. If God was truly loving and compassionate towards Adam and Eve, this line of reasoning argues, giving Adam such a large temptation in his midst is unkind. In fact, according to this question, it suggests that God *wanted* Adam to fail. Like the question of demanding obedience, the question of "fairness" must be carefully weighed in the context of who God is. He is the righteous and rightful owner of the garden. Adam and Eve were the regents, or the tenants, and they resided in the garden at the good pleasure of God. The entirety of creation belongs to God and is, therefore, God's to do with as he wishes. The very fact that they, too, had a rule to obey reminded them of their dependency upon God *and* functioned to teach creation itself the same thing: Adam and Eve ruled as God's regents, not as gods.

A similar pattern may be visualized in your local church. At home, the house rules are set by the parents: shoes off? So be it. See a spider? Introduce it to your size twelves. But when we gather as the church? Everyone sits to listen to the words of God proclaimed. Fathers, mothers, grandparents, friends, and mentors all submit to God. A child watching their father and mother submit to God learns a valuable lesson about the authority of God for their own lives. If the one who makes the rules that govern *their* life submits to a higher authority? Then that higher authority is worthy of the child's respect too. This is a fundamental principle of discipleship inherent throughout Scripture (Deuteronomy 6:1-9; Matthew 28:19-20; 2 Timothy 1:4-5; 2 Timothy 2:1-2). Thus, just as a child is impressed that mom and dad answer to someone, creation in the garden of Eden would realize that their overseers submitted to God. Such a chain of command gave everyone a sense of security because there could be accountability. This strengthened Adam and Eve's ability to successfully fulfil the Creation Mandate by exercising dominion over the created realm.

Do Not Eat

God's creation of Adam culminated in Adam's being placed in Eden as the regent and overseer of creation. He was a prince over creation, and he was to function as a priest in the worship of God in the garden. But he would also serve as a prophet because God gave him the rule: You can "take and eat" of any tree in the garden except the tree of the knowledge of good and evil.

God's command was explicit. It was clear. And it was given to Adam. Adam's subsequent responsibility was twofold. Firstly, don't eat from the tree. That's obvious. Adam's situation at this point was one of glorious freedom and privilege with only the mildest limitation imposed upon him. What appears to be surprising is that Adam's behavior was *not* like that of the mythical Pandora, whose gift of a bees-wax-sealed amphora was designed to intrigue and tempt her *into* disobeying Zeus. Unlike her inquisitiveness that led her to open "Pandora's box," Adam appears to have been content to accept the restriction. Instead of a morbid curiosity about the fruit of the tree, he set himself to the work of being a regent and began to name the animals.

The second aspect of his responsibility was to take the words of God, remember them, apply them, and be prepared to teach them. This is the work of a prophet. Prophets in the Bible sometimes specifically tell the future or warn about potential future judgement if certain actions don't change. But other times, prophets proclaim God's words to the people in that moment for that moment. It is the difference between *foretelling* and *forthtelling*. In this case, Adam had been given a command that required obedience and it would fall to him as the regent overseeing creation and as the priest overseeing worship of God to also be the prophet overseeing observance of God's rule.

Meanwhile, God had brought from Adam's side the mother of humanity. Adam's task as prince, priest, and now prophet, was to train Eve, who had not been present when God gave Adam the privilege to "take and eat" from every tree nor had she been there to receive God's specific restriction. Adam would, then, *image* God by sharing with her the same rule in the garden. And, as with creation, the fact that this was *God's* rule for *both of them*, Eve would not feel her stature as Adam's equal in nature was undermined.

In this context, God's single rule is extraordinarily reasonable. The point isn't quite so much a test of *love* but of *respect*. Some try to get around the presence of the tree and its apparent unreasonableness by saying that God *had* to give Adam and Eve the opportunity to *prove their love* for God and that, if God didn't, he would simply have made robots, incapable of freedom or choice. The tree, they say, allowed Adam and Eve to prove their love for God by freely avoiding the fruit of the tree. This view argues that God created them with the complete freedom to choose to love him (or otherwise) and the means by which they expressed their choice was through their behavior towards the tree of the knowledge of good and evil.

The fundamental problem with this idea is that Adam and Eve spent their time in the garden face to face with God. By nature, they only knew his grace and compassion. They did not have a nature of suspicion, mistrust, or disobedience. They didn't have temptation and couldn't conceive of *not* loving God. Their love *was* naturally towards God. They were created that way *because* they were created *without* sin. Their *natural* disposition towards God was not rebellion but devotion. To argue otherwise suggests that God is more concerned about offering humanity libertarian freedom than to preserve holiness in his sight. To argue that Adam was created *neutral* (as this view implies) is to misunderstand the full impact of Adam's sinless nature in the garden.

The test of the tree, therefore, was not that God was giving Adam and Eve the chance to prove their love, but rather it was to serve as a demonstration of their humility before him. It was to remind them of the Creator-creature distinction. This reminder was an act of love and grace from God towards them. This is because he is God: All loving, all powerful, all merciful, all gracious, all compassionate. Reminding his creatures that he is God was to remind them that he is the very essence of all that is good and beautiful and perfect. It wasn't a rule designed to *constrain* their freedom but to teach them that the exercise of their freedom is derived from God who created them and shared his very image with them. The rule ensured that they would be able to *enjoy* God. God's restriction flowed from the sheer magnitude of his infinite love. This means that the test of the tree didn't pit Adam's freedom against God's authority; it placed Adam's free exercise of his delegated authority alongside, and as an expression of, God's merciful love. So long as Adam remembered God's generous benevolence and honored this singular command, Adam would continue to have the freedom to operate as God's regent. This was the purpose of Adam's "working and keeping" the garden. Adam was a priest to serve God. Adam was not a usurper but a worshipper. Being reminded of his dignity and his position was an act of *grace* because of *who* God is: He was Adam's covenant Lord.

Was the tree "fair," therefore? Absolutely. It was God's rule for his regents and tenants to observe whilst in his garden. It was to remind Adam that God was God and Adam was working and keeping the garden as a sanctuary of and for God. It served to teach Adam and the entirety of the created realm that God was the sovereign Lord who reigned over all things. Even Adam, the image-bearer, was not God but was to be submissive towards God.

Adam and Eve, therefore, had the rule impressed upon them; Adam by God, Eve by Adam. So long as they obeyed, things would remain idyllic. The garden would flourish as they tended it. Creation would thrive under their regency. They themselves would procreate and grow in number so that the sanctuary of Eden itself would expand across the globe until, eventually, the entire realm was under the joyous and beautiful reign of God, mediated through his beloved image bearers. This was their purpose and plan and future. However, lest they be confused as to the *weight* of God's seriousness, the rule came with a warning.

You Shall Surely Die

God's warning was stark: "In the day that you eat the tree, you shall surely die." That is the definition of "*do not* take and eat." The idea of death in this context, however, has perplexed theologians for a very long time. In the book of Romans, Paul reminds us that "the wages of sin is death" (Romans 6:23). If we apply what Paul is saying here, that *death* is a *consequence* of *sin*, then to what extend did Adam, and then Eve, *understand* the idea of death? The implication is that, prior to sin entering the world, Adam and Eve weren't compromised by sin and therefore weren't going to die. Rather, because they were by nature made to be holy and reside in the presence of God, they would continue to dwell with God forever as his image bearers, made in his likeness. As with their understanding of obedience, to what level can Adam or Eve be said to *grasp* the conception of death?

There are a number of ways that "death" has been understood in light of their lack of knowledge. Some suggest that if Adam and Eve eat of the tree of the knowledge of good and evil, they would die immediately. That can appear to be the immediate and simplest interpretation of the command. God says that they shall die "*in the day they eat of it.*" Other interpretations suggest that if they eat of the tree, from that moment they will *begin* to die. This is an attractive interpretation because sin corrupts and destroys, and death is the *ultimate* consequence. It simply wouldn't be an immediate cessation of life.

A third interpretation says that the punishment would be that they would experience the *death of their innocence*. In this view, to eat from the tree would quite literally give them the knowledge of *evil*, and, in contrast, the *good* that they had once *only* known would be tarnished by this new knowledge of evil *and their participation* in it. This view is perhaps slightly more conceptual, but the idea isn't necessarily wrong. It does, however, lack the full thrust of the weight of the warning. If this idea is present in God's warning of "death," it's unlikely to be the main thrust.

A fourth way to understand the warning is to say that, at the moment the fruit was consumed, they would die *spiritually*. This means they would be living apart from God spiritually and would be under judgement rather than grace. This view is currently very popular because it seems to both allow for the natural reading whilst also allowing for the actual physical punishment of death to be postponed until the corruption of the flesh worked towards the natural conclusion.

A fifth interpretation has been given that dovetails with an early church view on sin itself. In this view, if Adam and Eve break the rule, they will start to die, and they will understand evil, and they will experience evil, but all of that is in direct correlation to their *lost relationship* with the Lord who gave, and gives, life. What this means is that, should Adam and Eve eat from the forbidden tree, they would immediately transition from being under the protection of God (who *is* life) to being under a curse of death. This movement from life to death is more than merely a spiritual death. It contains that element, but it highlights the deeper reality that their sin is more than having their nature transformed from holiness to sinfulness, but it is to literally reside in the darkness: It is leaving the palace to live in the dungeon. To eat of the tree is not merely disobedience, it is to choose to worship death rather than life. Consequently, this view suggests that Adam would be rejecting God and therefore life itself. His death would be immediate in that to eat of the tree would terminate his covenantal relationship with God and all the blessing that it brings, such as eternal life as God's regent, access to God, the ability to worship God appropriately, and harmony with creation.

My own view is that the fifth is the strongest interpretation that helpfully explores the full impact of what the idea of "death" in this curse implies. The weight of the punishment is such that *everything* Adam knows and has experienced to this point, from his communion with God, to his perfect relationship with Eve, to his pleasant interactions with the animal kingdom, to his own bodily health and immortality, would be corrupted and lost. Nothing would be the same ever again.

Yes, he would begin to die immediately, and would also actually die when his flesh is old and wearied, but it is so much more than merely the expiration of life. Yes, he would certainly lose his innocence because he would experience the knowledge of evil in all its fullness and horror, but it is more than a mere awareness of, and revulsion towards, corruption. Yes, he would die spiritually, but it is so much deeper than simply that. Yes, his nature would be corrupted, and he would in fact become enslaved to sin, but it is so much worse than that because the emphasis shouldn't primarily concern what he would *gain* (sin and death and slavery) but what he would *lose* (God's presence and God's favor).

If we have a correct view of God, as the early church fathers tried to demonstrate, then we must come to the conclusion that the worst thing that could possibly come from eating the forbidden fruit would be that Adam would leave the garden of life, turn from the very source of life, and instead live in a wilderness surrounded by death before he, himself, would eventually surrender to death. God is the owner and the creator, but he is also the source of life, love, grace, mercy, righteousness, holiness, justice, and goodness. Choosing to reject God would quite literally be the definition of suicide by treason.

Such was the warning that surrounds the rule in the garden. But lest we think Adam and Eve were living in a kind of prison paradise, remember that this was the *only* rule that as tied to such a severe punishment; the only way they would experience the consequence was if they decided that the perfection of Eden wasn't what they wanted. Eden wasn't a prison; it was paradise where they resided without sin and death and had a perfect and intimate relationship with God as his image bearers.

Application

This point about Adam's dependency is something that is reflected in the visible image of the invisible God, Jesus of Nazareth. In the Lord's Prayer, Jesus teaches his disciples, and thence every subsequent disciple, how to pray. For an agrarian culture like the majority of the ancient world, Jesus' prayer that God "give us this day our daily bread" made sense. For many, perhaps even most, this request would be a common refrain. Many laborers were paid daily. Their wages would barely be enough to feed their family, never mind the necessity of rendering to Caesar that which was Caesar's, paying the requisite temple taxes, and the other basic essentials of life.

Jesus' prayer, then, echoes something of Adam's condition in the garden. The situation of mankind had most certainly changed by 1st Century Roman Palestine, yet the fundamental reality for each and every human being is that we remain at the absolute mercy of God's benevolent provision. Adam was to rely upon God's sustaining of creation and to cultivate it so that he, his wife, and all under his charge could eat.

This sense of dependence on God's provision is something that appears to be lost in the modern Western world. The profligacy of our food waste, for example, betrays how divorced we have come from the sewing, reaping, and preparing of our food. According to the EPA, Americans discarded approximately 66 million tons of food in 2019.[3] This figure has risen steadily from 1960 and, unless trends dramatically change, appears likely to continue to do so. According to RTS, in 2023, each individual in the United States wasted approximately 325 pounds of food per year, despite the fact that almost 35 million people in the country suffer from food insecurity.[4] Shockingly, the amount of food *wasted* in the United States each year is roughly the equivalent of 130

---

3   EPA.gov, https://www.epa.gov/facts-and-figures-about-materials-waste-and-recycling/food-material-specific-data, accessed January 10th, 2024.
4   RTS.com, https://www.rts.com/resources/guides/food-waste-america/, accessed January 10th, 2024.

billion meals. To almost any other generation that has ever lived, such recklessness would be unthinkable. It's the result of decades of accessibility without risk.

Placing our current surplus of food in the Western world in juxtaposition with the Lord's Prayer almost feels like cognitive dissonance. They're so far apart that it can be very difficult to truly appreciate the difference between *need* and *want*. Is it, then, the case that the idea of 'daily bread' no longer applies to those of us who are fortunate enough to live in such luxury and excess?

I would argue the reverse is the case. As is so often true during plentiful seasons, we can end up forgetting the fact of our humanness and dependency because of a sense of self-sufficiency. This was often Israel's problem during the period of the judges: They would have plenty, they would become distracted by pagan gods, and then they would suffer the consequences for breaking the covenant. It wasn't during the years of plenty that Israel was devoted to her worship; it was the lean years that reminded them of their need for their God. We're not so different from the Israelites. Remember when the apocalypse of COVID-19 arrived? The fear of shortages hit almost every country and we collectively decided the most important thing that we couldn't live without was toilet paper! When the reality of our dependency on supply chains and global trading networks really hit us, we freaked out and panicked.

This is the purpose of the petition in the Lord's Prayer to "give us this day our daily bread." It's an opportunity to remember that we're always completely dependent on God for his provision for even our most basic needs. In the busyness and distractions of our world, we need to be proactive in constantly remembering our dependence on God for all our needs. God provided all the food necessary for Adam and Eve and the animal kingdom and He can meet our needs. Indeed, considering the food statistics above, God's provision continues today. This is true not only in the amount of food produced, but the general wealth we enjoy. There's a reason why Elon Musk was approached to spend $6 billion of his vast wealth to help end world hunger: The issue isn't that there isn't enough food on the planet; it's that so much of the harvest is hoarded and subsequently wasted. God's abundant provision for our daily needs continues and we are encouraged to remember that and praise him for it.

Considering Genesis 1 and 2, therefore, it seems that the implication in the garden is satisfaction rather than greed. In other words, Adam and Eve had all that they needed. Consequently, they were satisfied with what they had. They weren't to be gluttonous or exploitative. Creation was not their personal shop to abuse though selfish overindulgence. The language we keep coming back to is the idea of "cultivation" rather than "domination." Adam and Eve had a duty to care for creation. The consequent implications of this in our own era are vast and go far beyond the prior discussion of wasting food. From the ethics of farming to the rotation of crops and the processing of our foodstuffs, we must acknowledge that our regency over creation means that we must create food chains that avoid cruelty, violence, and unnecessary suffering. Whilst, as we shall see, we aren't called to be vegan, we are, nevertheless, expected to continue to exercise a Godly authority over creation. This means that we are to reflect the God in whose image we are made. Whether it be over the animals we like (domestic pets) or the animals we don't (spiders and snakes, anyone?), we have a duty and an obligation towards them. This obligation is grounded in the fact that we're regents of God and, as he displayed mercy and grace to us, we're to likewise exhibit those characteristics to the animal kingdom. It's a privilege to show compassion and thus to reflect God. Just consider, for example, the final few verses in the book of Jonah. God mentions the cattle as a rather unusual postscript to the reason why he doesn't want to destroy Nineveh. He cares about all of creation. And we have a delegated authority from our compassionate God to exercise our authority over creation with similar compassion. Indeed, as Christians, entrusted with the true knowledge of the character of God through both divine revelation and the Spirit's indwelling presence, ought we not to be the *drivers* of such ethical considerations? Is it not incumbent upon us to have consideration for the mistreatment of animals in our food chain? Whilst it may be hidden from our eyes, we are not naïve enough to claim that we are unaware of the forced feeding and intentional cross-breeding of animals that does so much harm to them.

Conclusion

In Genesis 1 and 2, God made humanity in his image and likeness to be his regent over creation, exercising a delegated authority over the created order to ensure that each animal knew its place and had what it needed to survive. God had, in the garden, promised to provide sufficient food for all of creation, and Adam and Eve were told to enjoy it and "take and eat" of his bountiful supplies so that they would have the energy and ability to fulfil their work and tasks in the garden. No matter where they went, there were plants and trees with sufficient nutritiousness for their daily needs. God's provision was more than enough: It was plentiful. And it was varied so that there would be different tastes, textures, and concoctions to delight the tastebuds and entice the senses. Eden was more than a sinless paradise; it was to be a *chef's* paradise. And God, as a smiling, doting, compassionate father, looking down at the creation he deemed "very good" said to Adam and Eve, "take and eat."

Adam, then, had been given a rule for his residence in the heart of paradise. We aren't told how long this testing would last, but it seems likely that the tree wouldn't be there forever. Rather, having demonstrated his loyalty, the probationary period would end, and Adam would reside in paradise forever. The fullness of the promise and potential for eternity would be unconstrained. They, as regents, priests, and prophets, would live in perfect communion and harmony with creation as the natural realm would glow in the righteousness of perfection and holiness. They would remain as covenantal heads over an expanding humanity, spreading the image and likeness of God across the world until, finally, the entire globe would be a single, glorious, planet of praise to the

Lord. But if they were to enjoy such a future, they would have to pass the test. They would have to obey the rule.

This is the image we're left with by the end of Genesis 2. God had created a perfect universe and placed a creature in the very heart of it that bore his image and likeness. This creature had almost universal freedom in the heart of God's material and earthly sanctuary. God had provided for his every need. Adam could eat from almost all the trees and vegetation in the garden giving him a limitless supply of nutrition, diverse tastes, and flavors. Adam had a mate and helper specially crafted by God just for him. They'd been given authority directly from God and a mandate to govern in his stead as his regents. He loved them, talked with them, and enjoyed them. God and his creatures were in communion and in covenantal relationship together. The picture is one of abundance, peace, perfection, and tranquility. This is as good as it could ever be.

All they were expected to do was to observe the single rule, and paradise was theirs for eternity.

3

"Take and Eat": Be Like God

But the serpent said to the woman, "You will not surely die. For God knows that when you eat of it your eyes will be opened, and you will be like God, knowing good and evil." So when the woman saw that the tree was good for food, and that it was a delight to the eyes, and that the tree was to be desired to make one wise, she took of its fruit and ate, and she also gave some to her husband who was with her, and he ate. (Genesis 3:4-6)

Introduction

I love pistachios. The salted ones are the perfect blend of crunch and saltiness. In what can only be described as an herculean achievement for humanity, you can even go to a store and buy a gigantic pack of pistachios that have already been shelled for you. What a wonderful world we live in. However, if you've ever purchased nuts, you'll know that occasionally you get one that isn't ripe. I've had a couple of instances where, in expectant ecstasy, I open my mouth and pop a pistachio in, only to crunch down and my mouth contorts in horror as bitterness spreads throughout my taste buds. It's all I can do to not spit them out. No doubt you've had those experiences also. Perhaps you go to the fridge, grab the milk, open the top, and take a chug. You don't bother getting a glass, because who drinks milk from a glass in real life, am I right? But as you chug, your taste buds revolt, because the milk's gone off! I'm sure you can think of numerous things that are comparable to those examples: Moments where the packaging looked so beautifully attractive and desirable but when you experience it, you find that the promises were a lie! There's a severe disappointment in that moment, isn't there? You *were confident* it would turn out right, but the promise was too good to be true.

Of course, these are silly, small examples. But this experience is something that we're all too familiar with, isn't it? Perhaps we've placed all our hopes in finding a spouse only to realize that they aren't perfect. We've often heard that the "grass is greener on the other side" of many a fence. Such a sentiment has led men to leave their families and cause untold pain to so many others. But it's okay, they say, because *now* they are happy. When we step away from the carefully crafted lies and portrayals on Instagram and TikTok, we realize that, for many of us, our lives are filled with idols that fail to deliver, lusts that fail to satisfy, and desires that fail to materialize. We're all intimately aware of the *disappointment* left by failed desires.

There is no greater example of this level of disappointment than Genesis 3. In Eden, Adam and Eve, who were living in the perfect paradise of Eden, became dissatisfied with who they were and what they had. And they desired something for which they weren't created. It looked so promising. It looked so inviting. It looked so delicious. And they were invited to "take and eat."

Genesis 3 opens with Adam and Eve in Paradise. God had created everything and declared that it was good. But not *all* was good. For, outside the realm of Eden and earth, a cosmic rebellion had already taken place. And from that rebellion would come the shattering of the peace and tranquility of Eden. This is the history of sin. Of death. Of man. Of paradise lost.

The Serpent's Arrival

We return to the beautiful garden of Eden to see Adam and Eve going about their business and their work. Suddenly, the idyllic and tranquil music of the Shire changed into the minor tones of danger and threat. The camera pans away from the holy couple towards a serpent. We aren't told the form of the serpent, but it seems that he appeared different to what we think of when we see a serpent today. Because many of us know the next act, we immediately jump into the narrative with our contextual conceptions of the serpent and the sense of *inevitability* with which we often approach this passage.

The serpent, we're told, was more cunning than the other beasts of the field. This word "cunning" has, in our parlance, a negative connotation. We tend to think of a cunning person as being intentionally duplicitous and manipulative. The word in this context can appear that way, also, but that isn't what is conveyed. The serpent would be known as clever and perhaps even coy, but Eve wouldn't have naturally been suspicious of the serpent. After all, Eden was a realm without sin or deception. Thus, when the serpent arrived in front of Eve, her reaction was likely to have been no different than any other animal.

He spoke to the woman. That sentence is rather amazing to contemplate. The serpent *spoke* to Eve. She understood him. Again, the text is frustratingly devoid of the details we'd love to discuss and think about. What did he sound like? Was Eve surprised? Did all the animal kingdom speak in such a way that Adam and Eve could understand them? If not, what on earth was Eve's reaction to the serpent? If so, then how did things change and when? Moses deemed those questions not important enough to answer because these questions aren't the point of the passage.

The Serpent's Query

The serpent arrived, and asked Eve: "Did God really say, 'You shall not eat of any tree of the garden'?" At face value this question, when read in isolation, appeared innocuous. As representatives of God's rule, Adam and Eve were his regents. It was possible that there had been misunderstanding between Adam or Eve and the serpent, and thus the question *could* be framed as merely one seeking clarification. In reality, the question had a different tenor to it. This was the first time that doubt entered the garden. The serpent's question was designed to introduce uncertainty. It was intentionally nefarious.

Why can we say this? Because the question *contains a misrepresentation*. Remember the command that God had given to Adam was *not* "You shall not eat of *any tree in the garden*," but that Adam could "take and eat" the fruit from *any* tree in the garden *except* the one that was in the midst of the garden. The rule God had given was noticeable for its generosity not its limitations. In contrast, the serpent's question sought to undermine Eve's understanding of the character of God. Rather than his benevolent, gracious, and generous provision, she was being manipulated to think of God as a malevolent and controlling tyrant. "Did God *really* say…" has the implication of surprise. It's like the serpent was actually asking "*Why* would God say such a thing as *that*?"

Eve's Response

Eve answered the serpent with what seemed like confidence and clarity. Her words echoed Adam's in many respects. She told this serpent that he was mistaken; God had said that they may eat from any tree in the garden except one. The fruit of that one tree was off limits to the regents. This was an answer that sounded good. However, the language had subtly shifted. Raymond Ortland notes this move: "God had actually said, "You shall *feely* eat from *any* tree, with only one exception." But Eve's misquote reduces the lavish generosity of God's word to the level of mere, perhaps grudging, permission: "We may eat from the trees." Already the garden doesn't look quite the same to Eve."[1] Indeed, Ortland astutely notes that the focal point of Eve's interest in the garden was not the Tree of Life, but the forbidden tree: "Now, in her perception of reality, the forbidden tree is at the center. Life is taking on a new, ominous feeling."[2] But then Eve continued:

---

1 Raymond C. Ortland Jr., "Male-Female Equality and Male Headship: Genesis 1-3," *Recovering Biblical Manhood and Womanhood* (Wheaton, IL: Crossway, 2006), p. 106.

2 Ortland, "Male-Female Equality and Male Headship," *Biblical Manhood and Womanhood*, p. 106.

"Neither shall you touch it, lest you die." This sentence explained that there *had* been miscommunication in the garden but *not* between the regents and the serpent; rather, the miscommunication was between Adam and Eve. But notice, too, that the warning from God, which had been given so directly to Adam, had also become somewhat muted. God's direct "in the day you eat of it you shall *surely* die" had become merely "lest you die." The confidence of the "surely" was reduced to something significantly less certain: "lest."[3]

It's like how the game of Telephone deteriorates. The message is given at the start of the chain, whispered from person to person, and by the time it gets to the last person, it has morphed, developed, and changed, ideally into something hilarious and bizarre. In Telephone, the more surreal the message is at the end the better. Sometimes things have been added or subtracted; other times the message has been lost in translation. In Eden, the message from God had changed by addition: Adam, it seems, had endeavored to *protect* Eve by adding his own rule to God's rule. God had clearly told Adam to refrain from eating from the single tree in the midst of the garden. But now it seems that Adam had added to this single rule by erecting a hedge around it. He told Eve that they couldn't even *touch* the tree. Adam's task in the garden, as a prophet who proclaimed God's words, was to ensure that God's message was correctly and *accurately* relayed to everyone so that they could be obedient. In this regard, Adam failed before Eve fell.

Eve knew that the fruit from this tree was not to be eaten. But she'd also been told that she couldn't touch it. What's critical to understand, however, is that it appears that Adam had told Eve that *God* had said they couldn't touch the tree. Often, we're guilty of similar behavior. Too often we try to build up hedges to keep us from getting close to sinning. Those hedges aren't always bad or unhelpful. In fact, many times, they can be helpful and useful *because* they keep us from moving towards sinful desires and

---

[3] Ortland, "Male-Female Equality and Male Headship," *Biblical Manhood and Womanhood*, p. 106

activities. The problem comes when we make our "house rules" equivalent to "God rules." When "house rules" are conflated with "God's rules," they cause misunderstandings about what God has *actually* said and what he *actually* wants us to do.

In this case, Adam's attempts to protect Eve served to weaken her. She was already at a disadvantage because her rebuttal of the serpent was predicated on inaccurate information. The serpent could challenge what God has said because her knowledge of God's rule was inaccurate. Her response was good in that she attempted to correct the serpent. Unfortunately for Eve, her efforts were compromised by the misrepresentation. Thus, the serpent's calling God's character into doubt appeared a little more credible. After all, the question *now* implied God is unkind. Why *can't* we touch the tree? To say that death is the consequence merely for *touching* a tree? The insidiousness of the query gave way to something even more dangerous: In the heart of Eden, God's sanctuary on earth, the serpent challenged God.

The Serpent's Promise

Eve's conversation with the serpent deteriorated from the start. The serpent continued with a harrowing statement. In the heart of the garden of paradise, the serpent directly attacked the authority and reign of God. What is often lost in this moment is the fact that, up until this point, however long Adam and Eve had resided in the garden, there had never been any challenge to God's authority, his word, nor his reign. The garden was perfect and peaceful. There was no challenge to his rule because there was no sin; likewise, there was no sin because Adam and Eve couldn't, to this point, *conceive* of so heinous a reality as to reject the benevolent, personal, and covenantal rule of God. Much is rightly made of the *lie* that the serpent presents. But it's essential to the narrative that we remember that Adam and Eve simply had no conception or experience of sin. This was, quite literally, an epochal, era-defining, moment of cosmic proportions and eternal consequences. In the very heart of the realm of heaven-on-earth, Satan was bringing rebellion against the rule of the Lord God. He told Eve, "You will not surely die. For God knows that when you eat of it your eyes will be opened, and you will be like God, knowing good and evil." Satan was calling God a liar in his own garden.

The first statement was the opening salvo in this four-part assault on the realm of God's rule and his regents. The serpent said to Eve: "You will not surely die." This was in direct contradiction to her repetition of God's clear warning. The serpent's prior query brought doubt. But the lie brought confusion. The serpent was calling God a liar and by doing so was both inviting Eve to agree with that assessment and inciting her to join his rebellion. God's warning was given as a means of protecting Adam and Eve by highlighting the importance of obedience to the creator. The serpent's lie introduced the idea that God was not worthy of obedience because he was, fundamentally, not worthy of her respect. The serpent not only denounced God's truthfulness but opened a path for Eve to switch her allegiance. Rebellion was brewing.

The second attack was found in the statement "when you eat of it your eyes will be opened." The language of "seeing" is visible throughout scripture as a means of delineating between spiritual awareness and spiritual blindness. That motif began here; the serpent was bluntly telling Eve that God had *not* given her eyes to see the *real* truth clearly. Thus, she was being made to believe that she was *currently* blind and that it was the serpent, not God, who could provide true perception.

The serpent's lie was rooted in a promise of deeper knowledge that only he could give to Eve. From offering her a pathway to a different empire, he was now encouraging her to seek knowledge, by which we can infer, *truth*, from another source apart from God. The knowledge that he was going to provide was grounded in a blatant rejection of God's character. By contradicting the words of God in the first statement, he now told Eve that not only would she *not* die; rather, she would be greater than she currently was. The serpent was promising her that the fruit would give her a different experience of, and vantage point for, life. If only she could see clearly, the serpent was saying, you could be *like* God in a different way – a way that elevated her to the position *of* God: Adjudicating good from evil.

Satan's third weapon was the promise that "you will be like God, knowing good and evil." This was perhaps the most perplexing of the statements from Eve's perspective because she and Adam *were already made in the image of God and in his likeness*. He created them to be image bearers that reflect his sovereignty through their mediated kingship and sonship. The serpent's lie was not merely an attack on God and God's character; it was also an attack on humanity's very essence as image bearers. By inviting Eve to participate in the rebellion, the serpent was duping her into thinking that there was *more* to being an image of God than what she already was. Just as the serpent was tricking her into *corrupting* the image of God in her nature, he was also enchanting her into slavery to a cruel and murderous captor.

Knowing good and evil has been interpreted in different ways. What the serpent sought to do, was to distract from the act of eating the fruit as an act of disobedience to God; rather, it was being packaged as revelation and even elevation. By treating the fruit as if it was a magic elixir, the serpent was implying that Eve would be able to both comprehend good from evil but also *be a judge like God*.[4] The attractive offer was to go beyond *bearing* God's image to *being* god herself. Knowing right from wrong, in this context, is tantamount to *determining* what was good and evil. Such power requires not only the omniscience of all things but also the holiness to gauge all things. Eve had neither of those attributes because she was a creature rather than the creator. The serpent was offering her promotion to the position of deity despite the fact that she was neither suited nor capable of even contemplating what that

---

4   Gentry and Wellum, *Kingdom through Covenant*, p. 217. Cf., W. M. Clark, "A Legal Background to Yahweh's Use of 'Good and Evil' in Genesis 2-3," Journal of Biblical Literature 88 (1969): 266-278; H. Blocher, *In the Beginning* (Downers Grove, IL: InterVaristy Press, 1984), p. 126-133.

would look like. Importantly, this was a position that the serpent is unable to provide.

This third attack was therefore one that encompassed God's character as well as God's creation. The serpent was aiming to drive a wedge between how God created Eve and how Eve saw herself. The image of God with which she was created was now being made to seem insufficient and unsatisfactory. The serpent was surreptitiously promising her that there could be more to her than meets the eye and the reason she had not yet attained that lofty grandeur was the very God who has supposedly blinded her to her own potential greatness.

The final piece of Satan's tactical attack was found in the phrase "for God knows." This implied that God had intentionally kept the truth, or at the very least the fullness of the truth, from her. Satan didn't explicitly say why this might be. In fact, it was better for him that he didn't; the suggestion was enough. Everyone could interpret motivation on their own. Eve was being encouraged to doubt God's motivations and therefore to believe that God couldn't be trusted to have her best interests at heart.

There was a craftiness to the serpent's ploy. The promise that Satan made to Eve in this barrage of deceitfulness was potent because there *was* a kernel of graspable truth in it. If Eve *did* eat the fruit, then she *would* see things differently; the eyes of her heart and mind and soul *would* be opened, just not in the way she was encouraged to expect. Rather than evolving and rising to godhood, sin would condemn her to being enslaved by the devil. Her experience of the world would change because she would be exiled from the father of light and life into the domain of darkness, of death, of damnation. As with all of Satan's promises, the gild of the promise soon tarnished to reveal not gold but a deceptively cheap knockoff.

The fascinating thing about this false promise of Satan is that it not only reveals his cunning duplicity and his methodology, but it also exposes the desires of *his* heart. Isaiah 14:12-14 gives us an insight into the hidden mindset that resides behind the father of lies. In those verses the prophet Isaiah shows us the innermost thoughts, not of *Eve*, but of the *serpent*: "I will ascend to heaven; above the stars of God I will set my throne on high; I will sit on the mount of assembly in the far reaches of the north; I will ascend above the heights of the clouds; I will make myself like the Most High." Satan's ploy goes deeper than simply tempting Eve; his offensive in Eden was nothing less than an expansion of his cosmic efforts to dethrone God. By entering God's garden and tempting God's image bearers, Satan was trying to deface and discredit God himself: An attack on the regent is an attack on God. But Satan could only *use* that which he *knew*; he tempted Eve with the very desire that captured *him*. The heart attitude of wanting to be like God means, by definition, God must be taken off his throne. If I am to be God, or if Eve is to be God, or if the serpent is to be God, then God himself can no longer be God. He must be replaced by a coup: A sinful heart is a god-killer.

It's this attitude that John labels the "spirit of antichrist": "By this you know the Spirit of God: Every spirit that confesses that Jesus Christ has come in the flesh is from God, and every spirit that does not confess Jesus is not from God. This is the spirit of the antichrist, which you heard was coming and now is in the world already" (1 John 4:2-3). To deny Christ is to dethrone Christ. Satan's rebellion has consistently followed this pattern. He hasn't changed. Unrepentant humanity continues to be the seed of the serpent (Matt. 13:38-39) and is used by him to choke the life out of the sons of the kingdom. All of humanity is a pawn in his dastardly game; the sons of the kingdom are just like Adam and Eve: Enemy combatants to be destroyed because they're image bearers of the real enemy. But the sons of the serpent are not important to him. He isn't their *god* as if he has some benevolent compassion and concern for them. No, they're simply useful tools to further enhance his own efforts at becoming god. They're not, however, collateral damage. They're willingly and willfully participating with him in the rebellion, despite the fact they will be cast aside as soon as their use expires.

But this fundamentally betrays a significant revelation about the nature of the serpent and his conflict. By the very fact that Satan *aspires to be God*, he is showing that *he is not God*. For all his posturing and strategic battlefield deceits, the serpent reveals himself as little more than another created being. Yes, it's true, he's demonstrating a cunning nature that can trick God's regents; but he's fundamentally *not* God's equal. Although the serpent may be more powerful than Eve, his grasping for the throne is just as ludicrous as Eve's because in the face of an infinite, all powerful, transcendent God, Satan is still a finite and leashed dragon. Certainly, he has the power to deceive the nations and to torment individuals. But on the cosmic level, the very fact he's trying to supplant God is a reminder that he himself is not God: He's an imposter, a deceiver, a wanna-be.

At this point in the narrative, the serpent had shown his intentions. He had contested God's reign in the garden by attacking his nature, undermining his character, and denouncing his grace. With bated breath, creation looked to Eve and anticipated her response. The serpent had engaged in character assassination. Will the regent defend God and expel the traitor?

"Take and Eat": Eve's Failure

Eve had a decision to make. The image that burns in the mind at this moment is that the serpent was gesturing towards the fruit. Like a sleazy salesman, he was slowly pushing Eve towards it. The invitation had been made: "Take and eat." Eve had been duped into doubting God. She had been deceived into distrusting God. She had been distracted from the task of exercising dominion over creation for God. And now she was being directed towards the single act that would demonstrate a conscious disrespect towards the sovereignty and authority of God in his own garden.

As the serpent was tormenting Eve's perception of reality and warping all that she had known with his lies, her eyes travelled towards the tree and settled on a single sumptuous fruit. She saw that the tree was healthy. Its branches were weighed down with their fulsome fruit. Her eyes were telling her that the fruit was healthy, ripe, and ready for picking. In the light of the sun, the fruit almost appeared to be dancing as the gentle wind rustled through the leaves. It *looked* delicious. Eve's eyes were the windows from which the heart of temptation was giving way to the action of sin: "Take and eat and be like God," she heard.

Her mind was ablaze with the promises that she'd received moments ago; merely eating a single fruit from this tree would make her wise beyond her imagination. She reached out her hand. Grabbing the fruit, she twisted it briefly and it fell into her hand. "Take and eat" reverberated in her mind. It might not have been audibly spoken, but the command, the temptation, was deafening. Transfixed, she raised it to her mouth and bit into it. The initial tanginess of the flesh and its juices tantalized her tastebuds.

And with that act, Eve had switched allegiances. From being a regent of God in the garden of God, this image bearer was now a servant of the serpent. And true to form, she looked across to her partner and fellow regent, Adam. She reached out her hand towards him and bade him "take and eat." Just as the serpent had deceived Eve, we now see that Adam was bewitched by the rebellion also.[5] Giving in to the same desires that had bested Eve, Adam took the fruit and ate. And Adam, too, betrayed God.

"Take and Eat": Adam's Failure

Whilst it is true that Eve was the one who engaged the serpent in conversation and was, subsequently, the first to eat the forbidden fruit, verse 6 gives us a vital clue about the larger setting.

---

5 Paul reminds us in 1 Timothy 2:14 that Eve was deceived by the serpent, but Adam was not deceived. Rather, having watched Eve eat and not die, and having likewise heard the poisonous promises of the serpent, Adam's sinful action of eating the fruit was deliberate, intentional, and conscious. He ate the fruit *as an act of defiance* against God. He was bewitched with the promises of becoming God, but he was not deceived. He knew what he was doing. And, just as a king brings his subjects into war on his behalf, so Adam's declaration of war against God forced the creation under his stewardship into the conflict with him.

Up until this point, the narrative has been retold as if Eve was alone. But we see at the end of verse 6 that Adam has been present. He'd listened to the serpent's query. He was there when Eve said the tree was forbidden even to be touched. He stood idly by as the serpent called God a liar, a tyrant, and a cruel master. Through it all, Adam remained silent. Not only that, but it becomes clear that Adam was just as hypnotized by the promises of the serpent as Eve. Instead of standing against the serpent, protecting Eve from an enemy and the garden from an intruder, Adam, like Eve, let the traitor lead him into treason: "Adam failed to rule, to have dominion over the Edenic kingdom, and to cast out the serpent as an intruder."[6] Eve's failure was dramatic, but Adam's was much worse. Indeed, it was his failure that left Eve as vulnerable as she was. Had Adam been obedient, he would have cast the enemy out. Instead, the addition to the command of God had left Eve vulnerable and, despite Adam's physical presence, Eve was spiritually isolated. Adam's silence condemned mankind to servitude in a different kingdom.

Now, instead of cultivating the garden as honored regents and spreading the image of God across the world as an expansion of worship, Adam and Eve would belong to a rival realm with competing goals and purposes. Rather than operating for the glory of the creator, they would find themselves running from him and in opposition to him. Their children, rather than serving alongside them into the eons of eternity, would understand the full weight of God's warning. And as the reality of Adam and Eve's treason hit them, their eyes rested on one another in horror. For the first time Adam noticed that Eve was covering herself from his gaze, her face contorted into a new expression. An uneasy and unusual feeling settled in the pit of their stomach: Guilt and shame.

---

6   Barrett, *Canon, Covenant and Christology: Rethinking Jesus and the Scriptures of Israel* (Downers Grove, IL: InterVaristy Press, 2020). P. 50.

Humanity's Shame

The immediate consequence that Adam and Eve experienced after their betrayal of God was that their eyes were opened. Although this is the same language as the serpent had used a few verses earlier, the sense is not *fulfilment* but *fear*. Adam and Eve were not rejoicing at the opening of their eyes. Instead, they noticed that they were naked, and this caused shame. The surprise of their nakedness was humiliating to them because they saw one another in a different light. Their eyes *were* opened, but what they *saw* was not what the serpent had implied. Adam and Eve's newfound knowledge didn't turn them into gods but rather revealed just how weak they really were. Having been tricked by the serpent, their self-awareness has increased because they realize their regal fragility and physical weakness. As in numerous places in the Old Testament, nakedness conveys a lack of innocence and a loss of autonomy over one's own life (cf. Job 1:21; Isaiah 58:7). Their complete dependence on God was grasped through a new lens for the first time because they realized that their relationship with him had become severely disrupted. Now they awaited his presence to see what their treachery would cost them.

Ashamed

Naked and ashamed, they found fig leaves and stitched them together to make loincloths to cover themselves. For the first time in their existence, Adam and Eve began to hide. At this point, they hid their bodies from one another in a scene that was diametrically opposed to the climax of Genesis 1 and 2. Their nakedness in 2:25 was seen in a good light; not to glorify nudity, but to express innocence, a sense of equality in nature and stature, and the complete absence of abusive coercion. With their eyes opened by sinful experience, Adam and Eve started erecting barriers to one another. The sewed loincloths are also symbolic of the sowed distrust and division between them. No longer in perfect union and unity, they were already preparing themselves for division.

UnGodly Gods

The manifestation of the awareness of their nakedness revealed their newfound selfishness. They were indeed autonomous from one another in that they were now unwilling to share their complete being with the other person. Their marriage relationship would no longer be as "one flesh" but as two people living together in various degrees of competition for control. At the same time, they were not going to completely reject the other. They were in rebellion *together*, and so we can glimpse the birth of a new form of idolatry through their marriage. As their eyes were opened in a new manner, they found themselves attracted to, and drawn towards, new temptations. For Eve, she would have a desire for her husband while Adam's gaze would lose the purity of desire for the prurience of lust. The essence of their vulnerability and the gentle naivety of their once-innocent relationship was corrupted. Their eyes weren't merely opened; their perception of everything had changed. Like the serpent, they *wanted* to be like God. But, just like the serpent, their aspirations outstretched their ability. Instead, they would merely become little gods of little kingdoms at war with everyone else.

Guilty

Adam and Eve experienced shame in their nakedness. Their shame led to distrust between them, and the production of garments was evidence that they had lost their innocence. A deeper significance can also be seen in that this was their first experience of *guilt*. The consequences for their sin was to be death. In this moment, they experienced the first tremors of their spiritual death; they became in some way alienated from one another. It's noteworthy that their guilt is expressed in terms that strip away innocence; their awareness of their nakedness was an admission of their guilt. It's no surprise that their reaction to the feelings of shame and guilt was to try to cover it up. They couldn't make amends for it, so they simply tried to keep it from being visible.

Just as they hid their bodies from one another, they next tried to hide the cause of their shame. Then, hearing the arrival of God in the garden, they hid from him. And waited.

On the Dock

God came to the garden to spend time with his image bearers. This custom had been one of peaceful communion and perfect relationship between creator and creatures. This time was different. Adam and Eve were hiding in the forest of trees, avoiding the penetrating gaze of God. He called out to them asking where they were. Of course, God knew, but his question was a word of grace, inviting them to come into his presence. Having finally found his voice, Adam responded first. He didn't speak up against the serpent earlier, but he was forced to speak to his God now. He told God that he was aware of God's presence, and, because he was also aware of his own nakedness, he sought refuge *from* God by hiding. In his response, Adam admitted his guilt. He let God know that his eyes had been opened to the experience of sin and shame through the action of disobedience (the only way this could have happened). And thus, by hiding *from* God, Adam displays the pathetic nature of man's condition. He is afraid of the God who, moments before, he had so proudly sought to supplant.

However, Adam had been crafty in his response. He had *betrayed* his sinful action; but he had not *confessed* it, nor, indeed, repented of it. Adam was the first to demonstrate the paradigm of sinners in the aftermath of their actions: We run *from* God rather than *towards* him. Adam told God that he was naked. The source of his hiding was not in his disobedience, but in the *consequence* of the disobedience. Adam may be *acknowledging* that he had sinned, but he wasn't *confessing* his sin nor directly expressing remorse for it. It had not taken long for Adam's innocence to be ruined by his sin. His sense of shame at being naked was the excuse he made for his desire to avoid God. In reality, it was the fear of the consequence of his rebellion that terrified him.

God cannot be tricked. He was aware of all that had transpired. Adam's efforts at misinformation and distraction would not work on the sovereign Lord. God enquired from Adam how he came to see himself as naked? In other words, God was asking Adam how he had lost his innocence. "Have you," God enquired, "eaten of the tree of which I commanded you not to eat?" God zeroed in on the act of disobedience. The only way Adam would fear God was if the relationship between them was ruptured through the treasonous breaking of God's command. Their nakedness was not the *issue*, but a *consequence*. God wanted Adam to confess his sin whereas Adam sought to obfuscate.

Adam's response was brutal in its shamelessness and misdirection. Being directly questioned about the tree, he blamed everyone but himself. He blamed Eve because she gave him the fruit from the tree. And, in an even more telling statement, he blamed God for giving him the woman in the first place. It was *God's* fault for putting the temptress in the garden. It wasn't Adam's fault that he was led astray because God brought Eve into the garden. In the Genesis account, this is only the second time we hear Adam speak. He was no longer *praising* God for Eve but *blaming* God for her. Where once she was a blessing, a helper, and a partner for Adam now she had become a burden, a hindrance, and a curse to him. It was *her* fault that Adam sinned. Deeper still, Adam says that it is ultimately *God's* fault. Yes, he reluctantly admitted he had eaten the fruit, but it wasn't *his* fault.

Yet, in this vignette between Adam and God we can see something beautiful about God's character and nature. Despite knowing exactly what had happened, God nevertheless chose to come to the garden and seek out his treacherous image bearer. As the offended party, he could simply have consigned everything in creation to the trash can and started again. Instead, he came to Adam and offered him an opportunity to confess and repent. Adam, however, had been confused and manipulated by the serpent so that he no longer knew whom to trust. And so, instead of throwing himself on God's mercy and grace, he tried to save himself, thereby only further condemning himself. A major theme of scripture is man's incapability to resist the overwhelming urge of his sinful nature. Adam exhibited this in the garden. Refusing to trust God, he tried to outthink and outtalk God. But his efforts only further served to highlight his isolation from God (and, one imagines, Eve, who was just blamed for everything).

God next questioned Eve. You can picture Eve's withering look at Adam as God's voice booms into the trees. It hadn't taken long for sin to divide the couple and breach the intimacy of their relationship. God asked Eve what she had done. Again, the offer from God was to acknowledge her failure and throw herself at his feet in repentance and mercy. Instead, Eve showed herself to be a quick learner from her cowardly husband. Instead of owning up to her sin, she, too, cast blame elsewhere: The serpent. Like Adam, she reluctantly acknowledged that she did consume the fruit, but she says that she was deceived by the serpent. Her defense was different from Adam's in content, but not in nature. Her claim was that she wasn't to blame because she was deceived by the serpent. Had the serpent been *truthful*, she implied, she wouldn't have been disobedient. Perhaps this was a subtle jibe at Adam. After all, Adam had failed in his task of protecting the garden from intruders and the result was that Eve, his partner, had been deceived. It was the serpent's lie, and it was Adam's silence in the face of that lie, that let Eve be deceived. Perhaps, even further, it was Adam's failure to ensure the words of God's command had been relayed to her accurately. Touching the tree when she grabbed the fruit didn't lead to any significant changes, after all. So, if *touching* the tree didn't kill her, what reasonably could she have expected by eating its fruit?

Despite the wrangling over who was responsible, Adam and Eve were getting lost in the minutiae of the debate. From God's vantage point their situation was heartbreaking. They were dealing treacherously with one another just as they had been treacherous towards him. Their words in their denial of responsibility proved that they had truly become children of the serpent. Their very efforts to hide their sin by their words only served to illuminate the depth of sin's hold on them, even at this early stage. Their relationship with one another was now riven by division. Their position before God had changed because their allegiance is now to the father of lies. By accusing each other, they unwittingly supplied evidence in this impromptu trial that they were guilty of more than merely eating the fruit; they were full-fledged citizens in the kingdom of darkness.

Interestingly, God doesn't question Satan. This provides further evidence that earth has simply become a new battleground for Satan's larger rebellion. Satan is already adjudged guilty of treason and is therefore not going to receive any mercy or grace; he will be judged at the appropriate time. God will reveal the mechanism by which this judgement will come in the very act of cursing the serpent.

Turning from lawyer to judge, God hands down the pronouncements of guilt in three distinct condemnations. As we move through these judgements, notice that there is both a physical and a spiritual aspect to each punishment. First, God turns to the serpent and curses him. Notice, also, that the serpent's desire is to be God yet he, too, stands silent in the face of the Almighty. For all his pretentions to grandiosity, Satan is little more than another creature facing judgement.

The Serpent's Curse

The first punishment was given to the serpent. It appears confusing because it contains two parts; one to the physical animal, the serpent, and the other to Satan who was the mind behind the mouthpiece. The Lord cursed the serpent specifically, which removes the serpent from the blessing given to all livestock in 1:21. It also seems to suggest that the serpent would lose its dignity within the animal kingdom because it, alone of all the beasts of the field, directly bears the curse of God. Whatever form it may have once taken, it would now spend its entire existence crawling on its belly, in perpetual humiliation. Like a captive brought into the presence of a conqueror or a king, the serpent would be constantly reminded of its position as a defeated suppliant.[7] Fitting with this new posture, the serpent will continually slither over the rough dust of the earth. As it does so, God decreed "dust you will eat all the days of your life." The dust of the earth is another portrait of the decline in its position; the serpent is humiliated by becoming the lowest of the beasts of the field in a literal and metaphorical sense.

Things would get worse for the serpent. In Genesis 3:15 we have the *protoevangelium*, or the first piece of the "good news," which has come to be known as the gospel. God told the serpent, although ultimately speaking to Satan, that he "will put enmity between you and the woman, and between your offspring and her offspring; he shall bruise your head, and you shall bruise his heel." With this curse, God highlighted not only condemnation, but also grace (not, however, for the serpent). There will be enmity between the serpent and the woman, and between their respective offspring. This is of incredible importance because Adam and Eve have just committed treason. And yet, despite their failure, God promised that there would be mercy shown from the divine judge because there would be offspring from the woman who would be faithful to God. What this looks like is shrouded in mystery, but it's the first mention of the promised *serpent crusher*. This promised offspring from Eve will bruise the head of the serpent, even though the serpent will strike at his heel. There will be traded blows, but the war will be won by Eve's offspring.

---

7   This is an enforced *proskynesis*. The idea carries a deeper connotation than simply "bowing" as a sign of respect; it suggests that the one bowing was in a position of utter abasement in the presence of a powerful official. For the application of *proskynesis* in Persian culture, see Herodotus, *The Histories* (London: Penguin Books, 2003), translated Aubrey de Sélincourt, Book I. 134 and Xenophon, *The Persian Expedition* (London: Penguin Books, 1972), translated by Rex Warner, p. 150, especially the explanatory footnote in this edition: "The Macedonians found it absurd but the Greeks took it as a demand for divine honours." Xenophon, *Persian Expedition*, translated by Rex Warner, p. 151n3.

In this promise, given by God, we see that the line of humanity will not come to an end with the judgement of Adam and Eve. There is more than only the promise of a serpent crusher. This is the realization that there are now two lines within humanity: A line of faith and a line of rebellion. Jesus himself alludes to this in the parable of the weeds in Matthew 13 where he tells his disciples that the sons of the Son of Man reside in the same "field" as the sons of the serpent. These two lines will share the world for a season before the judgement. God will work through Adam and Eve's descendants, through the line of faith, until the time is right for the arrival of the serpent crusher. Throughout the rest of human history as covered by the texts of the Old Testament, the question is repeatedly asked: "Is *this* the one?" And, repeatedly, the disappointing answer is "no."

The Rebellion on Earth

There are three points concerning sin that this curse teaches.

God Hates Sin Because It Is Ultimately Against Him

Firstly, God hates sin because it is against him. Too often we confuse the *heart* of the sinful nature with the *action* of the sinful person. Both are evil. But the heart betrays the attitude of the individual. The heart, to use an illustration, betrays the *condition* of the person, whereas the *action* is merely a symptom. A *sinner* is someone whose nature and disposition before God is one of rebellion. They're traitors against the holiness and goodness and power of God. A sinful action, therefore, is merely how a *sinner* lives out their rebellion. Both are deserving of justice (without repentance), but one is evidence of the other. By assessing sinful behaviors and patterns, one can identify the loyalties of the person in question. What this means, practically, is that sin is much larger and more significant than simply the committing of certain illicit deeds. Sin is the outworkings of a nature and a will that is in direct opposition to God. And God hates sin because it's a rejection of his gracious and benevolent rule. To live in sin is to reside in the house of the enemy, the liar, the dragon, the defiler, and the bringer of death. To be a sinner without repentance is to be unashamedly in the domain of darkness. There's no neutrality in the cosmos; one is either at peace with God through the serpent crusher's victory as the suffering servant, or one is at war with God through willful and intentional rejection of his mercy. All of humanity can be broken into two categories: Sons of the servant or sons of the serpent.

God hates sin, therefore, because it is against him first and foremost. We see this in the life of David. After his shameless abuse of Bathsheba and his efforts at covering up his sin through the murder of her husband on the battlefield, David is confronted about his actions. In one of the most moving Psalms, David writes: "I know my transgressions, and my sin is ever before me. *Against you, you only, have I sinned* and done what is evil in your sight, so that you may be justified in your words and blameless in your judgement" (Psalm 51:3-4). At face value, this looks like quite the slap in the face to poor cuckolded and murdered Uriah. And whilst it is true that David has certainly abused his position, it is nevertheless true that his *actions* against *Uriah* are *evidence* of David's sinful position *before God*. David's statement in Psalm 51 is a reminder that the *ultimate* expression of sin is not simply in the *actions* but in the *nature*. David's nature overwhelmed his behavior and consequently he allowed himself to be held hostage to his lust, then his fear, then his ruthlessness. In all of those things, his heart was laid bare for God to see and grieve. This is why God's judgement is considered blameless in verse 4. As in Eden, God is the truly offended party, and therefore God is the one who speaks of justice and judgement. Because God is good and holy, his judgement is blameless. In the face of his sinful nature and his sinful actions, David (eventually) bent the knee and admitted his guilt. Like Adam, however, David's prior attempts to cover up his sin only added further evidence for the guilt of his sinful heart.

Sin, then, is something that is deeper than mere action. It's part of who we are. In fact, following the sin of Adam and Eve, sin has corrupted the *imago Dei* such that we are different than how we were created. Sin is a corruption of our nature, and it has deformed every facet of our being. This doesn't mean that we're each necessarily as wicked in our actions as we *could* be, for which we can all be thankful. But it does mean that, in our nature, we're utterly incapable of becoming right with God on our own efforts because even our best efforts are wholly corrupted by the impact and influence and infection of sin. Because no part of us is untouched by our sinful nature, we're unable to return to God. Just like Adam and David, we cannot earn our way to God because the very source of humanity is enslaved to sin. Our loyalty to sin is total, even if, sometimes, our actions don't outwardly look that way. We might say, to continue our medical analogy, that we can be riddled with the disease without always displaying symptoms. Thus, infected and corrupted, the warning of God in Eden has become manifest: Our souls are dead in sin. And, unless God provides the medicament of grace, each of us will eventually taste death in judgement.

God Wants To Destroy Sin

The second principle about sin that we can see from Genesis 3 is that God wants to destroy sin. Again, at face value, this is often presented as harsh and unkind. After all, isn't God a God of love? To which the answer is yes, God *is* a God of love, and *therefore* God desires the end of sin. Remember that sin is treason against God. But God is not an arbitrary king seeking to protect his throne from the courageous bravado of some 18th century revolutionaries. God is the very source of life, and light, and love, and purity, and holiness, and goodness. To stand in opposition to God is to opt to live in death, and darkness, and hatred, and impurity, and evil, and wickedness. As God is life, he truly understands the horror and evil of sin. This is most poignantly displayed in John 11:33 when Jesus saw the grief of Mary at the death of her brother, Lazarus. Jesus was "deeply moved" at her brokenness and grief. The actual word is better understood as "outraged" because of the consequences of sin. Anyone who has stood by the graveside of a loved one, or almost as painful, witnessed the heartbreak and sorrow of someone else's grief, knows the outrage towards sin and death that Jesus felt. Death is common, but it's not the way things were meant to be.

God seeks to destroy sin, therefore, because it's a virus that causes pain and death. As the God of life and love, his holiness demands the eradication of all that seeks to break and destroy his creation. If God did *not* want to destroy sin and evil then, by the very definition of his nature, he would not be God. Contrary to the current ideas that God's war against sin is cruel and outdated, the fact that God is unrelenting in his holiness is proof that God is love. If I were to walk my dogs one night and see that my neighbor's house is on fire and I refused to alert him to his danger, I would not merely be *negligent*; I'd be *culpable*. If I knew there was an accident just around the bend and I saw a car driving at reckless speed towards the pile up, but didn't try to stop the car? I'd be guilty. It's like this with God. He's the source of life. Sin is the disease of death. If God is *truly* holy, then his very nature seeks to destroy the thing that would destroy everything. For him to do anything otherwise would mean that God either isn't God or isn't good.

God's promise of a serpent crusher is his promise that he will vanquish sin. By making this promise in Genesis 3, God is simultaneously continuing to curse Satan and at the same time preparing Adam and Eve for grace in the midst of judgement. There is, even at the moment of punishment, when God is speaking as the ruler of the cosmos, a glimpse of his heart. We see the contrast between Satan, who is silent, weak, and condemned, and God, who is grieved, firm, and yet, despite having been wronged, offering grace. He wants to destroy sin because sin is the absolute antithesis of who he is. In his kindness, he also offers a way back for the image bearers. It may be difficult to see at this point, but the first seeds of redemption are sown.

God Will Destroy Evil

Just as God hates sin because of what it is, and just as God wants to destroy sin because it is apposite to him and his nature, he wants to destroy evil itself, which is personified by the serpent. He's the devil, the prince and the power of the air, the great deceiver, the leader of the rebellion against God, and the root of man's fallenness. But just as God hates sin because it's the evidence of our treason, God hates the figurehead of the rebellion. Just as God seeks to destroy sin because sin is the thing which corrupts creation, God wants to destroy the one who revels in sinful disobedience. Satan is a snarling lion, seeking whomever he may devour, and sin is personified in like manner (Genesis 4:7). The righteous and holy desire to destroy sin must be accompanied by the destruction of Satan. This destruction will be achieved at the end of time when every knee will bow before God and confess that Jesus Christ is Lord (Philippians 2:10-11), but his *defeat* will be achieved much earlier (Colossians 2:15).

In the heart of God's curse for the serpent he provides a promise of redemption. The coming serpent crusher, although suffering some kind of grievous blow, will nevertheless crush Satan. For Adam and Eve, however, they're guilty of following the silky-tongued sedition of the serpent. And God, the holy and sovereign ruler, must display his righteous judgement over his creation. Treason cannot remain in the garden. The gaze of the judge shifts from the serpent to the woman.

Woman's Punishment

Following the sinful pattern of the reversal of the created order, God then directed his attention to the woman. Unlike the serpent's punishment, Eve was not *cursed* by God for her sin. This as, in itself, a remarkable act of grace from God. Despite the fact she was punished, this was an indication that the woman (and, later, the man) may be eligible for some kind of redemption, whereas the serpent was beyond salvation. Like the serpent's, Eve's punishment was twofold.

Pain in Childbearing

In the first part of the punishment, God told Eve that he "will multiply her pain in childbearing; in pain you shall bring forth children." Note that *childbearing* was not the punishment; *pain* in childbearing was the punishment. The immediate impact of this penalty has been felt by woman throughout the ages through the deep, convulsive, and torturous trauma on the body during delivery. From the ancient world through to the development of modern medicine, the standard statistics suggest that as many as one in three births resulted in the death of the mother[8] whilst infant mortality has been estimated to be as high as twenty-five percent![9] The pain of childbirth is something that is truly unique

---

[8] "It has been estimated that as many as one out of every three medieval women died in their first childbirthing." Clifford R. Backman, *The Worlds of Medieval Europe* (New York, NY: Oxford University Press, 2015), Third Edition, pp. 475-476. The medical issues of the Middle Ages were not significantly different to those experienced in Antiquity, especially in Europe where Greek ideas continued to dominate. Cf. Woods, Robert. "Ancient and Early Modern Mortality: Experience and Understanding." *The Economic History Review* vol. 60, no. 2 (2007): 373-399. Accessed February 16, 2024. www.jstor.org/stable/4502068.

[9] In the period of ancient Greece, Waterfield suggests the following statistics: "Women gave birth, on average, to 4.3 children in the Classical period and 3.6 in the Hellenistic period, while the infant survival rate was 2.7 in the Classical period and 1.6 in the Hellenistic period." Robin Waterfield, *Creators, Conquerors, and Citizens: A History of Ancient Greece* (New York, NY: Oxford University Press, 2018), p. 10. Roberts and Westad speak about the mediaeval world's mortality rate as being so "ferocious" as to calculate a man's *average* lifespan at around thirty-three years of age. J. M. Roberts and Odd Arne Westad, *The History of the World* (New York, NY: Oxford University Press, 2013), Sixth Edition, p. 512. Likewise, in the Mediaeval Era, Backman has said that the "strain of a childbirth on a body that was itself often still a child's had the expected result: A high mortality rate…as many as one out of every four children died before their first birthday." Backman, *Worlds of Medieval Europe*, p. 476.

to women; despite the unisex nature of it, however, it's a bodily trauma that is universally acknowledged. Indeed, the extent and extreme nature of this pain will be so well understood by people throughout history that the Bible can use it as an illustration of the deepest emotional, psychological, and physical trauma (cf. Isaiah 26:17-18; Micah 4:9-10; 1 Thessalonians 5:3). The bringing forth of the next generation will now be simultaneously joyous and painful. Her role in procreation will be marred by the pain that will be associated with it. Thus, the punishment will be a constant presence in the life of womanhood, but it will by no means be limited to the feminine sex; the impact of this punishment will be understood by both men and women even if only directly experienced by women. This can be seen in the fact that the pains are not only associated with the delivery of the child, but in the raising of the child. Teaching each subsequent generation the purpose of humanity, the words of God, and the obligations of the (now-)corrupted regency will be mired with pain and difficulty. Such challenges are not solely the domain of the woman.

There is an even larger dimension to Eve's punishment which is seen in the more subtle first sentence: "I will surely multiply your pain in childbearing." This last word is variously translated as "childbirth" and "childbearing." The word is וְהֵרֹנֵךְ (*wehêrōnêk*) and its root is variously translated in the Bible to refer to childbirth as well as conception more generally (cf. Ruth 4:13; Hosea 9:11). In striking at the uniqueness of woman's specific attribute in the Creation Mandate's command to expand (her role in childbearing), God not only increases the pain of child*birth* but, also, the pain of child*bearing*. In this significant phrase, God increases the pain associated with pregnancy and conception more generally than merely the act of delivery. The entire cycle of childbearing falls inside this punishment. Thus, the monthly menstrual pain of menses from menarche until menopause, difficulties in conceiving, and even the sorrows of miscarriage and stillbirths are grounded in Eve's punishment. This pain functions as a consistent reminder of the nature of our sinful disposition as created beings as well as the rebellion that is emblematic of our entire species. Fear of her own death as well as that of her children, the challenges and hardship in conception, and the pains associated with womanhood more generally, are all pursuant to the command of God in her punishment.

The climactic hope of the offspring of the woman, the serpent crusher, promised in the midst of the serpent's curse in Genesis 3:15, comes through this most intimate punishment borne by Eve. There's a glimmer of hope amid her pain because it's through the agonies associated with her femininity that woman would eventually deliver the offspring who would deliver her, her husband, and many of her children (cf. 1 Timothy 2:15). Based upon the later revelation concerning the birth of Christ, Mary's supernatural conception without intercourse can be understood to be the fulfilment of God's pronouncement of judgement on the serpent and the recapitulation of Eve's pain and sorrow.

Relational Disharmony

The second half of Eve's punishment moves from her biology to her relationships. God told her that her "desire shall be for your husband, and he shall rule over you." Although there are often intricate and detailed nuances, there are two primary views surrounding the general interpretation of this half of verse 16. The first view argues that Eve's disregard for the creation order in her initial act of sin (listening to the serpent rather than to the command of God as relayed through Adam) becomes an inherent attribute of her sinful nature. Now, instead of working *with* Adam to fulfil the Creation Mandate, Eve will seek to exercise her dominion *over* Adam.[10] She will now be working "against" or "contrary to" his leadership.

The natural reaction to such coercive and manipulative efforts will lead to her being subjugated by, and subjected to, the

---

10 Philip Barton Payne, *Man and Woman, One in Christ: An Exegetical and Theological Study of Paul's Letters* (Grand Rapids: Zondervan, 2009), p. 50.

domination of her husband. The sense of relational community and communion seen at the end of Genesis 2 has been completely reversed and warped by sin. In fact, if the *imago Dei* is understood to include relationality, higher reasoning, as well as exercising a delegated regal authority, then the entirety of Eve's image bearing nature has been corrupted. Instead of reflecting God through a wisely cultivated and respectful relationship with Adam so that they can rule over creation together, she will now turn her intellect into a weapon of relational conflict so as to rule over Adam. She has, in a sense, become just like the serpent. Adam was not enthroned over Eve in the garden as if he were her king, but, nevertheless, in this view she was made to be his *helper* and therefore he had a protective responsibility towards her that is predicated upon his leadership role. Thus, her "desire for Adam" means that she emulates the serpent rather than God.

The second view, however, interprets the word "desire" in a different manner. In this interpretation, a woman's desire will be for her husband in such a way that she is viewing him as the means by which she can have children, and therefore to fulfil an aspect of her purpose, particularly her redemption (verse 15). Her desire is not to *dominate* her husband but to *worship* him or, possibly, to desire his worship of her. The punishment is not to be *against* him in the sense of opposition, but instead to be *against* him as a ladder leans against a wall. Thus, woman is driven *from her God* and *towards her husband*, in whom she now finds the means and hope of passion, love, security, fulfilment, and satisfaction, albeit in an idolatrous manner.

There are complex nuances within this view. Some argue that Eve's desire for Adam here is not actually negative in the immediate context; rather, whilst she desires a *return* to the state of her relationship with Adam prior to the fall, her punishment is that her husband will dominate her and rule over her. The desire for perfect intimacy is spoiled by Adam's sinful subjugation of her.[11]

---

11   I am indebted to one of my students, Kristin Lassan, for drawing my attention to sources in this section. Denise T. Plichta, An Anguishing

Some go further and argue that "desire" specifically means sexual desire, and therefore "lust."[12] Still others accept that Eve's desire becomes negative in terms of conflict with Adam, just as Adam's headship over her is turned into tyranny. Regardless, the overarching point is made that Eve's desires are corrupted by her new state under the fall; whether her appeal to having been deceived is an attempt to hide from her disobedience or a genuine error, she is punished in two ways that strike at the very essence of her womanhood: Her feminine potential to produce life, and the yearning of her heart.

These two views are generally defined by how one views the difference between the two sexes. Were men created to be the head of creation, including Eve, from the very start? Were Adam and Eve created equals in every way, with competency their distinction (rather than headship)? The debate rages on and, ironically, seems unlikely to come to a satisfactory resolution. Relational disharmony, disengagement, and destruction continue to impact families, disrupt society, and even divide churches. The issue, of course, isn't negligible, especially in terms of spiritual health, vitality, and sanctification. That being said, as God has implied in the verse prior, the punishment can be redeemed. Whether one holds to a complementarian or egalitarian view of male headship, the answer isn't

---

Process: Genesis 3:16," Redemptive History and Theology, https://redemptivehistorytheology.com/blog/chapter-8-pain-and-desire-genesis-316-20/, accessed February 13, 2024.

12 It's worth pointing out that many in the ancient and mediaeval world assumed women had the more libidinous sex drive. Because of Mediaeval man's view on the composition of man, it was believed that sex was potentially harmful, particularly to a man: "A sexually voracious woman, it was widely believed, could literally drain the life out of a man, given enough time." Backman, *Worlds of Medieval Europe*, p. 475. It was *this* fact, allegedly derived from Eve's punishment in Genesis that was supposed to explain why women were considered more prone to emotional weakness and therefore needed to be "controlled" or "ruled." For a thorough treatment and debunking of this line of reasoning, see Eleanor Janega, *The Once and Future Sex: Going Medieval on Women's Roles in Society* (New York, NY: W. W. Norton & Company, Inc., 2023).

in winning the debate but in properly comprehending and living in light of that redemption. Of course, both sides will say that, in order to live in light of that redemption, one must be on the right side of the debate. In a sense, that is correct; but the debate should be carefully guarded lest it leads to a deepening of the very conflict that the redeemer came to rectify.

As a woman, Eve's side of the Creation Mandate was to be the mother of humanity. The means of accomplishing and living out this aspect of the Creation Mandate is now something to be feared because of the biological trauma. It's also jeopardized by conflict with the very person with whom she is bonded into a one-flesh relationship and with whom she is meant to procreate. In essence, her life has become paradoxical. But in the middle of her fear, her pain, her desire, and her subjugation, she has hope. Within the heart of the punishment resides the heartbeat of grace. Through Eve's childbearing, a woman will be born whose own child, miraculously conceived, will be the long-desired and yearned-for serpent crusher.

Man's Punishment

In his previous attempt to deflect God's assessment of his guilt (and simultaneously throwing Eve under the bus), Adam had confirmed not only his guilt but his failure of leadership and headship. Thus, at the beginning of Adam's punishment, God picks Adam up on his failure as the head gardener. He rejected Adam's efforts at deflection: "*Because* you have listened to the voice of your wife." Adam's primary role towards Eve was to provide her with the words of God and to protect her. As the gardener who had directly heard the command from God, it was his duty to correct Eve when she spoke erroneously to the serpent. Instead, when Eve was being manipulated by the serpent, Adam's silence seemed to *confirm* Eve's statements and subsequently *affirm* Eve's actions by participating with her.

Thus, when Eve bade Adam "take and eat" the fruit, he permitted the continued upending of the creational order by listening to her, accepting the fruit, and failing in his role. Most people remember this account with the evident knowledge that Eve sinned by eating the fruit and failed by giving it to Adam. But *so did Adam*. He failed in his duty to correct Eve and to protect her. This is why God begins his indictment of Adam by referencing his *failure* before mentioning his *sin*: Adam's failure *led* to his sin. Adam's attempted defense served as evidence for his larger guilt. The serpent had tempted Eve with the fruit: "Take and eat," he whispered seductively, "and you can be like God." Eve, in offering Adam the fruit, may not have spoken the words of the serpent, but she didn't need to say them out loud. Adam had heard them already. He, too, had been convinced by the serpent. Just as Eve had been led by the serpent, Adam had been led by Eve; but ultimately it was a volitional act for both. This is why God directly punished both individually. Ignorance is no defense in a court of law; in this case, however, neither Adam nor Eve could plead ignorance at all. They were both guilty. God punished them both for their guilt, but he directly *calls Adam out* for both his sin and his failure.

The Curse of the Ground

Perhaps the first thing to note about God's punishment of Adam is that the ground was cursed because of *Adam*, not Eve nor the serpent. As the head over all creation, it was Adam's task to be a prophetic, priestly, princely gardener. His failure to exercise godly headship over creation brought about the corruption of nature itself.

The first aspect of Adam's punishment, therefore, concerns his environment. As the gardener whose job it was to cultivate creation, God cursed the ground. It's significant that neither Adam nor Eve themselves are directly cursed; rather, the serpent and the ground are cursed. The serpent's curse is because he is beyond redemption. The cursing of the ground was, however, linked with Adam's nature, role, and need. In terms of Adam's nature, we must remember that Adam was formed from the ground (Genesis 2:7). Therefore, at a fundamental level, although Adam himself was not cursed, the material realm experiences Adam's punishment. The nature of humanity will be impacted by the changes brought to the ground by this punishment.

It was Adam's task to oversee the created order, protect it, and cultivate it as holy ground. As a sanctuary, it was Adam's task to keep it suitable for God's presence. He failed in this task, listening to the lies of the serpent. Thus, the curse of the ground relates to his role because Adam will be unable to tend the garden at all; instead of a cultivated garden, Eden will become a wilderness and nature will become difficult to inhabit. It will be overgrown with thorns and thistles. In fact, the ground will produce thorns and weeds "for" Adam. Because of his sin, the once-plentiful, resource-rich, and abundantly-producing soil is corrupted by the presence of vegetative interlopers. These weeds and thorns make the production of food and the cultivation of produce incredibly difficult. Because the ground is cursed, and now filled with weeds that compete for vital resources, Adam must toil in the fields for a meagre production of food. Where Eden had overflown with bounty, now Adam would struggle to harvest.

Interestingly, part of Adam's punishment was that he would get most of his food from the plants of the field rather than the trees. Prior to the Fall, God had generously told Adam that he could "eat of every tree of the garden" excluding the forbidden tree. Now, although not restricting Adam from eating from trees, God seemed to direct Adam to the fields for the primary nourishment he needed. This is why he would eat bread rather than the fruit of the trees. Consequently, he too was being forced to perform *proskynesis* before God. Whereas before, he looked up and reached out his hand to grab from a branch, now he bends over and scrabbles in the dirt. He may not slither like the serpent, but Adam had lost his royal bearing. Adam's sin corrupted his royal dignity so that he, like the beasts of the field, would eat from the ground. The consequence of the sin was to make Adam appear less like his God and more like the animals. This is exactly what sin does: It dehumanizes. God's punishment reminded Adam of his creatureliness.

Pain at Work

The second aspect of Adam's punishment follows from the curse of his environment. As the ground became the source of his food, he must look down and work the ground. Unlike in Eden, the fields were unkempt, overgrown, and difficult to till and farm. His seeds will compete with weeds and disease. His harvest will be consumed by bugs and animals. The yield would often be insufficient. The result of this competition is that his work as a gardener would become painful. His muscles would ache because of the intensive labor. He would also experience pain in his flesh as he pulls out the thorns and thistles and weeds. Throughout the heat of the day, he will be forced to sweat over the ground as he tills the land, digs canals for waterways, plants seed, keeps predators and bugs at bay, and then returns to pull his crops from the ground. The tranquility and authority that he had previously enjoyed in Eden was replaced by a time-consuming, painful, and laborious process of farming. His work had not become *meaningless*, but it would often feel pointless and boring, and it would be plagued with hardship and frustration because it had become *time intensive*. Where once he tended trees that grew on their own and whose yield was predictable, now he must toil all day every week in the fields. From being an overseer of a garden, he became a laborer in a field.

Adam's life was changed unalterably. Now his primary effort would be directed towards sustaining himself for the duration of his life; there would be little respite from his work. This helps us make a vital distinction; Adam's punishment is *not work itself*, but rather that his work became simultaneously essential and toilsome. God created work (and marriage) prior to Adam and Eve's sinfulness. Work (and marriage) was, therefore, an aspect of the "good" creation. Work itself had been good in the garden. Adam had already been working as the gardener. He had enjoyed his work. It had been fulfilling, purposeful, and God-ordained. His work, just like creation itself, had been "good." This is going to change in this new world.

The Fall brought about relational disharmony between male and female. Now we see that it brought disharmony between man and creation. The punishment was not *work*, but *pain*. Whereas Eve's femininity was punished with pain, Adam's ability to fulfil his duties would become more difficult. And, consequently, his relationship with Eve would suffer; he would be distracted. Their relationship would become strained as they sought to fulfil different parts of the Creation Mandate in different ways, with both causing them differing pains and trials. Further, Adam's relationship with God would suffer. Now, he would have little time to converse with God in the cool of the day. Again, he would be distracted. Worship would come *after* work. The entire order of his life was changed by this punishment. Indeed, *life* itself had changed.

Ashes to Ashes and Dust to Dust

The final aspect of Adam's punishment is the ultimate consequence of sin. God bluntly tells Adam that his entire life will be spent in toil, frustration, and hardship, eking out a living in pain and sweat until "you return to the ground, for out of it you were taken; for you are dust, and to dust you shall return." God told Adam that his sin has killed him (cf. Romans 3:23; 6:23). There was mercy in that Adam was not killed immediately; but he *was* dying and he *would* die. And he would experience separation from God which is spiritual death. From that moment on, Adam's biological makeup would begin to decline and decay. He would experience cellular death that would accelerate with age until, finally, he would breathe his last and his body would return to the earth. The elements that had been used by God to form Adam would return through decomposition. Creation would be reversed as death would follow life.

God's forceful comments about Adam's source and composition also sharply reminded him that he was a creation. The act of disobedience was disrespectful to God's reign, but it was grounded in the Satanic desire to "be like God" in a way that was to challenge God's very godness. They were dissatisfied with being like him; they wanted to replace him. It's for this reason that God reminded Adam that he as a creature. Indeed, at the very basic level, his composition was nothing more than matter. Adam had reached for the celestial throne only to be reminded that he had been formed from the dust of the ground.

This last point brings us full circle in Adam's condemnation. The ground was cursed because of Adam's sin. The ground would also become impure because it would swallow the dead. Throughout scripture, death is a horrific, unnatural, and evil thing. Under the Mosaic covenant, the regulations concerning ritual purity surrounding corpses and death were clearly laid out: Being *in the presence* of a corpse would make someone unclean (Numbers 19:14-15); *touching corpses* would make someone impure (Numbers 19:11); even touching *animal* corpses could make one ritually impure (Leviticus 5:12; 11:39). Part of the curse of the ground, therefore, is that it has become a repository for the impurity of the dead. When Paul speaks about the groaning of creation in Romans 8:22-24, he's pointing out that creation yearns to be free from its bondage to sin and to the tyranny of sinful humanity. But there's another sense in which creation yearns to be cleansed from the *consequences* of sin. In other words, creation is longing for the resurrection of the dead to be cleansed from the ritual uncleanness that exists in the ground.

There is something curious about the structure of the punishment. The creational order was upended in the Fall, and that is mirrored by the order of the punishments. The serpent (as an animal) came to Eve, who subsequently came to Adam; God addressed the serpent first, then Eve, and finally Adam. In this final punishment, God promised Adam's death as the representative for humanity. Eve would likewise die. But the pronouncement of death wasn't given to her directly; it was implied from Adam's punishment. Her sin condemned her because the penalty for eating the fruit was death. God, however, only directly mentioned death when delivering his pronouncement on Adam. As the firstborn of the old creation, Adam bore responsibility for the sinfulness of all three. Nature was cursed because of his failure; Eve would likewise suffer by the addition of pain and toil to her work; and all would taste and experience death. Adam had condemned humanity. His only hope rested in the offspring of Eve whose destiny was to crush the serpent's head.

Back to the Garden

Adam appeared to understand that his death was inevitable, even though it wasn't imminent. Thus, Adam continued his work of naming and gave the woman, his wife, her name: "Eve." In Hebrew, Eve sounds like "living" or "life giving," so Adam clearly believed that they both would live to procreate. It has been assumed in numerous traditions throughout history that sexual activity was not part of life in the garden; rather, it was a consequence of the Fall. This is unwarranted speculation from the text and has drawn some very peculiar ideas concerning the value (or lack thereof) of sex. Although we do accept that sexual intimacy did exist prior to the Fall, it's clear that no children were born to Adam and Eve until after they sinned. Adam and Eve would have children and thus Eve would be the mother of humanity; the unfortunate reality is that her motherhood would be tarnished by pain and her knowledge of future generations would be limited by the length of her days.

Death

While Adam was distracted by giving Eve a name, God had been at work. In what is certainly a contender for the most distressing of all scenes in the garden, God returned to Adam and Eve with an item of clothing. This was a gift of immense grace towards them because God was teaching them that he was still accessible and that he still cared for them. He desired them to be able to come into his presence, and so he provided a way for them to do so: He covered them.

But he covered them with something *specific*. Remember that Adam and Eve had made themselves loincloths from fig leaves. That was insufficient. God's provision was different. God's clothing was made from animal skins. This means that the first animal death in the garden was caused by God. One can barely begin to imagine the sadness this must have caused in the heart of God as he related to humanity in this way. The first blood spilled in creation was spilled by the hands of God. This act reveals the heart of God towards Adam and Eve. Whereas one could possibly consider the judgements of the previous verses as harsh and unkind, we can see that, although God was distraught by their sin and the rupture in their relationship that developed because of their sin, his provision of clothing was a promise to Adam and Eve that he wouldn't abandon them. But his provision of clothing made from *animal skins* was a reminder that everything had changed. Their access to God would be curtailed because they're wrapped in death and ultimately, they, too, would die. Hope remains, but it's a flickering glimmer when set in the context of the darkness, gloom, and death in this passage.

Exile

And worse was to come. God spoke to himself (possibly a subtle reference to the Trinity, but it could also be a reference to the heavenly council pictured in the book of Job) and decided that Adam and Eve must not now eat from the tree of life. The implications of their living forever under the corruption of sin was so horrifying that God decided to evict them from Eden. He acknowledged that Adam and Eve had changed. What did God mean by saying that Adam and Eve had become like God? Was the serpent's promise actually *true*? A deeper reflection is that the promise of the serpent does come true in a very particular sense: They *do* come to understand the difference between good and evil but through experience. Unlike God, however, they're not *good* with the addition of this experiential knowledge: They're morally *compromised*. In other words, Adam and Eve sought to *be like* God in a way that made them *less like* God. When they were created, they were made to be innocent. By the Fall, they became like God in that they *did* gain a new understanding of good and evil; but unlike God, they were *mastered* by that evil. And thus, ironically, there is a very real sense in which, by understanding evil experientially, they became *unlike* God: They *knew* sin, and they were now *able* to sin. Because they were so compromised as to be *unable* to be *righteous*, it was unthinkable that they should live forever as sinful beings; therefore, God determined to *protect* them by removing them from Eden.

Thus, God exiled the hapless couple from Eden; they would leave the bountiful blessings of the garden for the untamed wilderness of the world. By sending them out from the garden, their punishments would begin in earnest. They were separated from the presence of God. Their pain in the toil of work would begin as Adam scratched a living from the cursed soil. He would sweat over it in backbreaking labor. Eve would assist him until the throes of labor incapacitated her. They would blame one another and thus encounter the promised relational disharmony. They would watch as their children were born, experience sickness, and let sin have its way with them.

Not only was their exile the *beginning* of their curse, but it was also the conclusive *end* of their previous circumstances. They were exiled from the garden where they'd been tasked to work and keep the garden as priests of God. They were replaced as the mediators between creation and God; that role was given to the cherubim who took their position as guardians of the garden. In the bitterest of ironies for Adam, he watched as the cherubim guarded the entrance to the garden so that he and Eve could not return. Adam had once been the protector whose task it was to keep the sanctuary of God holy and clear of trespassers and enemies. He failed by allowing the silver-tongued serpent to speak. Now, as he watched the angelic sentries, he realized with a pang that, yes, he had been replaced, but, worse, they were keeping watch *for him*. He was the outsider and trespasser. His eyes might have lingered on the cherubim long enough for him to sense their grim stoicism. *They* took their duty seriously.

And so, with a heavy heart, a troubled wife, and an unfamiliar sense of fear and trepidation, Adam turned away from paradise, from the presence of God, from the home he had enjoyed, and begrudgingly trudged into the wilderness. They had eaten the forbidden fruit and realized, too late, that it simply wasn't worth it. God, from the midst of Eden, his sanctuary-turned exquisite desolation, watched them leave with a grieved heart.

Application

So much of our understanding of our world hinges on our first parents' sinful choice to "take and eat" the fruit. The four major points of application concern God, sin, humanity, and mercy.

God

Genesis 3 is a reminder that God is good and that his creation was good. As God is good in his nature and essence, he rejoices in good things. He created a world of perfection and abundance for Adam and Eve. His goodness overflowed throughout the garden and was intimately and uniquely delegated to his regents. They were content in their innocence and their dignity was grounded in the fact that they were made to reflect God. They didn't need to have any experience or knowledge of sin or evil because God had made the world so that all they had to do was enjoy him and his bounteous provision. The single rule was one way for them to demonstrate respect and acceptance of God's authority.

As a God of community, he walked with them in the cool of the day because he enjoyed them and their company. Genesis teaches us that God loves his creatures and, because he is the source of life and love and grace, he desired to give them access to himself. He didn't need to create anything, and certainly didn't need to create creatures like Adam and Eve. This shows his incredible grace and selflessness in that he shares himself so willingly with beings that are so far beneath his infiniteness.

We learn that God is a God of order, and structure, and reason. He provided all that Adam and Eve needed to fulfil their commission. Adam and Eve were invited to enjoy his abundant provision in a perfect world without anything wicked or evil or ugly. The garden was a utopic paradise of beauty. Each intricately designed element was placed in its location purposefully to declare the majesty and goodness and creativity of God. To be God's regents over creation, God had generously and graciously provided Adam with Eve, his helper and equal. They had a dignified purpose that reflected his sovereign rule over the cosmos.

We're equally reminded that God's love is revealed through his holiness: His is a holy love. Because God is holy in the perfect sense, it means that he is uniquely set apart from creation. He can certainly interact with creation, and consistently does so. But God is not created: He is transcendent. He stands above, beyond, and outside the created world. Unlike Adam and Eve and the created order, God is spirit and eternal, whereas everything else is temporal. He is completely unique. There's nothing like him. Whilst Adam and Eve *reflect* him, they are *not* him. Thus, God's holiness sets him apart. As God is love, his love is refracted through his holiness. His love and his holiness are two sides of the same coin. He looks at Adam and Eve with a love that isn't content to let them remain in sin and remain hopeless and helpless. Because he is holy, he must punish their sin and their wickedness. Because he is love, he desires a renewal of communion and a restoration of their corrupted relationship.

God cannot let sin run amok in his perfect world. It must be punished. God's holiness means that God is also just. To be just, God's judgement must be proportionate to the crime. But sin is an infinite crime. Our guilt is so severe because it is an infinite debt against and infinite God who has been wronged in an infinite way. We, in turn, are finite beings. There's nothing that we can do to pay an infinite debt. And so, we're left with an insurmountable problem. How can we be restored to God when we're utterly incapable of making amends?

Sin

In a world and culture where sin is often downgraded to mere actions, Genesis teaches us that sin is, fundamentally, rebellion against God. Sin is our disease, our captor, and our enemy, yet we are guilty of Stockholm Syndrome: We choose to remain in our sin. Sin is much larger than horizontal actions. Sin is missing the mark of living up to the standard of holiness that God desires and demands from his creatures. This is often considered harsh, even unfair. But when we think about it for a moment, we realize that we inherently grasp the ugliness of sin…when it's committed *against us*. When someone sins against me, I instinctively know that I've been wronged. I feel its wickedness personally and intimately because I understand injustice. There is an apparent innateness to some kind of justice that, although it can be manipulated by our environment, is nevertheless a witness to our natural appreciation for *sin*.

This means that we do understand that our sin is larger than our actions. As Adam and Eve learned, the *action* of eating the fruit was a sinful thing to do. But the *decision* to eat the fruit was a change of disposition towards God.[13] It was to reject his authority in the garden. It was to reject his claim to speak the truth about what he had taught them about themselves. It was to reject his provision for them as insufficient. It was to want to be more than he had made them, even though he had made them higher than every other created being. God had done nothing to deserve their treachery and yet they chose to turn on him and seek to dethrone him and enthrone themselves. When we think of sin as Genesis 3 teaches it, we can appreciate that God is the wronged party. His creatures have rejected his rule, disobeyed his command, expressed a selfish and petulant disregard for his generosity, and sought the actual demise of his reign.

---

[13] "It is obvious that sin began in the heart of Eve already before she actually ate the forbidden fruit." Hoekema, *Created in God's Image*, p. 130.

Sin is anti-God. It is a heart attitude and a willful disposition to reject the goodness of God for worship of self. Sin is an outright assault on the goodness, the word, and the law of God. It is an affront to his justice and an attack on his holiness. Martin Luther, the sixteenth century reformer, talks about the sinful person as being a man curved in on himself. This is an apt image because it bends us down and inward. To be a sinner is to refuse to look to God and it is to refuse to reach out to those around you; it is to be selfish, self-focused, and self-worshipping. To sin is to be like the fool in Isaiah 40 who takes wood and uses half to make a fire and cook with, and from the other half fashions a god to whom he prostrates himself in idolatrous lunacy. In the garden, Adam and Eve's perfection was polluted by guilt, insecurity, and shame. Their relationship with one another was now marred by disharmony and disunity.

In trying to come to terms with sin, we must accept that there is a hidden aspect to it that we don't understand. Why did Adam and Eve sin? Yes, their disposition towards God changed because of the wiles of the serpent. But *why* were they so impressionable? Some have speculated that this makes God the author of sin, at least in *potentiality* if not *actuality*. And it's true that God permitted sin. But to *permit* something is not to *cause* it. Further, we know that sin existed prior to Adam and Eve for the serpent was the agent who brought sin into Eden as the tempter. Although we can *define* sin itself as a spiritual and moral rejection of God, his holiness, and his character, we're not given enough biblical data to truly grasp its fundamental origin. As Augustine has said, to look for an efficient cause of the evil will be "as if someone sought to see darkness or to hear silence."[14] As I have tried to argue in this section, the disposition of sin is evil, the action of sin is evil, and the heart of sin is evil. Beyond the sinfulness of sin, however, is the stupidity of sin. Sin is the turning from life towards death, from light to darkness, from health to disease, from the source of good-

---

14   Augustine, *City of God*, vol. 2 in *Nicene and Post-Nicene Fathers*, First Series (rpt.; Grand Rapids: Eerdmans, 1983), p. 230 (Bk. 12, Ch. 7).

ness to the heart of wickedness. Perhaps a reason why we cannot comprehend *why* Adam and Eve were susceptible to sin is because there is no sensible reason for it; sin is madness: "We cannot make sense of the senseless."[15] What we can say is that, in Eden, humans were free agents; after the Fall we became blind slaves.

Humanity

Adam was the representative head for all of humanity and therefore his decision to reject God's rule has impacted every son and daughter of Adam. The entire human race is *imputed* with Adam's sinful nature such that we've all inherited a sinful nature from our first father. Thus, just as Adam's work is pain and vanity, we too experience it (although not all of us need to work in the fields to feed ourselves, the principle is very much the same). Just as Adam's destiny is ultimately to return to the dust from which he was formed, we, too, will experience death because we're in Adam, and we've sinned just as he has. Like Adam, we, too, have disregarded what God has said about holiness, righteousness, and goodness. Although we haven't eaten the same fruit from the tree, we have nevertheless made the same *decision* to reject God's reign and made ourselves gods of our lives. The consequence of this is the same for us as it was for Adam and Eve: Separation. They were exiled from the garden, and humanity has ever since been separated from the presence of God, with all the spiritual and material implications that that separation causes.

These implications have impacted every aspect of our lives. We live in a world where society openly acknowledges the depravity of sinfulness and yet cavorts in it, praises it, rewards it, and loves it. Marriages are riven by division and disharmony. Sons and daughters of Adam are responsible for abuses of all kinds, against their spouses, their children, their neighbors, and creation. Our mutual relationships are frustrated by conflict and competition. Both live in the tension of seeking fulfilment and yet experiencing the pains of their respective domains. Our work is corrupted and

---
15   Hoekema, *Created in God's Image*, p. 132.

made difficult, annoying, and seemingly pointless. Our dominion over creation has morphed into dictatorial tyranny. To be clear, this doesn't mean that every human being is as evil and wicked in our actions as we could be; rather, it means that every part of every human being has been corrupted by sin. By God's mercy, the absolute sinfulness of sin has a modicum of restraint in most people through cultural, societal, and even conscionable pressure. But, at heart, every human being's natural disposition towards God is one of hostility, animosity, and rebellion. And our sinful actions reflect our sinful disposition. This is what we call the doctrine of original sin. Sin has reordered not merely the action of our worship but the very means of both our secular and sacral activity. Everything we do is now corrupted by sin such that we act as high priests of our own self-oriented religion. The point is that humanity has been wholly compromised by sin.

The idea of Adam and Eve's knowledge of sin and evil continues to exist today. In the culture war that continues to rage throughout the Western world, the idea that one gets to "identify" as how they feel is eerily reminiscent of Adam and Eve's sinfulness. Our modern world echoes Henley's poem that "I am the master of my fate / I am the captain of my soul."[16] To reject the biological sex of our genetics is to literally demand to determine who we are.[17]

---

16 William Ernest Henley, "Invictus." Poetry Foundation. N.d. https://www.poetryfoundation.org/poems/51642/invictus Accessed 19 February, 2024. Lines 15-16.

17 This does not mean that gender dysmorphia does not exist. It does exist. But its existence is part of the Fall, not the design. It's something that needs to be worked through and beyond; the answer to gender dysmorphia is not to embrace it but to combat it with patience, grace, steadfastness, and, most crucially, the gospel. Not all who identify as transexual suffer from the psychological condition of gender dysmorphia; those who do need care, compassion, support, and assistance as the gospel is brought to bear on their life. This is just as true for someone who identifies as transexual as it is for the heterosexual person addicted to self-destructive and dehumanizing addictions such as pornography. Both are examples of how sin has damaged and corrupted our humanity.

It is the perennial sin of rejecting what *God* has said by choosing what *I* want to believe about the world, about God's commands, and about myself. Just as Eve desired to be like God by choosing to reject the lavish provision and the singular command of the garden, our generation is choosing to reject the authority and design of the Creator.[18]

Worst of all, humans of every ethnicity and culture are aware of the biting grief of watching a loved one take their last breath and then depart from this world, never to return. The stark paradox of death is that although it certainly feels unnatural, it's the only truly universal thing about every living creature: We will all die. Sin reigns in our lives, and death dominates our future. Our legacy, however great, will be diminished by the fact that we will eventually be gone. We're afflicted by the temporal nature of our lives such that, as we age, our bodies break down, change, and decay in front of our very eyes. Regardless of wealth, power, beauty, wisdom, or talent, all will return to dust because of sin. The poet Francis Beaumont captures this sentiment with a piercing melancholy: "Here's an acre sewn indeed / With the richest, royall'st seed / That the earth did e'er suck in / since the first man died from sin: / Here the bones of birth have cried-- / 'Though gods they were, as men they died.'"[19]

Mercy

Genesis 3 also directs us towards the truth that in the midst of God's justice, man's rejection of God, and sin's attempted coup, God nevertheless chooses to display mercy. In this sorry story, the only wronged person is God. And yet despite the outrageous and scandalous arrogance of the rebellion, God consistently responded with mercy. He was merciful in providing judgement; by doing so,

---

18 See Carl Truman, *The Rise and Triumph of the Modern Self: Cultural Amnesia, Expressive Individualism, and the Road to Sexual Revolution* (Wheaton, IL: Crossway, 2020).

19 Francis Beaumont, "On The Tombs of Westminster Abbey." *Key to Poetry*. N.d. https://keytopoetry.com/francis-beaumont/poems/on-the-tombs-in-westminster-abbey/ Accessed 16 February 2024. Lines 9-14.

he taught Adam and Eve what true goodness looked like. He was merciful in cursing the serpent; by doing so, he promised Adam and Eve that redemption would be possible. He was merciful in delaying their deaths; by doing so, he allowed Adam and Eve to live a life and have children so that they could see some of their offspring. He was merciful in limiting the duration of their lives; in doing so, he promised their broken and sick bodies rest from the weariness of sinfulness. He was merciful in providing clothes, even clothes made from animal skins; in doing so, he taught them that he still cared for them. He was merciful in permitting them some means by which they could return to him in due course; in doing so, he was committing himself to the crushing of Satan, the defeat of death, and the restoration of creation. The one person in Genesis 3 who had the legitimate grievance is the one person who truly sought to correct the carnage. Once we accept that God is the wounded party, we can grasp that this passage is bursting at the seams with his mercy. As Alexander Pope has said: "To Err is Human; to Forgive, Divine."[20] Although Adam dehumanized himself by becoming like the serpent in his rejection of what God had said about him, God mercifully refused to make Adam and Eve *only* animals. In other words, he refused to remove the *imago Dei* from them. They continued to bear his image and likeness, even though they chose to reject the God in whose image they were made.[21]

Conclusion

In Genesis 3 we encountered our theme for the second time. In Genesis 2, God had provided a sumptuous world for Adam to enjoy and then a wife with which to enjoy it. In our discussion of this third chapter, however, the temptation to "take and eat" the forbidden fruit proved to be too enticing for both Adam

---

20 Alexander Pope, "An Essay on Criticism." *Eighteenth Century Poetry.* 2015. https://www.eighteenthcenturypoetry.org/works/o3675-w0010.shtml. Accessed on 16 February 2024. Line 526.

21 Anthony A. Hoekema, *Created in God's Image* (Grand Rapids, MI: William B. Eerdmans Publishing Company, 1994), p. 17.

and Eve. With their choice to eat the fruit, they plunged all of humanity into a never-ending spiral of spiritual rebellion against God's rightful reign. This chapter moved from the decision to sin, through the activity of the sin, and into the judgement for sin. It ended with paradise in tatters. Adam and Eve were in relational turmoil. Adam and God were separated. The sanctuary of Eden was under new a new regency. Pain and sorrow were following Adam and Eve into the wilderness. They were exiled from the garden and forbidden to return to it. As they looked ahead into the wilderness, they saw the future that lay before them: Bleak, barren, painful, pitiful. They turned to look at one another and were struck anew at their appearance. They were clothed in bloody skins. Their very garments reminded them of their own inevitable, inescapable, inexorable fate. They too would pollute the ground when their eyes closed in death. Their worst realization was that they knew they deserved it. They understood their guilt. They accepted their shame. And yet they yearned for forgiveness and restoration. The only hope they had was the sliver of a great promise garnered from the maelstrom of the punishments: That someday the serpent who had taunted them, tempted them, and now tormented them, would be crushed.

Second Course: Seafood Soup

4

"Take and Eat": Food For You

And God blessed Noah and his sons and said to them, "Be fruitful and multiply and fill the earth. The fear of you and the dread of you shall be upon every beast of the earth and upon every bird of the heavens, upon everything that creeps on the ground and all the fish of the sea. Into your hand they are delivered. Every moving thing that lives shall be food for you. And as I have you the green plants, I give you everything. But you shall not eat flesh with its life, that is, its blood. And for your lifeblood I will require a reckoning: from every beast I will require it and from man. From his fellow man I will require a reckoning for the life of man. "Whoever sheds the blood of man, by man shall his blood be shed, for God made man in his own image. And you, be fruitful and multiply, teem on the earth and multiply in it." (Genesis 9:1-7)

Introduction

I'm a paradox. I love eating meat; whether it's eating freshly cooked goat in the mountains of Morocco or thick-cut rashers of Irish back bacon, there's something that scintillates my senses when I know meat is on the menu. I don't disparage vegetables or carbs. I enjoy them all in equal measure (except, as has already been discussed, onions). But everything else is very much the sideshow to the main character in my culinary theatre. That being said, I truly hate death. I'm not sure that I could be involved in the process of killing and preparing an animal for the grill. For me, the problem is that I hate the idea of my kill feeling pain. My one experience of fishing is testament to my ineptitude when it comes to being a hunter-gatherer.

On a pier in Ireland, my friend and I were fishing and, after what felt like an interminably long (and boring) wait, my line began to bob with the telltale sign that a fish had been foolish enough to take my bait. But I'd never fished before. I didn't know what to do. I began to turn the spool and, slowly, the fish began to leave the water and come towards me. But we were on a pier. A tall pier, about twelve feet from the surface of the water. And I didn't know what I was doing. For reasons unknown, I began to panic and, as I panicked, I started to jerk the fishing rod so that the poor fish was being bashed against the wall of the pier. By the time I managed to get the fish over the edge, I was traumatized, and I can't even imagine what the fish was thinking.

Once the fish was safely by my feet, flopping around, I looked at Richard helplessly. I didn't know what to do. We eventually managed to get the hook out of its mouth and it was my plan to release it back into the sea. I tried. But fish are slippery. I only threw it as far as the curb. Once, twice, and then thrice I attempted to get it over the curb and back into its habitat, only to fail each time. Finally, in a fit of pique, Richard stepped in to put the poor fish out of its misery and launched it back into the ocean (and as far away from me as possible). I'm sure the fish was more distressed than I was, but I remember the *guilt* I experienced after that event. It stayed with me for days. And yet I'm a paradox: We ended our disastrous fishing trip with fish and chips.

My own experience notwithstanding, we are carnivores. Meat contains nutrients that we need and our bodies eventually crave. Whether it's the elaborate dishes of the Roman aristocracy, who encased smaller animals inside larger animals, or the decadent cruelty of ortolan, humans have become proficient at exploiting the animal kingdom for food. This ranges from chicken farms that intentionally overfeed the birds to satisfy our burgeoning fast-food industries to the ridiculous nonsense of overpriced steaks in fancy restaurants coated in flakes of gold for no other reason than that someone will be foolish enough to pay to eat it. The food chain is an essential chain for all of us, but we've become diabolically proficient in our administration of it.

There's something important about the topic of meat for food because it involves death. It wasn't always the case that we were given permission to enjoy meat. When Adam and Eve were given the food of the garden to eat, it was delicious and sufficient for all their biological needs. But it was not flesh. There was no animal death in the garden and therefore they did not kill animals for food. Indeed, all the way through the lines of Cain and Seth, we do not read that God gives humanity permission to kill for food. It's certainly possible that wicked men did so; after all, Lamech was willing to kill a *human*, why would he not be willing to kill a hog or a cow or a goat? We know that Abel killed animals to bring an offering to God. This was acceptable to God because of its value, but we can infer that he didn't eat it, or, at least, he didn't kill it for that primary purpose.

But this is about to change. In Genesis 8, God will tell Noah that there will be a change in mankind's diet. We will not only eat the produce of the land but the beasts of the earth and sea and sky as well. This new permission will come at a frightful cost: Animals will possess a natural dread towards humanity. No longer will humanity and creation live side by side, but there will be creational disharmony. The regents of creation will become tyrants. Instead of exercising dominion over the animals in our care, we will become dictators; rather than cultivating creation we will become cruel in our conquest of the natural realm. It may be permissible to eat flesh, but every meal is meant to be a reminder of the prevalence of death and our violence towards creation: "We have become," as Oppenheimer famously said, quoting the Hindu texts, "death, the destroyer of worlds." Our very sustenance is dependent on death. God, in his mercy, permits this, but it's an indelible reminder that sin continues its own carnivorous digestion of creation. To get to this point where we can "take and eat" the flesh of

Noah

The life and experience of Noah is often pictorially portrayed as a pleasant scene of smiling animals making their way peacefully up the ramp whilst Noah and his kin look on with amazement. In reality, this narrative is one of epochal judgement. God, having reached the end of his patience, told Noah that he has determined to bring a righteous judgement on humanity. This is because the earth was "corrupted and filled with violence" (Genesis 6:11). A consequence of this judgement would be that all flesh, not simply all human beings, would be destroyed. The fact that the punishment impacted all the created order highlights the fact that sin has taken creation captive. It's not that only man has been enslaved, but all his domain with him. Thus, although the judgement of humanity might provide a brief reprieve from man's tyranny, it will nevertheless be judgment that will fall upon all beasts of the earth that breathe. But amid this pronouncement of judgement, God chose to make Noah a priest like Adam had been. Noah was to hear the word of God and obey it and be the means by which a very tiny remnant of all living flesh would survive.

God told Noah to build an ark; he was given very specific instructions as to the dimensions of the ship, what materials were to be used, and how to seal it. God then informed Noah that the judgement was going to be a cataclysmic flood that would destroy all flesh on the earth. But because of God's mercy, he would preserve Noah and his family. They would repopulate the earth in a cleansed earth. Noah was to prepare the ark for a menagerie of animals; it would be a veritable zoo for the duration of the flood, from the smallest creepy crawlies up to the largest of the great beasts.

Noah began his work in obedience. He cut the trees and shaped them. As commanded, he used gopher wood to make the three-storied structure and then sealed it entirely with pitch. There

(continued from previous page: animals, however, there will be other catastrophic changes on the earth. And it begins with Noah.)

was a single door on the side of the ark by which he entered and exited. It took a long time, as you can imagine. No doubt he endured the scoffing voices of his contemporaries who believed their self-righteous, pious, holier-than-thou neighbor had finally lost it. Noah, they mocked, was building a *boat* in the *desert* because the voices in his head told him a storm was coming. Their derision was not tempered by the arrival of animals: Creatures of every shape and kind all marched up the gangplank somehow. There were seven pairs of all clean animals and two pairs of all unclean animals, male and female, so that they could reproduce. There were seven pairs of each bird nesting on the ark.

After the ark had been prepared to God's specifications, God spoke to Noah again and told him that the storm would arrive in seven days. With the animals safely on board, Noah was to enter the ark with his family, and wait. And as Noah finalized the details, ensured the animals were secured, took a last inventory of the supplies, he took a final look around his homeland. Life was going on as usual. He saw people he knew and loved. Friends he had grown old with (he was six hundred years old at this point) walked past and continued to throw jibes at him. With a fearful sigh, he turned his back on them all and entered the ark. He had obeyed the Lord. The ark was ready.

The Flood[1]

As promised, the seventh day dawned from when God had told Noah to prepare the ark, and the first pitter patter of rain fell from the skies. Moses records it thus: "In the six hundredth year of Noah's life, in the second month, on the seventeenth day of the month, on that day all the fountains of the great deep burst forth,

---

1 There are many flood narratives from around the world. Of these, the most well-known is that of Gilgamesh. There are many incredibly fascinating similarities to the Noahic account of the flood, although there are also significant differences. It's well worth reading because it appears that the flood narrative was part of the corporate consciousness of the ancient world. Other accounts contextualize it to their culture, and Moses reclaims the truth.

and the windows of the heavens were opened. And rain fell upon the earth forty days and forty nights" (Genesis 7:11-12). Noah and his wife, with his sons and their wives, entered the ark as the rains began. As they found a place to sit, the interior suddenly grew dark as the Lord closed the door.

And the rain continued to fall. The initial light shower soon turned into a deluge. The rains pelted down against the roof of the ark. Rivers burst their banks as the waters rose. Underground chambers that had been closed since creation were opened, releasing millions upon millions of tons of water. The storm didn't abate. Then, to Noah's horror, over the sounds of the terrified animals, he heard screaming. He couldn't open the door, for God had sealed it.

He heard voices he knew. Friends, family members, acquaintances. Though muffled, and despite the competing cacophony of terrified squeals, squawks, and brays, he understood them to be apologizing for their years of mockery, teasing, and abuse. Above all, he knew they were begging to be given entrance to the safety of the ark. But Noah was powerless to open the door. This was God's judgement: He was wiping the earth clean and returning it, almost, to the state of primordial precreation.

The worst was yet to come. The banging and pleading, the crying and screaming, continued for hours. Maybe even for a day or two. But then, suddenly, Noah and his family looked around at each other as realization hit them. They strained to hear. You can imagine one of them putting their ear to the wooden frame trying to listen for another thump on the exterior. But there was none. The silence, broken only by the fearful animals and the fierceness of the storm, was itself deafening. The ark had been lifted from ground and was being thrown around by the waves. But that meant that the waters had risen so high that all who were outside the ark had died. No more screaming. No more pleading. No more crying. No more pounding on the ark. God's judgement had come and all that remained of mankind sat huddled, grief-stricken, and terrified, inside a wooden ark, jostling amongst the waves perhaps some 17,000 feet above sea level. As Genesis records: "Everything on the dry land in whose nostrils was the breath of life died" (Genesis 7:22). And still the water levels rose. For forty days and forty nights the rain fell, and the waters rose. The ark continued to bobble over the waters, but the structure held its buoyancy.

Eventually, the storm passed. The boat, an isolated island amidst the tempestuous seas of judgement, ran aground on the mountains of Ararat, though we don't know the exact mountain cleft it rested on. Noah waited and watched. The waters slowly began to recede, and Noah sent out a raven after forty days. Thereafter he sent out a dove. The first time, the dove returned to him, tired and empty handed. The second time the dove had a sprig torn from an olive tree. This indicated that the waters had receded sufficiently to allow vegetative life to grow. Seven days later, he sent forth the dove for a third time, and it didn't return. This signaled to him that his cruise had come to an end. God told Noah that he could leave the ark and bring his family and all the animals with him. He'd been on the ark for around a year, safe from the judgement, but cramped and frightened. Now they could step on dry land once more and begin anew. They would repopulate the earth.

A New Covenant

This new start was confirmed by the establishing of the covenant between Noah and God. God made a covenant with Noah specifically because, in this re-creation moment, Noah had become the head of humanity. He was fulfilling the Adamic role as the descendant of Adam through Seth's lineage. Noah entered this covenant with God as creation's representative because he was the patriarch over creation. God explained that he would establish this covenant with Noah, his offspring, and with the birds, the livestock, and every beast of the earth, and all that came out of the ark. Although it was made *with Noah* it concerned all of creation. A covenant is a means to unite people into an intimate relationship. Covenants often have obligations that are to be observed by one or both parties, and if those obligations are not kept, there are punishments clearly laid out that will be applied to the offending party.[2] In this case, God was making a covenant with Noah (arguably he was actually reiterating the covenant already made with Adam) and he took upon himself the obligations of the covenant. It was a Royal Grant form of covenant. He promised never to destroy the world again by means of a flood nor to curse the ground.[3] The covenant obligation was the promise to permit humanity to flourish and thrive until such a time as creation will flow into eternity. The promise of its survival is going to be predicated on God's sustaining hand (Genesis 8:21-22) and his merciful grace. If ever creation doubts God's intentions, he provided a sign for the covenant to remind them of his promise: A rainbow.

This covenant was made between God and Noah on behalf of all humanity,[4] but it's an everlasting covenant because it binds God forever.[5] This means that God promised to refrain from global judgement in this manner ever again; God was not limiting

2 For more detail on covenants, cf. Gentry and Wellum, *Kingdom through Covenant*, pp. 129-145.

3 This may fulfil Lamech's prophecy in Genesis 5:29 where Noah would bring relief from the curse of the ground. This certainly would make sense of his ability to farm a vineyard and reach some prosperity so swiftly after the flood. However, it does not mean that God will stop judging humanity for its wickedness; the form of punishment may be different, but God has not abdicated his responsibility as sovereign judge.

4 "See the Lord's loving kindness: not only with your generation, he says, do I form my agreement, but also in regard to all those coming after you I give this firm guarantee." St. John Chrysostom, *Homilies on Genesis*, 28.4, taken from *Fathers of the Church*, 82:186.

5 "Who "binds up the waters in the clouds" (Job 26:8)? The miracle of it–that he sets something whose nature is to flow, on clouds, that he fixes it there by his word! Yet he pours out some of it on the face of the whole earth, sprinkling it to all alike in due season. He does not unleash the entire stock of water–the cleansing of Noah's era was enough, and God most true does not forget his own covenant." Gregory of Nazianzus, *Theological Orations*, 28.28, taken from F. W. Norris, *Faith Gives Fullness to Reasoning: The Five Theological Orations of Gregory Nazianzen* (Leiden and New York: E. J. Brill, 1990), 241.

his power nor his wrath but was choosing to change tack in how he interacts with creation. He reiterated the Adamic covenant by making this new covenant with Noah and opted to bind himself to it on the basis of his very nature. Because God is the absolute and only good, pure, and righteous being, he *will* keep his word.

This covenant obligates God to patience and, in a sense, peace, rather than war, with creation. It does *not* mean that sinfulness would go unpunished, of course, but it does mean that God would seek a different way to deal with sin, should it remain on the earth after the cleansing of the waters. God was not suggesting that he would *ignore* sin, nor sinfulness. The idea that he's hanging up his warbow is simply incorrect; after all, he is at war with sin and Satan. Rather, the rainbow is a positive sign of the covenant that binds God to the preservation of his creation. And it's this covenant that gives us hope. After the wickedness of the lineage of Cain and the evil of humanity that caused God so much grief, we stand with Noah, at the base of the mountains of Ararat and look at creation. It had come through the wash. Noah was the father of a new era. Creation had been renewed. It continued to be vibrant and beautiful. Wicked people were purged from the earth. But a glaring question remained: Had the flood destroyed the curse?

But Sin Remains

The next section breaks the hopeful reverie. Despite the waters of judgement, sin had not been washed away. The curse remained. This is demonstrated in two examples which, curiously, are eerily like the Fall. Here, Noah was tempted by the fruit of the vine. After the horrors of the judgement, Noah set himself to work the land. He planted and tended a vineyard from which he produced the first vintage of the post-flood world. We often overlook the psychology of what Noah went through and jump to judgement of his actions. Sin is sin, it's true; but, at least from the human perspective, Noah had witnessed the holy wrath God. And yet Noah lived with the fact that he survived. This guilt, now termed "survivor syndrome," was induced by the trauma as well as the fact that he and his family survived. This was loss on a global scale. Everything and everyone that he had once known no longer existed. God had saved him, but the emotional cost and the psychological burden must have been extremely heavy for him to bear.

That being true, we're nevertheless saddened to realize sin still pervaded creation. Like Eve, Noah was unable to resist temptation and he got drunk on the wine of his vineyard. And, like Adam, in whose headship role Noah stood, he failed. We have, then, a paradox of a man. Prior to judgement, God looked upon Noah and found favor in him because of his obedience and, we might say, worship. In contrast, after the flood, Noah was a broken man. God may have purged sinners from his creation, but sin continued its cruel campaign. This first example of sin's continuation covers Noah's failure to exercise his responsibility by having dominion over creation. Instead, he fell prey to its enchantments just as Adam and Eve had done centuries earlier.

The second example is much more insidious. Whereas Noah's drunkenness was sinful and evidenced his failure to be a better Adam, this second was a *consequence* of his drunken failure and highlighted the ongoing relational dysfunction caused by sin. For Adam and Eve, sin caused them to be ashamed and turn from loving one another to conflict. Noah, however, appears to have been the subject of a serious breach of respect and trust. The passage is notoriously difficult to fully comprehend, but despite the various interpretations, the overarching premise remains clear: Sin's corruption remains in the re-creation.

Noah got drunk and passed out naked inside his tent. His son, Ham (the father of Canaan), entered the tent and saw his father's nakedness. He then went to his brothers and told them about his father's shame. There's some ambiguity as to whether Ham merely looked at his father in scorn (or lust), or whether there's an incestuous component inside the tent. It's worth noticing the pattern previously identified with Eve, however. Both *looked* and *saw* that something was desirable before acting. It seems likely that Genesis

9:24 implies something had been done to Noah. Indeed, the curse rained down on Ham by Noah in 9:25-27 appears to be extremely excessive if the crime were mere mockery.[6] Irrespective of whether illicit activity took place or not, the point is that we have, in the re-creation world, sinfulness that reflected the sin from Eden: Noah had been found incapable of ruling creation in a holy manner, and the relational problems of the Adamic family continue. As in Genesis 3, this failure descended into pronouncement of curses and enslavements. The parallels with the Adamic experience are frighteningly similar. The post-flood world is as wicked as the pre-flood world, which was identified by the damning indictment of Genesis 6:5: "The LORD saw that the wickedness of man was great in the earth, and it grieved him to his heart."

In contrast to the curse of Canaan, Noah blessed his other sons such that Shem is identified as a worshipper of Yahweh while Japheth would live in the tents of Shem.[7] Thus, as before the flood, we appear to have another lineage of hope (Shem) living along-

---

[6] It is curious why Noah cursed Canaan rather than Ham. One argument might be that, as Noah has been shamed by his son, so Ham's son would be shamed because of Ham. It's a poetic means by which to punish Ham. For this view, see St. John Chrysostom, *Homilies of Genesis*, 29.21, taken from *Fathers of the Church*, 82:212-213. It should also be noted that Ham's curse was *not* justification for slavery of Africans, contrary to some preachers in the 17th and 18th centuries. For such a view, see Alexander H. Stephens, "Doc. 48—Speech of A. H. Stephens," in *The Rebellion Record: A Diary of American Events*, ed. Frank Moore (New York: Putnam, 1861), 46 and George D. Armstrong, *The Christian Doctrine of Slavery* (New York: Scribner, 1857). For one, a healthy exegesis speaks only of Canaan, the son of Ham, being enslaved by Shem and Japheth. It could be inferred that this includes descendants, but even then, the New Covenant in Christ would abrogate and conquer all such curses.

[7] By looking at the table of nations, we can see that Shem would ultimately be the line through which Abraham would come, and thence Jesus. Therefore, the descendants of Japheth would be those who were "outside" ethnic, corporate Israel during the era of the Mosaic covenant, but who will dwell "in the tents of Shem" during the post-resurrection era when all are united into Christ through faith.

side another lineage of rebellion and wickedness (Ham). Unlike before, however, the intermingling of the two lineages would lead the world into deeper and deeper sinfulness. The twin hopes at the conclusion of Noah's life remain small albeit persistent echoes from the past: Their promise of a serpent crusher and the oath that God will not destroy the earth again. These promises are the faint flickering of a faith-filled yearning in the midst of the dark and wicked rebellion.

Noah himself was a failure. His father, Lamech, had predicted that Noah would be the one to bring relief from the toil of working on the cursed land. Despite finding favor with Yahweh and surviving the judgement, Noah proved that he was not the serpent crusher. He was, rather, compromised by sin. And, consequently, as we zoom back out from this specific story, we hear the drumbeat of death from Genesis 5 echoing still: "Noah lived a total of 950 years, *and then he died*" (Genesis 9:29). The wages of sin persisted into the re-creation. This tells us that things haven't changed. The wait for a serpent crusher continued.

A New Reality: "Take and Eat" Flesh

As part of the re-creation event under Noah, God provided Noah with a reiteration of the Creation Mandate. God commanded Noah that he and his descendants were to be fruitful and fill the earth. But, unlike Eden, the animal kingdom would not submit to humanity as it once had. Instead, God told Noah that "the fear of you and the dread of you shall be upon every beast of the earth and upon every bird of the heavens, upon everything that creeps on the ground and all the fish of the sea" (Genesis 9:2). Animals are now delivered into Noah's hand rather than into his care. God continued: "Every moving thing that lives shall be food for you. And as I gave you the green plants, I give you everything" (Genesis 9:3). From this point on, God has given divine permission to consume meat. This may well simply be a concession to what humanity had already been doing, though it seems more likely that humanity changed because of the Fall and the flood. Thus,

God said "take and eat" even though it requires death. We are, in the Fall, sustained by the very thing that will ultimately claim us all: Death. The poignancy of that irony ought not to be lost on us. Just as Adam's shame was covered through the death of an animal, now, again, God provides for Noah's needs by permitting animal death. There is, nevertheless, the feeling that this is a concession rather than a good progression. We can infer this from the fact that death is a result of sin itself and to eat flesh is, in a sense, impurity of the utmost order. God, by permitting the killing and eating of animal flesh, was acknowledging and accepting the corruption of our very nature.

Consequentially, Noah was told that the animal kingdom would no longer trust humanity as regents and guardians but would fear men as tyrants and hunters. They would be afraid because the hunter's arrow brings death. The animal kingdom may not be made in the image of God, but animals understand fear and feel pain.

God did prescribe restrictions to Noah, however. God told Noah that the consumption of flesh with its blood was forbidden. The idea appears to be that blood is the source of life (cf. Leviticus 17:11) and therefore God retains authority and sovereignty over life itself.[8] It's a throwback to the tree of the knowledge of good and evil. God is reminding Noah that the true knowledge of righteousness belongs to God alone. The fact that this restriction continued through the Mosaic diet (cf. Leviticus 3:17; 7:27; 17:10-14; 19:26 and Deuteronomy 12:15) and into the New Testament (cf. Acts 15:20) teaches us that God considers this lesson one that transcends the various covenantal epochs of redemption. The fact we get to eat meat is something to be appreciated rather than taken for granted. Humanity may be permitted to kill ani-

---

8   "An animal's blood is its soul… [God] is teaching them in these words that as long as the blood as been set aside for me, the flesh is for you. In doing so, however, he is intent upon resisting in advance any impulse towards homicide." St. John Chrysostom, *Homilies on Genesis*, 27.13, taken from *Fathers of Church*, 82:172.

mals for food, but we are not permitted to forget that God is the giver of life.

This lesson is reinforced by the next verse. God told Noah that, whilst all life is valuable, human life is specifically unique: "And for your lifeblood I will require a reckoning: from every beast I will require it and from man. From his fellow man I will require a reckoning for the life of man" (Genesis 9:5). God was introducing a direct law against murder. The repetition of the word "require" draws attention to the principle in question. God was using this technique to ensure that Noah and his descendants understood the gravity of his warning. If we remember that the Fall was swiftly followed by Cain's murder of Abel, this was a wise prohibition. God, as the overseer, giver, and defender of life, was making clear that the spilling of blood in murder would be held to account as a direct offence against his position as the Lord over all things. This law established the principle that murder was to be punishable by death. It was, however, also a law of mercy. If you recall Lamech's boast, he proudly killed a younger man for the crime of wounding him. Lamech's "justice" was, at root, unjust (Genesis 4:23-24). God was correcting that by establishing the pattern of the *Lex talionis* (an eye for an eye). It's right for God to condemn a murderer to death. The punishment will fit the crime, and, because God is the judge, there can be no miscarriage of justice. By introducing this clause, God was telling humanity to avoid *unnecessary* killing, especially of fellow human beings. And he warned everyone that causing the death of his image bearers will lead to judgement for that murder: He will demand a reckoning. This warning was given to *all* creation, highlighting its importance.

God continued yet further: "Whoever sheds the blood of man, / by man shall his blood be shed, / for God made man in his own image" (Genesis 9:6). This stanza echoes Genesis 1:27 and provides more evidence that we're to see the entire flood event as a re-creation. Even so, it's notable that, although it's paralleled with Genesis 1:27, the image of God is considered from a very different perspective. In Genesis 1:27 it was praised as a means of unifying male and female in their relationship so that they could fulfil their purpose. The contexts of Eden and Ararat are vastly different; here, the image of God was used as a warning against murder. This difference reflects the undeniable reality that the re-creation was by no means a return to Eden. Sin continued to plague humanity and mankind continued to seek a savior.

Conclusion

The gift of eating flesh is a poisoned chalice. Meat enhances our diet, but is a direct consequence of sin. The created order continues to be in disarray and that disarray is now heightened and given a point of reference. Not only is there relational disharmony between man and woman, but it also exists between parents and offspring, and even between siblings. Creationally, however, there will be disharmony between Noah, the second representative for humanity, and the animal kingdom. In a twisted turn of events, to "take and eat" flesh is the means by which this creational disharmony is manifested and comprehended. With every steak or fried chicken sandwich, we're to remember that we are literally feasting on death. And while the death we eat sustains us, it ought also remind us of our broken nature and our own inevitable demise. Sin remains.

5

"Take and Eat": Covenantal Diet

Then the LORD said to Moses, "Behold, I am about to rain bread from heaven for you, and the people shall go out an gather a day's portion every day, that I may test them, whether they will walk in my law or not. On the sixth day, when they prepare what they bring in, it will be twice as much as they gather daily. (Exodus 16:4-5)

This is the law about beast and bird and every living creature that moves through the waters and very creature that swarms on the ground, to make a distinction between the unclean and the clean and between the living creature that may be eaten and the living creature that may not be eaten. (Leviticus 11:46-47)

Introduction

The first (and only) time I've eaten goat was during a mission trip to Morocco. The team had been travelling all day through the Atlas Mountains and we were exhausted. We had stopped at numerous villages to deliver gospels and to try to share the message of Jesus. Everywhere we went, people were transfixed by our red-headed team member (she even received an offer of marriage with a very generous dowry of 2000 camels!). By the end of the day, we were exhausted. One small community deep in the mountains offered to let us stay with them. The men brought in their television and turned it on so that we could watch Arabic newscasters and act like we understood what they were saying. At about nine at night, they produced an amazing meal for us: Curried goat on a bed of couscous with nuts and vegetables sprinkled throughout. To this day, I speak of that meal as one of the best meals I've ever eaten. And it certainly was delicious. But there's a part of me that wonders if it was my desperate hunger that made the meal taste that *little* bit better.

When we pick up our narrative again, the descendants of Israel had been living in Egypt for centuries. During that time, their numbers had grown so dramatically that a new Pharaoh came to fear them. They were, after all, *outsiders* even if they *appeared* to be loyal to the crown at the moment. Consequently, Pharaoh ordered that the Israelites were to be enslaved as a means of keeping them too busy and too tired to orchestrate a coup. This, however, would bring Pharaoh into direct conflict with the God of Abraham, Isaac, and Jacob. A test of wills between God and Pharaoh would result in the Israelites leaving Egypt for good. And on their journey towards the land promised by God, they, like me, dined in the desert. But before they could take their seat and eat from heaven's kitchen, they had to first witness God's war against the god-king, Pharaoh. This war brought about another creation event which we call the Exodus: When the people of Israel received a covenant from God that made them a nation.

"Take and Eat" the Passover

After Joseph's death, the children of Israel grew in number. As God had promised Abraham much earlier, the Israelites remained in Egypt for a long time. Eventually, a new Pharaoh (possibly even a new dynasty) came to the throne who "did not know Joseph" (Exodus 1:8) and wasn't sure if he could trust the Israelites living inside his realm. As a result of this distrust, he decided that the safest thing to do would be to oppress the Israelites and force them to do menial labor. His fear was that these "foreigners" would become so numerous that they would rise up and overthrown the Egyptians. If this Pharaoh was indeed leader of a new royal dynasty (rather than simply a new king), his fear about the Israelites would be well founded based upon his own experience of palace intrigue.[1] Thus it comes to pass that the Israelites were enslaved in a land not their own for four hundred years. Yet in their collective memory was the God of Abraham, Isaac, and Jacob, and the covenant promises that remained unfulfilled.

Pharaoh's plan backfired, however. We read in Exodus 1:12 that the "more they were oppressed, the more they multiplied and the more they spread abroad." This paradoxical growth caused the Egyptians to fear the Israelites even more. They increased their oppression until they were effectively enslaved and forced to work long hours on hard labor. The aim was to break the spirit of the Israelites, benefit from their labor, and cause them to be so exhausted that the idea of rebellion would be not only impossible but also inconceivable. Even still, however, the Lord blessed Israel with progeny. Pharaoh and his advisers concocted another plan; they reached out to the midwives of the Israelites, Shiphrah and Puah, and ordered them to kill any male child born to the Israelites. Pharaoh was plotting a gender-specific genocide. Most likely, his plan was that the female children would be more likely to integrate into Egyptian society because they would marry Egyptian men.

But Shiphrah and Puah were too wily for Pharaoh. Instead of murdering the infants, they told Pharaoh that the labor he had inflicted on the Israelites as a means of oppression had made the women sturdy, so that their children were delivered before the midwives reportedly arrived. These children were therefore seen to be alive and could not be quietly murdered. Pharaoh was incensed at this third failure at population control. In a final fit of pique, he commanded that the Egyptians be watchful; when they saw a male Israelite child being born, they were commanded to cast the infant into the Nile to drown. Female children were to be spared.

This is the context of the arrival of the next major figure in the narrative of redemption. The Israelites were the people of the promise. But they were also the people who were impoverished

---

1   The dating of the Exodus is very contentious and there is little agreement amongst scholars. It's likely to be earlier than Rameses the Great, however.

and enslaved in the land of Egypt. Baby boys were to be killed in a savage act of hostility driven by Pharaoh's paranoia that he had an enemy in his realm who could assist the enemies of Egypt.

A man from the family line of Levi took a Levite woman to be his wife. They conceived and a son was born to them. The mother was able to hide this child for three months, but as babies get older, they grow, and they begin to make themselves more and more known. At some point, she decided that she would entrust the child to God. She made a bassinette out of bulrushes and covered it with pitch and then placed the infant into the baby-boat. With a deep grief and sadness in her heart, the mother set the tiny little ark into the river and turned her back on him. Whatever would happen to the child would be known only to God. And to a pair of beady eyes hiding by the river's edge. This was the infant's older sister. She was to keep watch and tell her mother what happened to the boy. The sister, probably Miriam, watched as the little boat bobbed with the gentle current. Then her heart froze in horror as she saw the commotion of a royal gathering come to the river. It was a princess of Pharaoh. The princess saw the basket and, after it was brought to her, looked down upon the crying baby boy. And her heart had pity on him. She raised him out of the basket and identified him as a child of the Hebrews.

Miriam, the crafty sister, presented herself before the princess and asked if she wanted the child to be nursed by a Hebrew woman. After getting permission, Miriam brought her mother to collect the boy. Unbeknownst to Pharaoh (probably), the boy was reared by his own mother who was paid for the privilege by the very palace that had sought to kill him. At a specific age, however, the boy was given to the princess in the palace, and she adopted him as her son. She named him Moses, for he was drawn up out of the water.

If we're thinking biblically theologically, we should hear, again, hints of another re-creation event. For Adam and Noah, life came from the waters receding; in Moses' case, the waters didn't recede, but he was drawn from it. In a kind of parallel, the preservation of Moses culminates in the birth of the covenant nation, Israel, just as the garden and post-flood world resulted in the covenant promises between God and specific individuals. Humanity came through Adam and Noah and a covenant people was promised through Abraham. Moses would be the leader of a covenant nation bound to God through mutual oaths of loyalty and fealty.

Moses was raised in the palace and would have benefitted from the superb education of the highest levels. He would not have been trained to be a Pharaoh, but certainly would likely have been prepared to act as a high official. Due to the extreme fear of outsiders and the Pharaonic paranoia about the preservation of the family lines, most high positions of government tended to be kept "in house" and filled by family members. Moses, although not an heir to the throne, would nevertheless have been trained to oversee financial, legal, social, religious, and cultural institutions in order to serve the Pharaoh and ensure that *ma'at* (divine or cosmic order) was maintained. God thus sovereignly used even the horrific behavior of a murderous Pharaoh to prepare Moses for the tasks that lay ahead.

In time, Moses was tasked with overseeing the Hebrew slaves. We aren't told if or when he was aware that he was not a biological part of Pharaoh's family, nor do we know if that caused him concern. What we do know is that he did identify with the Israelites to the degree that he jumped to the defense of one slave who was being beaten to a bloody pulp by an Egyptian, killed the Egyptian, and buried him in the sand. Moses, a murderer, had hoped that his crime had been unseen; it soon came out, however, that people knew what he had done. Terrified, he fled from Egypt to the land of Midian. There, after some heroics, he was able to join the family of the priest of Midian by marrying Zipporah.

While Moses was enjoying his new life in Midian's wilderness, Pharaoh died. The slavery and oppression of the Israelites, however, didn't die with him. The Israelites groaned in their agony and in their slavery. They cried out to God, and he heard their cry. He remembered the covenant he had made with Abraham.

God would fulfil his promise to lead the Israelites out of Egypt and bring them to the land that he had shown Abraham. The time had come when the children of Israel were to become the nation of Israel. But they needed a nation builder. This is why God had been preparing Moses: To be the leader of a new covenant nation.

But Moses was in Midian working as a shepherd over his father-in-law's flock. He decided to take the flock to Mount Horeb (also called Sinai). As Moses was walking with the herd, he noticed a bush on fire. Walking over to look at it, Moses was amazed that the bush was not burning away. It was on fire, but it wasn't burning. As he inched closer, a voice called out to him from the bush: "Moses." Startled, he responded that he was present. The voice told him to remove his sandals for he was approaching holy ground. After Moses complied, the voice spoke again with a sentence that would forever change Moses' life and the history of the world: "I am the God of your father, the God of Abraham, the God of Isaac, and the God of Jacob" (Exodus 3:6). Moses hid his face in fear as God continued: "I have seen the affliction of my people who are in Egypt" (Exodus 3:7). God told Moses that he was going to bring them to the land that had been promised to them four hundred years prior in the covenant promise given to Abraham. Perhaps surprised or maybe even elated, we can only wonder what Moses was thinking at that revelation. The next sentence, however, shocked him. God told Moses that God would use Moses to lead the people away from Pharaoh and to the promised land. Moses prevaricated. He didn't want to go back to Egypt. He was on the run from the Egyptians as a murderer while his own people viewed him as a traitor. But God was not to be denied. Moses even tried to hide behind what appears to be some kind of speech impediment, but God was adamant that Moses would lead his people out of Egypt and into the promised land. God informed Moses that his younger brother, Aaron, could be the official spokesman but God had chosen Moses and therefore it would be Moses whom God would use.

Despite his uncertainty and some unwillingness, Moses obeyed. The trepidation he felt in telling his wife, his father-in-law, and his community in Midian was no doubt significant. But that trepidation paled in comparison with the fear of standing before Pharaoh in the halls where he had once walked as a prince of the realm. A new Pharaoh was on the throne, but there's no reason to think that this new Pharaoh, probably a sibling Moses had known, would be happy to see the murderer return. Especially once he delivered God's message.

Nevertheless, Moses and Aaron went to the throne of the most powerful man in the Ancient Near East and made their position clear: The Israelite God was demanding that the god-king of Egypt give up his claim on the slaves and let them leave. Pharaoh was unimpressed. He refused. This refusal started a fight between Yahweh and the gods of Egypt that would last for ten rounds: The ten plagues. Each plague was to put further and further pressure on Pharaoh, not only as the political ruler, but as the god-king whose primary duty was to preserve *ma'at*. His claim to the throne as the Pharaoh over Egypt was predicated upon the fact that he was the incarnation of Horus and was therefore God-made-flesh. If Pharaoh suffered defeat in war or ruled over severe climate irregularities, it indicated that his power was weakening. Other claimants to the throne might start to wonder if it was time for a new leader. The return of Moses, therefore, was certainly viewed by the political and religious elite as nothing short of an incitement to rebellion and possibly even an effort to introduce a coup. With each new plague, the façade of Pharaoh's power and control over the elements eroded further and further as Yahweh was consistently victorious.

The magicians of the Pharaonic court were able to keep up with Moses and Aaron's God for a few rounds, but by the ninth plague they'd tapped out. As God had promised, however, he hardened Pharaoh's heart so that all watching this battle royale would know that Yahweh was supreme. First, the Lord turned the Nile to blood. The Nile was the heart and soul of the Egyptian state; the silt deposits left behind after each inundation provided Egypt with the fertile soil it needed to grow the annual harvest that would sustain it. It was a specific task of the Pharaoh to oversee the inundation and the Nile waters because the agricultural surplus from the receding flood waters was essential to Egyptian life and survival. Yahweh therefore struck right at the heart of Pharaoh's image and Egypt's soul. The animal life in the Nile suffocated and died and began to decompose. Under the heat of the sun, the stench must have been horrific and would have hastened the spread of disease.

The second plague saw Yahweh provide an infestation of frogs from the Nile. They were to be found everywhere, from beds to ovens. Although Pharaoh's magicians could replicate the arrival of the frogs, they were unable to get rid of them. Pharaoh offered to let the Israelites go into the wilderness to offer sacrifices to their God (though he was not willing to release them). It was a compromise borne of necessity rather than willingness. The time was set for Moses to pray so that all would know that it was Yahweh who had both brought the plague of frogs and terminated their hopping reign of tyranny. So it was that, after Moses prayed to God, the frogs died and were piled up into huge mounds of decomposing flesh. Yet more stench. Yet more death. Yet again, Pharaoh hardened his heart, thinking that he had duped Yahweh into relieving the plague. He refused to let the Israelites go.

Thus, Yahweh brought the third plague. This time the dust of the land was changed into gnats who swarmed all over the region, biting people and animals indiscriminately. Sleep became impossible whilst work would be almost unbearable due to the unpleasant distraction. But Pharaoh remained unmoved.

The fourth plague was another infestation, this time of flies. They would swarm throughout the land such that every house knew the turmoil of their unpleasant presence. These dense swarms invaded every home, shop, field, causing havoc on the livestock and quality of life in every Egyptian. Trying to do something as simple as eating was impossible without biting a mouthful of flies along with your bread. For this plague, Yahweh demarcated the region that would be attacked by the flies. He said that the flies would not infest the homes of the Israelites; by this distinction, Pharaoh would know this was not a freak accident. And so it was. The flies came and harassed the Egyptians, but the Israelites were unbothered by them.

God upped the ante with the fifth plague: The livestock would be attacked with diseases. Many Egyptian animals would die, damaging the Egyptian economy, but also dramatically hurting the immediate lives of many Egyptians who relied on the milk and meat from their animals as well as for travel and trade. In another poignant display of God's sovereign control, he again ensured that the diseases only impacted the livestock of the Egyptians. Suddenly, the personal wealth of the Israelites increased dramatically: They now held the majority of the healthy livestock in all of Egypt. But still Pharaoh continued to harden his heart and he continued to refuse to free the Israelites.

The plague of boils came next. These festering sores were debilitating. The pain was so fierce that Pharaoh's own magicians were unable to stand before Pharaoh, never mind replicate the miracle. Yet God hardened Pharaoh's heart so that Pharaoh continued to refuse to let the Israelites go to the promised land. After the boils had been relieved through Moses' intercession, God responded to Pharaoh's hard-heartedness by sending the worst hailstorm Egypt had ever seen. This plague came with a gracious warning. God told Pharaoh to bring any surviving livestock and harvestable crop in from the field and to remain under shelter lest the hail would crush human and animal and crop alike. The leaders and officials of Pharaoh who had seen enough of the contest to trust Moses' warning did as they had been told: They brought their possessions in from the fields. Under the shelter of their houses and barns, those who had heeded the warning were thankful to see that their meagre possessions were safe. Those, however, who had rejected God's warning watched in horror as their crops were destroyed, as their remaining sickly animals were pulverized, and as their Egyptian slaves and servants collapsed by the heavenly barrage of icy cannonballs. Yet again, the land of Goshen, where the Israelites resided, was untouched.

This time, Pharaoh acknowledged his sinfulness and told Yahweh's ambassadors that he would let the people go. Moses, by this time, realized that Pharaoh was obdurate and unyielding. He explicitly stated that he knew Pharaoh did not truly fear God. Nevertheless, Moses would take Pharaoh at his word and went out of the city to appeal to God to stop the storm. When it stopped, Pharaoh was informed that the ripened crops of the land were destroyed. The crops that had not yet ripened, however, appeared to be fine. Thus, although the flax and barley harvest would be discounted, the nation would avoid famine because the wheat and spelt had been preserved.

At least, that was what he had hoped. After hardening his heart yet again, God prepared the next plague: Locusts. The Lord told Moses and Aaron that he was personally destroying Egypt so that the Israelites would be able to trust God's sovereignty and power over all other gods, kings, and powers. Moses and Aaron then approached Pharaoh warning him that, unless the Israelites were permitted to leave, what little was left would be devoured by huge swarms of locusts. After Moses and Aaron stormed, Pharaoh met with his advisers. The fight had been kicked out them and they told Pharaoh that it would be better to get rid of Moses and the Israelites than to continue with these plagues until Egypt ceased to exist. Pharaoh recalled Moses and told him that only the men could go, leaving the women, children, and possessions as Pharaoh's hostages. Such terms were unacceptable. God sent the locusts. And they devoured all the crops that had survived the hail. Egypt was now facing a full-scale famine with a weak and sickened population. Pharaoh, the supposed guarantor of Egyptian strength and prosperity, was powerless in the face of such relentless warfare waged by God. After appealing for mercy once again, Moses prayed, and the Lord used the wind to carry the locusts away. But Pharaoh, driven now by an intense pride and violent hatred, hardened his heart yet again.

Thus, the Lord prepared to show Pharaoh just how dark his heart had become. Yahweh turned out the lights in Egypt, literally. The sun didn't shine over Egyptian territory for three days, though life continued as normal in Goshen. The darkness was blinding. And *heavy*. It was darkness unlike any pitch-black night. The Egyptians could *feel* the weight of the darkness. They were unable to see anything. Feeling their way to candles, they would light a torch but couldn't see the flame even though they heard the telltale noises of flickering fire. Somehow, Pharaoh was able to reach Moses and asked him to appeal to God to once again get rid of the plague. This time, charitably, he offered to let the Israelites go into the desert to worship God and to take the women and children, but they must leave their animals behind. This was another calculated move; they would be restricted in how far they could go without their pack animals, and, if Pharaoh was right and the Israelites didn't return, then the Egyptians would have the tangible wealth left by the Israelites to make up for their absence. Moses countered by saying they needed to take their herds and flocks with them for Yahweh demanded sacrifices. Pharaoh's charity ended. He told Moses to get out and if he returned to stand before Pharaoh's throne, he would be put to death.

It appeared that there was an impasse; Yahweh's power was indisputable and uncontested. But Pharaoh's arrogance was unyielding. He was willing to destroy Egypt for the sake of his pride. Thus, God would break Pharaoh by striking at the very heart of his paranoia and position.

God told Moses that the final round was coming. The Israelites were to go to their Egyptian neighbors and ask for items of silver and gold. These were duly given because the Egyptians feared the Israelites. Moses, particularly, was highly regarded because he was the mouthpiece for such a powerful God. Having been given the wealth of a nation, the Lord told Moses that he would kill every firstborn son in Egypt. This would be a righteous punishment mirroring the earlier decree by Pharaoh that all Israelite boys were to be killed either by the midwives of by being drowned in the

Nile. Importantly, even the child of Pharaoh would not be spared. Pharaoh's own son, the crown prince and heir apparent, was to suffer death because of Pharaoh's pride. The ensuing cries of anguished grief would haunt the Egyptians for generations. Moses delivered the message to Pharaoh, but he knew Pharaoh wouldn't listen.

Moses then spoke to the Israelites and told them how to avoid the angel of death. Each family was to take a lamb at a year old and with no defect. These animals were to be killed at twilight and their blood smeared on the lintels and posts of the doorframes of the house. The people were to "take and eat" the meat after it had been roasted over a fire. This was the first Passover meal. It occurred on the night when the Lord visited his wrath on Pharaoh and Egypt but any house who had honored the Lord by following his instructions escaped judgement. It was a collective judgement and a collective mercy. Israelites were to remain in their homes all night until the fullness of God's punishment had come to pass.

At midnight, God struck the firstborn of every family in Egypt who had not followed his instructions. The sins of Pharaoh, as had the sins of Adam and Eve, and Noah's peers, brought death. When the bodies were discovered, there was a cry throughout the land of Egypt as mothers and fathers held sons to their breast, as siblings cried over the bodies of their brothers, before all turned to the Israelites and begged them to leave. No Egyptian house had been untouched by death. The Israelites, however, had been faithful and had witnessed the might of God's justice from their individual arks of safety.

Pharaoh was grief-stricken and his stubbornness finally collapsed. He called Moses to him and told the Israelites to go, taking everything they had, and worship the Lord as they desired. And he asked them to bless him also. The Israelites took the gold and silver gifts from their Egyptian neighbors, their flocks and herds of healthy animals, and they followed their covenant-keeping warrior God out of the land of slavery towards the land of promise. They had taken and eaten the sacrificial lamb of the Passover, and they had been freed by God's mighty arm. They took their flocks, their wealth, their clothing, their unleavened dough, placed everything on their pack animals and wagons and carts, and made their way towards the Sinai Peninsula.

Unsurprisingly, Pharaoh had a change of heart. He chased the Israelites after they had departed. His army drew up against them. But Yahweh had already proven this pretender wanna-be god-king was no match for the almighty sovereign ruler of the cosmos. Moses appealed to God for help and the Lord opened up a channel of dry land through the sea for the Israelites to walk across. When Pharaoh's army chased them, however, Yahweh proved his superiority yet again: The waters that he had been restraining were let loose over the soldiers, their cavalry, and their chariots. The mighty army of Egypt was wiped out. The historic might of Egypt was humbled in humiliation. And the people of Israel stood on the other side of the water, secure and dry, watching it all happen in amazement.

They'd been freed from Pharaoh's grip and from the whips and chains of slavery. They had had to be obedient to the commands of God; but those who had eaten the Passover meal and daubed the blood around their doorposts had learned a vital lesson about God: Deliverance would come through an innocent and pure sacrifice. Redemption, they learned, was brought about by being sheltered under and covered by the blood of the sacrificial victim. This pattern of sacrifice would be established as part of their cultic expression of worship in the wilderness and in the land of Israel.

Each Passover, this meal would remind the Israelites of their miraculous deliverance from Egypt by their mighty and powerful God. But it was also to remind them of their *need* for deliverance. When the sacrificial system would be fully established, it was for more than remembering the Exodus; it was to remind them that they were in covenant relationship with God yet were also corrupted by failure to observe the strictures of the covenant terms and conditions. Each time they consumed the Passover meal, they were reminded of the larger problem. Each individual, not merely Israel, remained enslaved to a larger, more dangerous, enemy than an Egyptian Pharaoh: Humanity remained enslaved to sin. And the only means of redemption was to kill an innocent victim as a substitute. The innocent blood shed by the sacrificial lamb would be the means of demonstrating humility and repentance before the holiness of a good and righteous God. The Passover meal reminded the Israelites of God's merciful compassion and his redemptive power whilst the sacrificial system taught them that God was holy, and humanity was sinful. To approach God was a serious thing and to do so appropriately was something that mattered to God. The sacrifices in the tabernacle and in the temple would be a continual illustration that access to God, which had once been so freely enjoyed by Adam and Eve, remained elusive to humanity. Every celebration of the Exodus was a reminder that the condition of humanity remained perilous: Sin's poisonous tentacles still stretched throughout the world in rebellion against God. The Exodus had delivered Israel from the cobra of Egypt. But, as we shall see, the Israelites were still enslaved to the serpent.

Manna and Quail in the Desert

After the dramatic victory over Pharaoh, the Israelites sang songs of triumph and joy as they marched towards the promised land. Their excited enthusiasm swiftly turned sour, however, when their bellies began to rumble. For all that they had seen of God's might and power and commitment to their rescue, they were swiftly distracted by the gnawing feelings of hunger and thirst. It didn't take long before children began to complain that they wanted to eat, and parents realized that their rations were running low. They were a people on the move so they had no fields from which they could expect a harvest. They were in the desert so the likelihood of being able to trade for goods was limited to travelling nomads who tended not to have significant reserves of essential supplies. Such a large body of people as this would drink rivers dry. The situation seemed disastrous. And the people started to grumble against Moses and Aaron and then God himself.

"Why," they asked, "has God rescued us from Egypt simply to bring us into the desert to have us die of hunger and thirst?" Before long the memory of slavery had waned to such a degree that they lamented and even *resented* their redemption. They pondered if their life had been *better* in Egypt. Yes, they'd been slaves, but at least they'd been able to eat and drink. They'd known a sense of stability. Slavery, it seemed, had become preferable to freedom.

Moses asked God to respond to their complaints. God complied, though he expressed frustration at their lack of faith and the ease with which they felt enabled to complain. It was a dangerous foreboding of their future behavior. Nevertheless, as the people wandered through the wilderness, they were growing antsy at the lack of water. Moses records that they were searching for three days to find water but failed. When they *did* find a spring, their elation turned to angry fatalism when it was reported that the water was too bitter to drink.

Moses cried out to God for help and the Lord showed him a piece of wood. After throwing it into the pool of water, the water became suitable for consumption and the people's rebellious grumbling dissipated. For now. But in response to their grumbling God told the people that he would continue to bless them and keep them from experiencing the diseases that he had inflicted on the Egyptians *if* the Israelites continued to listen to his commands and do what is right by his decrees. He was testing them to see if the Israelites were merely fair-weather followers.

After they left the region of Marah (where bitter had been made better), they entered the Desert of Sin (this does not mean 'sin' as we understand it; it's simply a placename). In this desert, they grumbled again, going so far as to say to Moses that it would have been better if God had simply killed them in Egypt rather than bringing them out of their slavery only for them to starve in the desert. God heard their grumbling and set about to feed his people, but also to test them: Would they listen to his command?

God told Moses that he would rain down bread from heaven. There'd be sufficient each day, for each day; when they woke in the morning, they were to go out and collect what they needed for the day. They were not to store food overnight, except on the sixth day, to cover the sabbath. The sabbath was a unique day in which the people were excused from work; thus, God permitted them to double their gathering to ensure they had food for their day of rest.

That night, the Lord sent a feast of quail to the Israelite host so that they had meat in the evenings and, in the mornings, after the dew had evaporated, thin wafers of bread called manna remained on the ground. Each person gathered all that they needed and had enough food to eat until they were satisfied. God had miraculously provided for their needs. But the command remained: "Take and eat" only what you need; do not disobey God by storing food from today for tomorrow (except concerning the sabbath).

But some Israelites didn't trust God and didn't listen to the command given to them. Instead, they stored manna and quail "just in case" God failed to honor his promise. The test God had set was fundamentally *not* a test about *food*; it was a test about *faith*. Would the Israelites, after all that they witnessed God do for them, trust God to provide for their needs? Or would they refuse to trust God? The next morning, some went to find their hidden stash of manna and quail and found it had become revolting: Maggots had burrowed into the rotting food during the night. They'd failed this test.

Yet God continued to provide for them *despite* their failure. A new rhythm developed in the Israelite camp. They'd wake up and collect their manna, enough for their daily needs. Later, after some more grumbling, God provided quail for the Israelites who would then also wait patiently in the evening as the quail came to their tent, ready to be caught, killed, cooked, and consumed by the hungry multitude. When the sixth day came, the people gathered double so that it would last through the Sabbath. Some Israelites, however, didn't gather double. Perhaps they were put off by what happened before with the maggots and stench. Regardless, they were disobedient. They didn't gather enough. When those Israelites woke up with hunger in their bellies, they followed their regular routine of going out to gather their food, even though this was the sabbath, the day of rest. To their dismay, the ground was barren. These, too, had failed to listen and heed the words of God. They went hungry that day. It was a lesson learned for the Israelites about the character of God; but it was also meant to be a lesson for the Israelites about themselves. Their propensity for sinful rebellion, despite being a uniquely chosen people with a special covenantal relationship with God, was just as noticeable as Cain's or Lot's. The Israelites failed their testing in the wilderness.

The application from this part of our exploration of the "take and eat" motif is self-explanatory. The Israelites failed to trust that God was the God who provides for his people. Their hearts were hardened towards God despite his continual gracious activity. God had fought for them in Egypt and fed them in the wilderness. Yet, despite his magnificent and munificent grace, the Israelites were consistently unwilling to trust their God.

Too often, like the Israelites, we take God's commands for granted and demand from him things that he hasn't actually promised. How many times are we guilty of the thought process that our sins aren't really *that* bad, even though we know that God hates our sinfulness? No doubt each of us can point to times when we've tried to defend ourselves from sinful behavior by comparing ourselves to *other* people, implying that *our* sins are rather insignificant. We aren't murderers, after all, right? But the principle that God was showing the Israelites during their desert dinners was that God cares about the obedience of his people. He wants his people to obey his words and his commands because to do so reveals a deeper truth: We *trust* him. Even if we can't understand his commands fully, to obey them is to acknowledge that God is God.

When we fail to obey God in our own lives, the fundamental issue is not *merely* the actual act of disobedience (which is a symptom) but the heart of faithlessness. In those moments of sinful rebellion, we're saying to God that we don't trust him. When we steal, we're saying to God that we don't trust him to provide for our daily needs. When we act out in lust, we're saying to God that we don't trust in his created order for sexual communion with a single spouse. When we lie, we're saying to God that we don't care about his valuing honesty and hating falsehood. Lying, further, dehumanizes the person to whom we're lying because we're saying that we think *they* are not worthy of our best, most godly, behavior. Rather, we're setting ourselves up as greater than they. To lie is an archetypal act of hubris and arrogance. The Israelites were meant to learn that they could trust God because he showed himself trustworthy. Instead, the reality was hammered home that the hearts of the Israelites remained cold. They were not worshipping God; they were simply following him because they had no other option. They were not trusting God; they were simply looking for any tangible benefits he might give them. The Israelites had failed God. But God wasn't finished with Israel.

The Covenantal Diet in the Promised Land

After their wanderings continued for a while, the Israelites *finally* arrived at Mount Sinai, the destination mentioned much earlier in Exodus 3:12. God had brought them to the place where they could worship him as their own uniquely personal God through the inauguration of a covenant relationship. It's at this point that we begin to speak of Israel as a *nation*.

Our expectation is that when the Israelites come to the holy mountain to worship God, there would be a sense of excitement, anticipation, and reverence. To finally reach this point of redemption after all they'd endured for four hundred years, we can be excused for thinking that they would be ecstatic to be on the verge of such an historic moment. And yet, despite the miraculous power and mighty deliverance that they had experienced, their constant grumblings, failures, dissatisfaction, and general antipathy has been jarring.

Nevertheless, the Israelites *were* about to embark upon a new era of redemptive history. They were going to come before their God and enter a covenantal relationship with him. This type of covenant is called a "suzerain-vassal" covenant, which simply means that it's a covenant relationship between two peoples who have different authority. In this case, God was the superior party, and the nation of Israel, corporately, were the inferior party. The Israelites would take upon themselves obligations to God who would reward them or punish them based upon whether the Israelites observed them or not. From this point onwards, these covenantal obligations become known as the "Law" or "Torah" (which means instruction) of God. These conditions were specifically for those who were under *this* covenant; to be in covenantal relationship with God *through* Israel was to be under the regulations God imposed *on* Israel.

We would be mistaken if we think that the *purpose* of the covenant was purely to force the people to be obedient. These covenant obligations served two clear purposes. Firstly, these obligations were designed to give the Israelites the opportunity to choose to be obedient to God as a demonstration of their faith in him. By acting in faithful obedience to the stipulations of the covenant, the Israelites would receive tangible blessings from God. These blessings included peace from enemies, prosperity in trade and produce, and healthy progeny who would be able to confidently oversee the inheritance of the family land from generation to generation. Just like in the Creation Mandate, Israel's obedience was meant to be a starting point whereupon the rest of the rebellious world would slowly come to see the benefits and blessings of returning to God and desire to join Israel inside the covenantal community.

Secondly, they were meant to set Israel apart from the rest of the world. As the world looked at Israel, they were meant to see a people who looked, sounded, smelt, acted, thought, and worshipped differently. Because this covenant was a *conditional* treaty, whereby the Israelites would be blessed *if* they obeyed God but would be disciplined and punished *if* they disobeyed God, the expectation was that they would live in the blessings of God as obedient covenant partners. Because these blessings included peace, prosperity, and a sense of a just and righteous life, Israel was to be a "city on a hill" for the world. When traders or armies entered or passed through Israel, they would see what life *should* look like when in right relationship with God. Because Israel's geographic location was at a critical crossroads between the Ancient Near Eastern world, there'd be plenty of traders, diplomats, soldiers, and migrants moving through Israel's Eden to bear witness to the utopia God would bring to this promised land. At least, that was the intention.

There were, however, consequences for covenantal disobedience as well. If the people faltered from obeying God and turned instead to the worship of false and pagan gods, they would face discipline and punishment.[2] The punishments would directly correlate to the blessings: In disobedience, God would raise up enemies to attack the peaceful borders of Israel; he would cause famine and disease to disrupt their prosperity. And, if those punishments failed to bring about genuine repentance and a return to covenant fidelity, the ultimate punishment would be their expulsion from the land: He would exile them from the land of Canaan and spread them throughout the face of the earth.

Clean and Unclean

At Mount Sinai, the Israelites came before their rescuer and provider. He had made grand promises to the Israelites about their place in the world and his plans for them as his special people. Those promises would be brought into legal authority through the inauguration of a covenant. Covenants are personal commitments that draw two or more parties into a specific relationship with mutual obligations and privileges. The primary way we think of cov-

---

[2] The covenant blessings and punishments are laid out in Deuteronomy 28. The book of Deuteronomy was the covenant treaty between God and Israel.

enants today is through marriage; two otherwise unrelated people are joined together into a relationship that binds husband and wife together closer even than previous biological relationships. And, from that marriage, a new family unit is formed.

When the Israelites came to the holy mountain, they were aware of what was happening. They may have been enslaved in Egypt, but the concept of covenant oath making was an established practice throughout the Ancient Near East. After arriving and pitching camp, Moses climbed the mountain to speak with God. Moses was the intermediary between the people of Israel and God, just as Adam represented all of humanity in the garden. God reiterated that his people would become something new and different as a consequence of this covenant. Israel, above all the nations, would become God's "treasured possession among all peoples," and their duty was to live as "a kingdom of priests and a holy nation" (Exodus 19:5-6). The people of Israel were being constituted into a nation. When Moses descended the mountain to bring the terms of the agreement to the Israelites, the people all responded: "All that the LORD has spoken we will do" (Exodus 19:8).

This moment is of the utmost importance. In our world, we get terms and conditions with thousands and thousands of words and then a simple little box at the end: "Tap here if you have read and agree." The Israelites, likewise, were carefully informed of their duty as covenant parties. This generation signed up for *all* Israel. This is why, in the actual covenant text as recorded in the book of Deuteronomy, God demanded that each generation teach their children the covenantal obligations because each generation was bound to the covenant until it would be fulfilled: "These words that I command you today shall be on your heart. You shall teach them diligently to your children, and shall talk of them when you sit in your house, and when you walk by the way, and when you lie down and when you rise" (Deuteronomy 6:5-7). Neglecting to properly inform the next generation of their responsibilities would lead to their disobedience of the covenant, making them recipients of divine punishment. And, crucially, that punishment would be *righteous* punishment. God took upon himself the obligation of blessing Israel for obedience as well as the responsibility for disciplining Israel for disobedience. If he failed to provide either the blessings or the discipline, then *he* would fail as the covenant partner, which is unthinkable.

The covenant ceremony took place in a maelstrom of cosmic cataclysm: Thunder and lightning heralded the imminent arrival of God as cloud covered the mountain. When God descended, he did so in a cloud of smoke billowing from a holy fire. At the Lord's presence, the earth shook in a majestic quiver of excitement: *God had returned*. Trumpets were sounding and echoing throughout the cosmic conflagration, their tinny notes crescendoing to a dramatic climax. In the midst of the cacophony, Moses cried out to God who warned the Israelites not to rush the mountain; God must be treated with a respectful, worshipful, caution. He would kill any who tried to advance towards him without being consecrated. Moses and Aaran, the chief priest, went up the mountain to meet with God as intercessors for the people of Israel.

The Ten Commandments are what is commonly understood to be the main tenets of the covenant with Israel, at least, at the lay level. Historically, however, theologians have acknowledged that the covenant treaty of Israel is much broader and far more detailed than merely these ten stipulations. Rather, when the book of the covenant is considered in its entirety, the covenant obligations for Israel were extremely detailed and far-reaching. Everything from clothing to moral and ethical concerns to food regulations to legal judgements were laid out for the Israelites to refer to in the future. This has often led to what is called the tripartite division of the law. In this view, the covenant stipulations could be separated into three distinct categories, all of which Israel was bound to observe, but, perhaps, not all of which future covenantal peoples are bound to obey. These three categories are the moral stipulations, the ceremonial stipulations, and the civil stipulations. By carefully delineating which aspects are civil and ceremonial, these theologians believe that they can explain how the Israelites were to be governed (civil) and how they were to worship (ceremonial) within the historical confines of their covenantal agreement. The *moral* stipulations, however, can be applied much more broadly (beyond merely Israel) because they reveal the heart and mind of a moral and holy God. All who want to come before God must *still* observe the Ten Commandments because they reflect God's moral character, not Israel's temporary consecration. This view is appealing, particularly to us who reside in the litigious and legally minded West. The problem with this view is that the Bible nowhere divides the covenant like this. There's no hint throughout scripture that the moral stipulations were designed to be detachable from Israel's covenant.

A second view argues that the *entirety* of this covenant was only for ethnic, corporate Israel. All Israelites, at least until the arrival of Messiah, were to observe every stipulation of the covenant; anyone who sought to come to God through Israel must align themselves with the covenantal agreement. In essence, to worship God, one became an Israelite, which was to become part of a kingdom of priests, a holy nation, and God's special possession. This meant that any convert also became a devoted observer of *all* that God had commanded, be it moral, ceremonial, or civil. When Christ came to fulfil Torah, he *abrogated* the entirety of the Mosaic covenant (meaning all three categories). Under the New Covenant, moral, civil, and ceremonial matters are redesigned for worship and discipleship. Rather than picking and choosing bits that we think can carry across the epochs of redemptive history, this view argues that the New Testament specifically establishes the new stipulations for those who live under the New Covenant. This explains, for example, why one can find nine of the Ten Commandments reiterated in the New Testament, but the commandment about observing the Sabbath is not restated for the church.

This book leans towards the second position. The covenant with Israel was uniquely for Israel to function as a national "city on a hill" so that the world could come to see what life lived in covenantal relationship with God should look like. It was designed this way to make the nations of the world jealous of Israel's unique blessings because of their unique relationship. This is why the narratives of Rahab and Ruth are so poignant, and why Israelites like Jonah feel so repugnant to us; Israel was meant to be a flame that drew the pagan moths of the world towards the light. Instead, Israel would become insular and bigoted. They believed that Yahweh would specifically be *their* God, owned and controlled by Israel, rather than seeing that *they* belonged to God. Israel's uniqueness was never meant to keep the world at bay but was meant to show the world how to return to God. The tenets of the Mosaic covenant, therefore, were unique to Israel as the means of demonstrating Israel's special position before God and cannot be divided into three categories because such a division is inherently alien to the covenant itself.

For our purposes, the Mosaic covenant had several unique requirements surrounding food. These stipulations were given to the Israelites to set them apart from the rest of the world. There may be certain health benefits to avoiding some of these foods, especially those at the bottom of the food chain. If this is the case, it is nevertheless *not* the primary point. These restrictions were not given to enhance the Israelite *diet* but to provide an Israelite *demonstration* of their obedience to God. The division between "clean" and "unclean" foods in this era of redemptive history was to show the world that Israel was different. This is why, in Deuteronomy 14:7, these foods were considered "*ceremonially* unclean for you." These restrictions were about worship and covenantal obedience because Israel was to be a nation of priests. Thus, they were consecrating themselves to his service by avoiding things that he, at that time, declared to be unclean for them.

The dietary stipulations are laid out in Leviticus 11 and Deuteronomy 14. What is perhaps interesting is that the majority of these stipulations fundamentally limit the overall amount of death humanity would cause on the animal kingdom. Certain animals were considered suitable and acceptable to eat, and therefore obviously to farm and to kill; but by providing restrictions on any land animal that does not *both* eat the cud *and* have a divided hoof, or any aquatic animal that does not have fins and scales, or any bird that itself feeds on carrion, drastically limits the overall consumption of meat for the Israelites. There was a symbolic nature to this: Death was still death. The Israelites were to avoid *unnecessary* death and they were to avoid *cruel* death (hence the command to avoid cooking a young goat in the milk of its mother). The nature of this cultural and social distinction can be found in Deuteronomy 14:21 where dead animals found by an Israelite was considered unclean *for Israelites*. An Israelite who found such a carcass was permitted to cook it for a foreigner or even to sell the corpse to an outsider so that *they* may eat it. But Israelites couldn't eat such food. This may partly have ceremonial reasons, such as that they couldn't be sure the blood was properly drained (Genesis 9:4 and Deuteronomy 12:16), but more likely it was because the Israelites were to be a "people holy to the LORD your God" (Deuteronomy 14:21). The point, again, was that the Israelites were to live and act uniquely in the eyes of the world so that they could bring people to God as the explanation for their cultural and societal unusualness. In a sense, these restrictions were meant to be a means of evangelism.

The Israelites were brought into a covenantal relationship with God and were given clear permissions to eat certain animals and very clear rules about avoiding other animals. The reason that God chose specific animals to be clean and others were declared unclean is not quite clear, though it's likely to do with the wider principles about valuing life and the purity of the animals in relation to their own existence within the created order. The regulations would visibly and demonstrably set Israel apart as different than the nations of the world. These differences were meant to be unusual, even unsettling, to their neighbors so that they would reflect on Israel's position in the world, take note of her spiritual prestige, consider Israel's material prosperity, and ultimately draw the inevitable conclusion that Israel's oddities were the cause of her blessings. Thus, by living according to the covenant, the nations of the world would be drawn to Zion and her God.

The purposes of the Mosaic covenant were to make Israel distinct in the world and therefore to make Israel's God known throughout the world. In many ways, this succeeded. Even Julius Caesar and the Romans respected the religious heritage of a people that the Romans considered to be atheists.[3] However, this covenant for Israel, which had been accepted by all the Israelites in Exodus 19, had stipulations that were to be obeyed by all future Israelites. We know that Israel failed. What's perhaps most surprising is how swiftly they fell into rebellion.

A Calf in the Wilderness

The test immediately came to the Israelites. Moses sacrificed young bulls and read the Book of the Covenant to the Israelites. Again, they affirmed that they would do all that was in the covenantal treaty with their God. Moses then took blood from the bulls and splashed the people with that blood as their covenant signature.[4] He then climbed to meet with God with a group of leaders. As was typical after a covenant ratification, they shared a meal. Moses was then called up to the top of the mountain and he remained at the top of the mountain, covered by the clouds of God's glory.

While Moses was in the presence of God atop the mountain, the Israelites at the bottom grew restless. Instead of waiting patiently for Moses to return, they circled Aaron. Because of his sacral duties, they appealed to him to make gods for them. These would be visible, controllable, and, they claimed, were the

---

3   Josephus, *Antiquities*, Book xiv, Chapter 10.

4   The splashing is likely to do more than simply act as a signature. It probably carries similar connotations to the Abrahamic covenant of Genesis 15 whereby the visual spectacle of the animals laid out in halves were a promise of what would happen should the covenant be broken. Whoever walked through the channel was accepting that they, too, would be torn apart. The blood of the sacrificed bulls here likely is a reminder of the consequences of disobedience.

"Take and Eat"

real gods who had rescued them from Egypt. In a very stark and shocking moment, they renunciated Moses by stating that they don't know what had happened to him, suggesting that they didn't much care either. Even more egregious was Aaron's willing complicity. He smelted the gold down and used it to fashion a calf. The people were ecstatic. Aaron was guilty because it was his sacred duty to ensure that the first two of the Ten Commandments were observed: "You shall have no other gods before me. You shall not make for yourself a carved image, or any likeness of anything that is in heaven above, or that is in the earth beneath, or that is in the water under the earth" (Exodus 21:3-4).[5] Aaron failed.

The Israelites sacrificed to this monstrosity and they took and ate and drank until they were energized to participate in sinful revelries. It was a damning moment for Moses to hear from God that the Israelites "had corrupted themselves" (Exodus 32:7). This revealed the daunting nature of his task and that of his successors. He had put up with grumbling and even vicious rejection of his leadership. But he now descended to see the full depth of Israel's stiff-neckedness. And he burned with anger.

Despite this treachery, Moses interceded for the Israelites. God desired to punish them with destruction (which was within the terms of the covenant treaty) and start afresh with Moses. Moses was also a descendent of Abraham so God wouldn't have been failing his covenant with Abraham. However, Moses successfully appealed for the Israelites and God held his vengeance. Instead, Moses threw the tablets of the covenant against the bull, destroying them. He burned the calf, ground the gold into dust, put it into their water, and forced the people to drink it. An unusual usage of our "take and eat" motif, perhaps?

After Aaron's pathetic excuses were heard and rejected, Moses gathered faithful men who executed the blaspheming ringleaders. These followers were from the tribe of Levi who became the priests

---

5 It's worth reflecting on Gentry's discussion on the numbering of the Ten Commandments in various traditions to note that there is some debate as to what is a commandment and what is a theological statement. Gentry and Wellum, *Kingdom through Covenant*, pp. 330-336.

of God in the tabernacle and temple. Moses returned to the summit of the mountain whilst the camp experienced a very different mood. Despite their sin, Moses again appealed to God for mercy and, in response, God promised not to destroy the whole people.

This is a large event when we consider the narrative of redemption. Israel was meant to be a city on a hill, set aside for her devoted obedience to the Lord. Israel's birth was, in many ways, another re-creation event. After the sin of Adam, in Genesis 3, there was increased sinfulness leading to a sort of exile and judgement: The flood. After Noah and his kin exited the ark, we saw a sort of re-creation event, but with some significant differences. After the flood, sin remained, and the death of animals for food was permitted. Here, Israel, after being constituted as a kingdom of priests, failed. Sin's fundamental rebelliousness was again made manifest in Israel's rejection of God and by Aaron's failure to observe the very first commandment in the book of the covenant. Israel had failed.

But God was faithful. Although he could have destroyed the Israelites according to the covenant, he refused. Instead, in Deuteronomy 34, when Moses again stood before the Lord, God inscribed two new tablets with the covenant to replace those that Moses had destroyed in his fury. The covenant was reiterated to the Israelites through Moses. But the omens of failure were laid out for all to see. Israel had already failed. They'd seen the mighty wonders of God in Egypt. They'd been invited to "take and eat" food straight from the kitchens of heaven. Yet it wasn't enough. For all that God had done for them, for all that he had provided for them, the Israelites continued to be a thankless people. If this was the attitude of the generation who *entered* the covenant with God at Mount Sinai, and who witnessed the glory of his presence on the mountain, how much worse might future descendants reveal themselves to be?

Application

There are five key applications that flows from this section of Israel's relationship with God. Firstly, access to God must be on his terms. God's mighty victory over the Egyptians was to be the basis for Israel's faith in God's power and the source of trust in his provision. The subsequent covenantal stipulations and restrictions imposed on the people were to set them apart for God. For the Israelites, this meant refusing to eat certain foods, to wear certain types of clothes, to worship at a specific location, and in a specific way. It also meant to have strict rules that governed social, civil, ceremonial, and public laws and ethics. For their obedience, they would be tangibly rewarded with the threefold benefits of peace, prosperity, and progeny. When the world saw these blessings, they would seek out the God of Israel and desire to worship him.

To come before God, however, was a privilege, not a right. This was made clear during the wilderness covenant oath at Sinai. Even though the Israelites were entering into a special relationship with their God, they had to be consecrated in a certain manner, and they were not permitted to come into the personal presence of God. Access to God, although now permitted in some cultic, ceremonial, sense, was still heavily restricted and guarded. The only person to see the glory of God up close was Moses (Exodus 33:8-23). The critical application from this section is that God remains somewhat distant, even from his covenant people. They are *closer* but access remains limited. The Israelites were invited to "take and eat" from God's bounty, but they were not brought into the intimate presence of their God.

Secondly, God's people are to be set apart. Although this book rejects the idea that the Mosaic covenant is still in operation, the principle of God's people being set apart continues. It looks different because the kingdom of God is not an earthly kingdom (John 18:36) with regular borders. Indeed, the blessings of the New Covenant are different than the very specific blessings laid out in the Mosaic covenant (which *should* be the death knell of our modern prosperity gospel heresies). Nevertheless, the idea that we're to be set apart for God as a community of believers continues to be true. And the dangers of becoming isolationist and parochial are equally present for the church as for Israel. It can be too easy for the church to become insular and inward focused rather than seeing the weekly gatherings of the church as a training ground for the warriors of Christ to go out into the world with the message of his gracious kingship.

God's holiness demands that his people emulate him and grow to reflect him. To be like God is to become holy as he is holy. This is the beauty of what God promised the Israelites through this covenant; they become more than simply a scattered people from twelve tribes. God took this wayward, enslaved people and transformed them into a kingdom of priests whose duty was to mediate his covenantal blessings to the whole world. If you hear echoes of the Creation Mandate in that, you're correct. They were also given a unique position amongst all the peoples of the world as a treasured possession of God Most High. But with such privilege came obligation. The people were to *be* holy in their behavior. In Israel's case, that included obeying all the various dietary regulations, as well as the civil and moral rules. To be set apart under the Mosaic covenant was to "take and eat" what the Lord permitted, and to reject what the Lord rejected.

Thirdly, humanity continued its abhorrent love affair with sin. The Israelites complained, grumbled, and even sought to attack Moses. But in the very act of waiting for the final ratification from God through Moses, they immediately turned against God and Moses, seeking instead a god of their own making that they could *see*. They gave up their wealth (that God had won for them from Egypt) to construct this idol of their spiritual harlotry in a parody of worship. Despite God's many miraculous actions for Israel, their eyes and hearts remained unchanged. Sin's torrid control of the hearts of man, even those in covenant relationship with the holy and all-powerful God, remained dominant. Because of the depth of sin's power over humanity, we realize that something even greater is needed than regulations. The Mosaic covenant, for all its lofty ideals, was ineffective to save humanity from its greatest enemy: Sin.

This profoundly upsetting reality brings us to the fourth key application. God, aware that the law established by the Mosaic covenant was insufficient, also established a pattern of redemption through sacrifice. This can be seen from the Passover in Egypt, but also can be witnessed throughout the book of the covenant. In the Passover meal, God used the blood from an innocent lamb to demarcate his own people in the midst of a hostile nation. Using innocent blood, his own people were spared his judgement whilst those who remained uncovered by the blood of the lamb experienced his terrible wrath. Likewise, written throughout the covenant stipulations were rules for forgiveness of sin through sacrifice. The death of an innocent in the place of the guilty was required. Such a sacrifice would be acceptable to God if correctly offered. This is poignantly acted out for the people on the Day of Atonement through the ceremonial treatment of the scapegoat (Leviticus 16:20-22).

Finally, God continued to use blood as a symbolic artefact for life, innocence, and purity. The blood of the lambs on the doorframes in Egypt was innocent blood shed for the preservation of the people who hid themselves under its protection. The blood of the sacrificed bulls was splashed on the altar and the people to consecrate them and remind them of the consequences of covenant disobedience. The covenantal restrictions concerning eating certain animals and the stipulation that they could not eat animals whose blood had not been drained was to ensure that the people respected life as a gift from God, be it human or animal life. The blood spilled after the treachery of the golden calf debacle served to teach the Israelites that covenant idolatry was a serious decision with fatal consequences. The blood of the sacrificial system was a constant reminder of the weight and horror of their sins in the eyes of God. All combined, blood itself became a reminder of the sacredness of life and the cost of redemption. Sin continued to hold sway over humanity; but God had revealed that there would be means for reconciliation to him. The Mosaic covenant was a signpost for what would be to come. If the people of Israel failed, which they've already shown is very likely, then the answer humanity needs is an obedient servant, not *more rules*. What the Israelites need is a True Israelite who can perfectly observe the covenant obligations and, like Moses, stand as an intercessor for the people. But, when we combine this with the original purpose for Israel to be the means for God's reign to go throughout the world, we see that this True Israelite will be a greater Moses (Deuteronomy 18:14-22) who will bring a new covenant for the entire world, not merely ethnic, corporate Israel. He will create a New Israel with followers from every tribe, tongue, and nation who find their salvation by hiding under his innocent blood shed on their behalf.

Conclusion

The invitation to "take and eat" in Egypt was to result in their redemption from slavery. The Passover meal was to be an annual reminder that salvation was possible, but the blood of the sacrificial lamb was also a reminder that the cost of redemption was extraordinarily high. Death was required, and not just any death. The victim had to be innocent and pure, which, as we walked with Israel through the wilderness, was going to be difficult to find. To "take and eat" of the holy meal was to acknowledge the need for redemption as sin continued to be a barrier between God and humanity.

The restrictions imposed on Israel by the covenant made in the wilderness were given so that Israel would be set apart from the world to such a degree that people would be curious. When questions came their way, the Israelites were meant to respond with a "come and see" attitude, bringing people into the presence of their God. The blessings were not solely for the Israelites but were to be another means of proving the faithfulness and power of Israel's God to the entire world.

The problem was that Israel was a faithless partner. Time and again the Israelites failed to honor their covenant obligations. They repeatedly turned to idols and pagan gods who had done nothing for them. Israel's fickleness may not have been seen in the overt failure of the eating and dietary restrictions (unlike their explicit acts of idolatry); however, even these dietary restrictions showed the insidious nature of sinfulness. In a perverted twistedness, these acts of obedience became a *means of salvation* rather than simply a *demonstration of covenantal faithfulness*. Obeying the laws soon became the very thing that they felt made them safe; the covenant blessings, they soon believed, were theirs so long as they obeyed the tenets of the law, irrespective of their worship and heart condition before God. This would be why God would later reject their sacrifices as inadequate and unacceptable because the people were an unloving, unethical, and ungodly people (Hosea 6:6-7; Micah 6:6-8). The Israelites had forgotten that beneath the acts of obedience was the covenant heart of worship. Coming into the presence of God was not based upon how well they had avoided eating certain animals; they could only come before God because of the spilled blood of the sacrificial system which acted to cleanse them from sin. Those sacrifices would become meaningless if they were offered out of ritual and duty rather than faith and worship. The Israelites, despite dining in the desert and despite receiving their covenantal diet, were covenantal idolators and adulterers. The problem of sin continued into and throughout Israel's covenantal era. Their failure meant that humanity needs another option: A faithful covenant partner.

Third Course: The Main Course

6

"Take and Eat": The Tempter Strikes Again

> *Then Jesus was led up by the Spirit into the wilderness to be tempted by the devil. And after fasting forty days and forty nights, he was hungry. And the tempter came and said to him, "If you are the Son of God, command these stones to become loaves of bread."* (Matthew 4:1-3)

Introduction

When I was around the age of thirteen, I had to have my appendix removed. Over the previous few years, I'd suffered from repeating bouts of a rumbling appendix. This happened like clockwork around December so eventually the doctors decided to cut me open, tear it out, and see what happened next year. That may not be the exact medical terminology but fits my memory of the general experience. Thankfully, the problem has not (to date) resurfaced. And I have a pretty little scar that makes me feel like I've been in a fight.

On the day of my surgery, I was not allowed solid food and then, for the next few days, I was on a restricted diet until my wound healed. Thus, for about a week, I was told to eat minimally, and what I did eat tended to be more along the lines of soup than steak. I love meat and I love carbs; the absence of both was an extremely unpleasant experience. At thirteen, I'm not sure I'd have been so eager for the removal of my appendix had I known the dietary tyranny that would be forced on me for that interminably long week!

Nevertheless, as I was hungry, my mind drifted often to something that I craved. For about a week, all I could think about, dream about, fantasize about, was getting my hands on a tube of salt and vinegar Pringles. I could almost taste them when I closed my eyes and pictured them. My stomach rumbled as I tormented myself with memories of the good old days when I could eat whatever I wanted. I don't mind saying that, at times, the thought of Pringles consumed me. In my mind, I wasn't simply *craving* them; I felt like I *needed* them. There was an insatiable desire that was not satisfied until I was finally able to get some. And I confess, when the moment arrived, I *inhaled* them.

It might sound like a silly illustration; but in this chapter, we're going to see that my seven days of limited diet pales into insignificance with the forty days and nights that Jesus fasted in the wilderness. We all know how powerful a deep, aching, temptation can be. We've all experienced the long tunnel of temptation, to feel that we *need* whatever our soul, our mind, our flesh, demands. My frailty was on display after a few days; how much more vulnerable was Jesus when the Spirit of God brought him away from his friends and family into the wilderness, with no provision? When Satan entered the scene, Jesus was at the limits of his human endurance. I did not *need* Pringles to survive; but Jesus was in desperate shape. He needed food. He needed sustenance. And Satan, knowing the depths of his hunger, was prepared to exploit it to bring Jesus down.

Context

Prior to the commencement of his Messianic ministry, Jesus had to undergo two critical experiences. The first, his baptism, involved him submitting to the waters of the river Jordan under the ministration of his cousin, John the Baptist. At the climactic moment, the Spirit of God descended upon Jesus in a dramatic expression of holy anointing. Alongside this divine consecration, the voice of God the Father boomed from the heavens with the majestic words: "This is my beloved Son, with whom I am well pleased" (Matthew 3:17). The technical term for this divine expression of favor is called a *bat kol*, or the "voice of God." The voice of God can be heard at critical moments in Jesus' life and ministry. The beginning of Jesus' ministry is therefore marked by the *identification* of Jesus as the son of God by God the Father. But this wondrous baptismal event also serves to *anoint* Jesus with the calling that will assist him in his ministry. To be clear, Jesus is not being *adopted* as the Son of God at this point; nor is he receiving access to God the Father and God the Spirit for the first time as if this were some kind of conversion experience. Those ideas are both heretical. Nevertheless, there *is* something dramatic and powerful about what happened to Jesus. We might be best to call it his "commissioning" moment. It's by this action that Jesus was being publicly commissioned to begin the task of declaring that the kingdom of God was at hand (Mark 1:1 and Matthew 4:17). Messiah was on the march.

Before he could start preaching, however, the mountain top experience of his commissioning took a nosedive into a traumatic and spiritually difficult valley. The same Spirit who descended on him in Matthew 3:16 led him into the wilderness where he was to undertake a cosmically consequential feat of arms against the serpent. Jesus wandered and fasted in the desert for forty days and forty nights, preparing for his faceoff with the enemy. This was not a sumo wrestler "bulking up" for the weigh in; rather, this was spiritual preparation for the upcoming bout. Matthew acknowledges that Jesus was hungry after his extended period of fasting. The tempter had bided his time. Seeing Jesus hungry and isolated, the enemy slithered into the presence of God's anointed and commissioned Messiah with an all-too familiar intention: Break the obedience of this new Adam.

From the Fall, the story of humanity had been crying out for the promised serpent crusher. With every advancement in the redemptive arc of history, the faithful followers of God looked to the hero of their age to see if *this* one might be the promised one. Adam gave way to Seth who, in turn, would give way to his son and so on. The anticipation continued through the line of the faithful until Noah who, it was hoped, would "bring us relief from our work and from the painful toil of our hands" (Genesis 5:29). As we saw, however, Noah was compromised: He was not the serpent crusher. His failure would eventually lead to the infamous Tower of Babel and another climax of human rebellion. God, refusing to break his covenant with creation, chose not to destroy the world again; instead, he forced the people to obey the Creation Mandate by confusing their language and spreading them across the face of the earth.

The next hero in the redemptive arc, Abraham, was likewise insufficient. For all his mighty deeds and his diligent faith in the promises of God, he, too, failed. After a series of unfortunate events, Abraham and Sarah had their promised son, Isaac. He, in turn, would have two sons who would quarrel over birthrights and authority, highlighting the ongoing presence and power of sin even in the line of the promise. The ultimate victor in this fraternal rivalry was Jacob, whose name eventually changed to Israel. From his highly unorthodox family planning contest came twelve sons who gave their names to the twelve tribes of what would be the foundation of the people of Israel. Yet, for all their spiritual heritage, their lives were filled with arrogance, and rebellion as we witnessed in chapter five.

Despite the privilege of a covenant between Israel and God, the hope of restoration to Edenic paradise was not to be. Neither Moses nor the people of Israel were faithful covenant partners. Instead, even as Moses was in the presence of God receiving the covenant tablets, the people of Israel were engaged in an orgiastic display of adulterous idolatry, and this pattern of covenantal disobedience continued with brazen regularity. The book of Judges portrays their cyclical failure in increasingly gruesome detail. Finally, the people demanded a king.

Saul was chosen because of his stature. But he, too, failed. His behavior towards God smacked of self-important hubris. It was as if God was Saul's servant, not the other way around. Consequently, God raised up a new line of kings through a courageous shepherd boy, David. All eyes were on this "man after God's own heart" to see if he could slay the serpent just as he had killed lions, bears, and even Goliath. Sadly, for Israel, the Davidic covenant given in 2 Samuel 7 made clear that the serpent crusher was *yet* to come; the Messiah would be *like* David, but David was not the Messiah. David revealed his own sinfulness by cuckolding Uriah the Hittite, and then, when his sin was going to be revealed because Bathsheba was pregnant, he had Uriah deliberately killed on the battlefield. Later, in a desire to destroy Israel, Satan caused David to take a census of the people under his reign. Satan's ploy for David was just like his manipulation of Adam and Eve: David began to think that his success was of his own making.

Consistently, throughout the rest of Israel's history, from the might of Solomon's empire through to the exile of the people by Assyrian and Babylonian princes, to the restoration of Israel by Cyrus of Persia, the Israelites were desperately yearning for the arrival of the serpent crusher. But brief moments of ecstatic hope were swiftly dashed as the inexorable march of sinful rebellion plagued every individual and marked every hero as a failure. The serpent crusher had not arrived. From Adam through to Joseph the carpenter, every plausible candidate, whether recorded in the canonical witness or not, proved to be a failure. The silvery tongue of the serpent was too seductive for even the greatest of the biblical heroes to resist. This is why Satan approached Jesus in the wilderness with such confidence: Throughout all human history he had never met a single person he could not break. Satan was unaccustomed to losing.

The Temptations[1]

Satan approached Jesus with the swagger of confident arrogance. Jesus had been fasting in the wilderness for forty days and nights. In his humanity, he would have been weak and desperate. The parallels between these temptations and those of both Adam and Israel are poignant. We're meant to see Jesus as another Adam and another Israel. Satan's desire remained the same: To thwart the will and purposes of God. By breaking Jesus, just as he broke Adam, and Noah, and Abraham, and Moses, and David, Satan would continue his sinful rebellion over and throughout the material realm. This is why we find Jesus in the wilderness, just as Israel had been in the wilderness before the covenant ceremony. The gospel accounts are making the case that Jesus, the Messiah, is the greater covenantal head, truer Israel, and sole faithful covenant partner. But first he must prove it.

A Wilderness Picnic

Importantly, it was only when Jesus was vulnerable that Satan made his first appearance in the wilderness. No doubt he'd been stalking Jesus like a hunter; but he's a trained killer. He waited until the flesh was weak. Finally, he entered the scene. Face to face at last the Savior met the serpent. And Satan spoke first. He began: "If you are the Son of God, command these stones to become loaves of bread" (Matthew 4:3). This is Satan's *modus operandi*. Just like in the garden when he encountered Eve, Satan sought to cast doubt on Jesus's claim. Remember, God himself had just anointed and commissioned Jesus through a public *bat kol*. But Satan, once again, brought doubt to God's pronouncement: "*If* you are the Son of God, Jesus, then *prove it*. After all," Satan teased, "You're hungry, aren't you? Turn those stones into delicious, steaming,

---

[1] It's interesting to note that the only witnesses to this spiritual combat were Jesus and Satan; the gospel writers would therefore have received their information from Jesus himself. This helps us understand how Jesus himself saw his own ministry.

fresh loaves and satiate your human needs. In fact, *doing* so would *prove* that you're God."

The similarities with Adam are poignant, but so are the similarities with Israel in the wilderness. God had commanded the people not to store manna overnight (except in preparation for the Sabbath). Satan's temptation was to doubt God's promises. God had said the people would be provided for from the kitchens of heaven. But *could God be trusted?* Why not keep some safely stored away *just to be sure?* Satan was trying to get Jesus to doubt the word of God and be suspicious about the promises of God. Satan aimed to turn Jesus into a skeptic. Notice that Satan's plan wasn't to immediately get Jesus to *reject* or *denounce* God; he merely wanted Jesus' confidence in his heavenly Father to waver. Jesus was physically weak, emotionally isolated, and spiritually vulnerable and Satan attempted to taunt Jesus into *proving* he was God. But in doing so, Jesus would be indicating that he didn't trust God. It seems, at surface level, an inconsequential demand: Just make some bread. But it would be done through a willful rejection of God's provision and an abuse of his own power. By bending to Satan's taunts, Jesus would be just like any other king, rejecting God's authority, and acting solely in self-interest.

Satan saw Jesus' hunger. He pointed to the rocks and enticed Jesus to turn them into bread and "take and eat" in defiance of God's natural order and God's sovereign provision. But Jesus refused. Instead, he quoted from Deuteronomy 8:3: "Man shall not live by bread alone, but by every word that comes from the mouth of God." Jesus reminded Satan that there's *more* to life than mere physical sustenance. That was important for his human flesh; but "what will it profit a man if he gains the whole world but loses his soul (Matthew 16:26)?" For Jesus to *truly* live, he must "take and eat" from the bread of life.

Jesus rebuked Satan and proved himself superior to the Israelites who hid manna in their baskets overnight. He trusted God that he would provide what Jesus needed to accomplish the ministry for which he was so recently commissioned. Likewise, he proved himself obedient in scarcity where Adam was disobedient in plenty. Jesus knew the words of God and *trusted* them. Unlike Adam and Eve, there was no editing, changing, denying, doubting, or updating the words that God had given. Jesus quoted Deuteronomy 8:3 as a means of denying Satan's tactical ploy to doubt God.

The point of this temptation is *not* that it's sinful to eat (though, of course, without excess). Nor is the point that we should deprive ourselves of what God has so generously provided. In the garden of Eden, God had given Adam and Eve plenteous provision; after the flood, God even permitted the killing of meat for nutrition. The point is that Satan's diabolical offer of "take and eat" was once again meant to bring about a denial of God's words and a rejection of God's kingship. Satan was asking Jesus, as the commissioned Messiah, to do things *his* way, not God's. This becomes clearer with the second and third temptations.

Trust falling in the Temple

For the first time in human history, Satan's efforts were met with a stalwart strength of faith and purpose. Thus, he quite literally upped the ante and continued his efforts to break the iron will of Jesus by taking him to the pinnacle of the temple. Here, he demanded once again that Jesus prove his claim to be the Son of God: "If you are the Son of God, throw yourself down, for it is written, 'He will command his angels concerning you,' and 'on their hands they will bear you up, lest you strike your foot against a stone'" (Matthew 4:5-6).

Notice, again, that Satan began by doubting Jesus' claim to be the Son of God. He was trying to rile Jesus so that he felt he must prove his claim for it to be legitimate. As before, Satan's initial ploy was to get Jesus to doubt God's pronouncement at the baptism and to react with frustration. But this time Satan plays dirty. He told Jesus that he could perform a dramatic feat by throwing himself off the pinnacle of the temple complex and *prove* his faith in God's words. Why? Because God had said that he would protect his anointed one. In the first temptation, Satan had urged Jesus to use his power selfishly. But here Satan was suggesting that Jesus confirm his sonship by *fulfilling prophecy*. The cunning nature of this temptation is that Satan identified that Jesus was trusting God's words, and so he embarked upon a plan that *used* scripture. As in Eden, however, Satan took what God said but deliberately *misinterpreted* it. He twisted God's word, but because he used God's word, it had the veneer of religiosity.

By quoting Psalm 91:11, Satan was suggesting to Jesus that God would "command the angels concerning you" so that the freefall from such a height wouldn't result in his death (which is the obvious normal consequence). But this is not the point of Psalm 91. Psalm 91 is a song of confidence in God's protection. The one who trusts in God, the Psalmist states, will be delivered from the snares of evil, and disease, and danger. Psalm 91's message is about trusting God to protect those who have taken refuge in him. It's *not* about testing God's promise by placing yourself in harm's way.[2]

Satan was trying to get Jesus to test God the Father's words at the baptismal event by placing himself in mortal danger; if *God* was true to his word, he would protect Jesus. But the very act of testing God like this would flow from a heart disposition of distrust. Desiring God to *prove* his protection is to inwardly doubt that God can, or will, save him. Satan was trying to manipulate Jesus. By exploiting a human tendency to *doubt* God, he was try-

---

2 A common interpretation of this temptation is that Jesus would *prove* his Messiahship and receive a large public following if he were to miraculously survive such a great fall. This would be, perhaps, a means of circumnavigating much of the difficulties and challenges of his future ministry. But it would be to avoid the ministry that Messiah was meant to observe and follow. He must fulfil the prophecies that include miraculous healings, teachings, exorcisms, and reaching out to the Gentiles. This interpretation is unsatisfactory when correctly read through the lens of Psalm 91. Satan was not tempting Jesus with a crowd gathered by his showmanship; rather, he was tempting Jesus to test God. By jumping from the building, Jesus would be defying God's purposes for his ministry and demanding that God reward his foolish behavior.

ing to make Jesus *prove* he trusted God by testing God's promise; but in doing so, he'd be admitting that he didn't trust God at all. This temptation wasn't about Jesus' obedience so much as it was about his willingness to publicly put his own Father to the test. Satan was trying to confuse Jesus by offering him a *false* promise. By misquoting Psalm 91, Satan was implying that the Psalm promised Jesus that bad things wouldn't happen to him, even if he was reckless, because God would save him. But the Psalm doesn't promise that; rather, it's theme is that anyone who trusts in God and hides in his protection will be cherished like a child.

Once again, Satan was confounded when Jesus refused to bite the lure. Jesus quoted Deuteronomy 6:17: "You shall not put the Lord your God to the test." There's likely a double implication in the use of this specific quotation. On the surface, Jesus was again telling Satan that he won't test God *because* he trusts him. But there's likely a more subtle, deeper, layer. Jesus was aware of who he is: *God* the Son. Therefore, by quoting this verse, Jesus was simultaneously saying to Satan "don't test *me*." Jesus was not deceived nor manipulated; he, who authored scripture, was not led astray by the misappropriation of these holy words. Jesus knew the true context of Psalm 91. And in that Psalm, the one who is ultimately prefigured is the Messiah who, by trusting in God, would have victory over the evils of the world. Specifically, in verse 13, the Psalmist states: "You will tread on the lion and the adder; the young lion and the *serpent you will trample underfoot*." Jesus knew that the true context of Psalm 91 pointed to the destruction of the serpent by the obedient Messiah.

A Crown Without A Cross

Exasperated, Satan decided to go nuclear. Satan, we have seen, has read scripture. He knows the work that Messiah will undertake by God's command. Passages such as Isaiah 53 speak of a servant who suffers. Satan was aware of these promises (even though it's unlikely he fully grasped their significance). Suffering is unpleasant, and it would be especially so for the incarnate Son who had never experienced suffering for all eternity past. Thus, he brought Jesus to the top of a large mountain and provided him a vision of all the kingdoms of the world in all their glory, pomp, pageantry, power, wealth, and seduction. The vista was a magnificent sight. All the nations of the world dangled in front of the eyes of the Messiah who had come to claim them and deliver them from the kingdom of darkness into his glorious light (Isaiah 9:2; Luke 1:79; 2 Corinthians 4:6; Colossians 1:13; 1 Peter 2:9).

Satan gestured towards these kingdoms. He leaned in and seductively whispers: "I will give you all these if you fall down and worship me" (Matthew 4:9). This temptation was particularly mendacious for three reasons. Firstly, Satan only showed Jesus the veneer of these kingdoms; he hid their sinfulness and rebellion from him. Jesus was being encouraged to see them as he thought they ought to be, but not as they really were. Satan was projecting splendor but hiding sin. This was like the garden of Eden, where Eve was encouraged to look at the fruit as she was being temped so that she "saw that it was good to eat." Here, Jesus was being forced to gaze at the cities, but the mirage attempted to blind him to their true state and therefore distract him from his true mission: Redemption. He didn't come to earth to become another tyrant but to be the liberator.

The second reason why this temptation was especially treacherous is that Satan set himself up as God, or, at the very least, as God's equal. He stood on the mountaintop as if he was the great king and ruler of all that was visible. The implication was that the entire material realm belonged to Satan, and he could give it to whomever he desired. Satan was acting like his rebellion had won and overthrown God's throne. But that, too, was a deceptive illusion. Satan had no more power to give Jesus the kingdoms of the earth than you or I. He wasn't a king over creation but a fellow rebel. He may be a roaring lion whose tyranny terrifies and tortures creation under his temporary dominion; but he owns nothing and he's most certainly *not* God's peer. In Eden, the serpent's offer to Eve was a gilded promise. He told her she could be like

God (ignoring the fact that she already *was* made in his image). This was not something Satan could give. Likewise, this offer to Jesus was not something that Satan had the power to provide. The nations of the world, no matter how neatly wrapped and presented, were not Satan's to give. He may be the prince and the power of the air, but he's not the landlord. Just as the Canaanites didn't own the land that God had given to the Israelites, neither does Satan own the land over which he exercises his temporary violence.

Thirdly, and most significantly, Satan's third temptation desired to offer Christ a kingdom without the cross. This is the greatest temptation: To be a savior without suffering. Satan played on the frailty of humanity and told Jesus that following God's plan would lead to suffering, pain, shame, humiliation: "But, Jesus, you are *God*. Gods don't *suffer*!" It's as if Satan was bartering for Jesus' services as a mercenary soldier: "God will give you kingdoms through suffering; but I will give you kingdoms if you simply bend your knee to me. Work for me and I'll give you *all* the nations of the world. And I'll do it *without* demanding your suffering. Just worship me." Satan tried to prevent the gospel by getting the Messiah to forsake the mission. Although Satan likely didn't foresee the cross (and especially the victory within it), he nevertheless knew that this temptation would sink into the very core of Jesus' humanity. We, in hindsight, can see the depths of this conniving temptation in the garden of Gethsemane when Jesus was horrified at his impending suffering.

Yet Jesus refused to bend his knee. This offer of Satan's, although tempting, was an empty promise because he had nothing to give. Jesus instead continued to place his trust in God. The offer of Satan should be contrasted with God's promise given in Psalm 2 where the reign of the Lord's Messiah is discussed. The nations that Satan showed Jesus? David says that they rage against God and his anointed one: They desire to break the bonds of the creaturely divide and overthrow God, making themselves gods of their own lives. In contrast, God will "speak to them in his wrath, and terrify them in his fury" (Psalm 2:5) because he will "set [his] king on Zion, my holy hill" (Psalm 2:6). This king is none other than his Son, and God's promise is that, "I will make the nations your heritage, and the ends of the earth your possession" (Psalm 2:8).

God's promise in Psalm 2 directly contrasts with Satan's promise in Matthew 4 in three ways. Firstly, God shows the Son the true status and nature of the world: They're in rebellion. Secondly, God alone claims ownership; the nations and kings rage against him, but God laughs at them from his throne. He's sovereign even over their rebellion. If they repent, there will be mercy; if they refuse, there will be justice. Thirdly, because God alone is the ruler over all creation, and God has shown their true condition, the Son will be given a people who "take refuge in him" (Psalm 2:12). That refuge, Jesus knows, comes through his work as the suffering servant. There can be no kingdom without the cross.

Instead of bending his knee in worship to Satan, Jesus trusted God's promise and followed God's plan which, although marked with suffering, ultimately led to his exaltation, such that *every* tongue will one day confess his true lordship (Philippians 2:11). Jesus responded by quoting Deuteronomy 6:13: "You shall worship the Lord your God and him only shall you serve." Jesus would not worship a creature; only God is worthy of worship. He then commanded Satan "Be gone!" The irony of Satan obeying Jesus when he had just been acting as God ought to be comical. The way in which he left, however, was anything but comedic. In the Greek, it might be better rendered that Satan left *until another opportunity* arises. Satan may have lost the battle of the wills in the wilderness, but he wasn't conceding defeat. Like a rabid wolf, he would continue to stalk his prey until Jesus could be attacked and defeated. The Messiah now began his ministry, but the conflict was far from over.

A point must be made about the use of scripture here. Jesus did not defeat Satan because he had memorized scripture and quoted it as if it were a spell or some kind of superstitious talisman. We know this because Satan himself could quote scripture (albeit with ill intent and out of context). Jesus quoted scripture not as some kind of magical formula but as the grounds and basis for his rejection of the lies Satan was presenting. Scripture memorization is not, in and of itself, going to make any individual less prone to sinful behavior; rather, scripture is how we comprehend what God has promised (and, just as crucially, what God has *not* promised). Jesus knew the words of the Bible *and believed them*; this is why he could resist Satan. He knew what God had actually said, and he knew that God was more trustworthy than Satan.

This principle is extremely important to grasp because very often we can treat scripture like some kind of spiritual amulet or charm as if the words themselves, when written or spoken, are powerful, irrespective of context. This is not the case. Scripture empowers believers by teaching them about the nature, character, and promises of God. It's meant to give us courage and strength to trust God in the face of the evil one. Merely quoting a verse won't terrify the devil and make him flee from us in terror. It is not about *him*, but about *us*; we need scripture to build up our faith and remind us that God is trustworthy because he is faithful. Satan can read the Bible and he can listen to us quote it all day long. It's not until we respond in faith to it that he cares. When we apply scripture by faithfully obeying it, trusting God's promises, Satan's deceptions are brought crashing down.[3] When we *trust* scripture as the revelation of God, it's powerful in our personal lives.[4]

Jesus Is Greater

Because Jesus was victorious over Satan in this dramatic contest, we're meant to understand that Jesus is greater. He succeeded where all others had failed. Unlike every other human, he remained utterly and totally sinless. Adam failed in a paradise of plenty, but Jesus succeeded in the withering wilderness. Noah had

---

[3] Note that obedience does not provide salvation but is a response for salvation.

[4] This does not mean scripture is only applicable as we experience it. What I am arguing is that how use scripture matters. Sanctification from sinful attitudes and behaviors begins when we trust that God is better than our sin.

failed after the trauma of the flood, but Jesus succeeded despite the waves of temptation. Abraham failed to trust the word of God that Isaac would come, but Jesus succeeded by trusting God's word without flinching. The Israelites failed to trust God's provision, but Jesus succeeded by accepting that we need to trust God to truly live. David failed by using his power to murder his friend after stealing his wife, but Jesus succeeded by refusing to use his power to serve his own needs or abuse others.

Humanity not only failed prior to the arrival of Jesus, but we continue to fail God's holy standards today. We fail when we listen to the lies of the serpent, give in to the desires of the flesh, refuse to trust that God is sufficient, resist God's holiness, and reject his rule, choosing instead to worship ourselves in moments of sinful rebellion. We fail when we listen to the tempters' promises that *this* time our sin will satisfy. We fail when we look at the temporary pleasure of sin and think that it will quench our spiritual thirst. Every human has failed. Jesus alone walked through the suffocating tunnel of temptation to the end, never deviating to the right or to the left. He alone knows how to truly defeat temptation because he alone has consistently and completely overcome it. Satan's attempt to break Jesus had failed. And now Jesus, the greater Adam, the greater Moses, the greater Israel, the greater David, was going on the offensive. The kingdom of God is at hand and the king started his march. He would begin the process of winding back the breadth of Satan's illegal empire so that all Satan had tried to bribe Jesus with would now become Christ's, not by dent of illicit worship, but by the right of conquest!

Application

A primary application is to note that Satan waited for Jesus to be isolated and hungry before beginning his temptations of Christ. Satan knows our vulnerabilities. He's spent millennia successfully analyzing humanity and knows how to maximize our sinful desires and tendencies. He gears his temptations towards our desires; he will know what our sinful hearts yearn for and then offers us temptations that will scratch that rebellious itch. Satan isolated Jesus and waited for his human nature to grow weak. It was only then that he pounced. It is often so with us; the fires of lust rage hottest when we are isolated and where uncontrolled passion can find freedom. Gossipers tend to find themselves privy to much secret information. The envious and jealous soul is tempted with constant disappointment and fantasies about the other side of the fence where the grass always appears greener. Those prone to bouts of anger will be made to experience many inconveniences and frustrations that bubble and simmer under the surface until they erupt in an explosion of wrath. The list of temptations is endless: Idolatry, lust, anger, theft, jealousy, bitterness, adultery, coveting, murder, intoxication, dissension, lying. And Satan is a master at exploiting every one of them.

This is why we must be diligently on guard. We must know and understand our own sinful predilections so that we can guard against the fiery arrows of the tempter by applying the means of spiritual protection. Satan desires to torment our minds with thoughts and desires when we are tired, alone, bored, sad, or resentful of others. We must avoid spiritual isolation which only increases our vulnerability; this is why the household of faith where we can confess our sins one to another is of vital importance to the Christian. We're an army of broken and wounded saints in need of the holy ministration of the gospel from one another. When we're isolated, we're prone to a barrage of temptations and an onslaught of lies from the deceiver. Fellow believers are tasked with being priests to one another by repeating the truth of the work and power of Christ so that the serpent is defanged and silenced.

A second application is that Satan will make wild and delightful promises as part of his deceptions. Of course, as we saw with Jesus, the things Satan offers are going to be fraudulent; either he has no power to give them in the first place, or they'll be false promises. Just as he had no power to *actually* give Jesus the world, he nevertheless tried to entice Christ to *believe* that he could. He does this with us; he cannot (and, indeed, would not) satisfy our deepest spiritual needs. Anything and everything he offers is a pale and boring alternative to the true reality that comes from God. God made marriage to be a place of safe and intimate vulnerability climaxing with the sexual expression of union between a husband and wife; Satan's paltry alternative is loveless and valueless sex. God provided community through friendship and relationship; Satan's pathetic offer is a narcissistic domination of others. God's gift of work was given to humanity as a means to reflect him and his glorious creativity; Satan has turned the idea of work into meaningless mundanity. Human beings were made in the image of God, distinct but valued; Satan has torn that unified *imago Dei* apart through disease, dysmorphia, and division.

A third application is to remember that Satan *knows* scripture and is more than willing to play along with a pretention of holiness if that can be exploited. He was willing to abuse and misuse the words of Moses to try to entrap and entice Jesus. He will do the same with us. How many Christians become haughty and arrogant because of their salvation and their victories over sinful behavior? How many look down on brothers and sisters who have stumbled in sin with airs of disgust and disdain? The tendency towards self-worship is often not far from the household of faith, especially when individual acts of obedience are held up as a litmus test of faith, rather than the humble worship of Jesus as Lord.

Just as Satan used scripture to tempt Jesus, he can use it to coerce us into sinful behavior. This can be illustrated through the frequently abused passage in 1 Corinthians 7:3-5: "The husband should give to his wife her conjugal rights, and likewise the wife to her husband. For the wife does not have authority over her own body, but the husband does. Likewise, the husband does not have authority over his own body, btu the wife does. Do not deprive one another…" Satan can take those words and introduce them into a marriage with devastating effect. A man who feels rejected will be tempted by Satan to use those verses to bludgeon (dare I say, even assault) his wife into intimate relations, neglecting her desires or needs. This is, of course, the *modus operandi* of Satan:

Cherry picking verses at whim. This is reminiscent of the consequences of the Fall where Adam and Eve's desires became contrary to one another. Through the gospel, however, husband and wife are meant to submit to one another, as Paul explicitly states in Ephesians 5:21-31. Satan, by tempting someone to misuse 1 Corinthians 7, is deliberately avoiding the larger context of restored romantic relationships as presented in Ephesians 5. A wife should submit to her husband as to the Lord. A husband should *sacrifice* his desire for his wife as Christ sacrificed his rights for his bride, the church. Because the pattern of sacrifice is Jesus who "did not count equality with God a thing to be grasped but made himself nothing, taking the form of a servant, being born in the likeness of men...he humbled himself by becoming obedient *to the point of death, even death on a cross*" (Philippians 2:6-8), husbands are to reflect Christ through sacrificial love, not sinful selfishness. By exploiting a spouse's sex drive, Satan can reintroduce the disharmony of sin into a marriage *by misusing scripture*. Satan's skill can blind us to the holiness of obedience by the perversion of scripture; we can *feel* like we're *righteous* even when we're deceived into sinning.

Conclusion

Satan tempted Jesus to "take and eat" in defiance of God's will and purposes for the Messiah. The temptation was not about *eating* any more than Adam and Eve's sinful behavior concerned the mere ingestion of the fruit. The fundamental principle beneath both the sin in the garden and the temptation in the wilderness was disobedience to God's words and a refusal to trust God's provision, protection, and purposes. By attempting to get Jesus to turn the rocks into bread, Satan was trying to exploit his human nature to operate as any other human would; doing what it took to satisfy himself, even if that meant undermining God's creational order and serving himself rather than submitting to the will of God. By ordering Jesus to jump from the temple ledge, Satan attempted to manipulate Jesus into testing God by distorting the words of scripture. In offering him the kingdoms of the earth,

Satan was intentionally trying to prevent Jesus the Messiah from being the prophesied suffering servant. In every case, however, Jesus demonstrated his humble faith in God the Father and quoted scripture as the basis for his trust. He did not employ scripture as a magic formula but wielded it as a sword that struck a death blow to the lies and deceptions and charades of Satan's temptations.

In an amazing turn of events, Jesus, the incarnate Son of God, ordered Satan to leave and, for the very first time in all human and redemptive history, Satan was forced to retreat without having gotten his man. Jesus, instead, had walked through the entire tunnel of temptation, facing desperation, deception, isolation, manipulation, and desire without giving in: He had passed where Adam had failed. Because of his success, he would begin his march through hostile territory, proclaiming the dynamic immanency of the kingdom of God. But although Satan had been forced to retreat, his war against the anointed one would continue. Jesus had been invited to "take and eat" from the feast of the fallen and refused; in time, he would provide his own invitation to "take and eat."

7

"Take and Eat": Passover in the Upper Room

> *Now as they were eating, Jesus took bread, and after blessing it broke it and gave it to the disciples, and said, "Take and eat; this is my body." And he took a cup, and when he had given thanks he gave it to them, saying, "Drink of it, all of you, for this is my blood of the New Covenant, which is poured out for many for the forgiveness of sins."*
> (Matthew 26:26-28)

Introduction

I love Christmas. It might seem odd to talk about Christmas to introduce a chapter about Maundy Thursday, but hear me out. When we think of Christmas, we typically think of some variation of the same five things: the incarnation and nativity, jolly ol' Saint Nicholas, cold weather, presents, and...turkey! In our household, growing up, Christmas dinner was the meal of the year. We had turkey, ham, sausages wrapped in bacon, brussels sprouts cooked with bacon bits, cauliflower in a cheese sauce, Yorkshire puddings, potatoes in countless variations, and a munificence of other garnishes, sauces, and traditional nibbles. The Christmas dining table held a cornucopia of delicious treats! There were many other scrumptious meals throughout the year, but when the immediate joy of unwrapping the presents dissipated, the next thing to anticipate was the Christmas feast. Christmas dinner holds a nostalgic joy in my heart.

But I married an American. An Hispanic American at that. My American friends tend to have their annual traditional meal at Thanksgiving. We in Britain don't celebrate Thanksgiving so we throw everything into our large Christmas dinner. When we got married, my wife and I "had a conversation" about our traditions. For me, Christmas dinner was *the* centerpiece of the day. The family, gathered around the table, eating ourselves into a joyous, tryptophan-induced food coma, before napping by the tree, is a Dunn family staple. My wife, on the other hand, preferred her turkey binge at Thanksgiving and didn't care so much about the Christmas meal. In the end, our little family compromised: We would not choose *either* celebration but incorporate *both* into our own tradition. Now, we have a smorgasbord of Hispanic spices and British cuisine (I know, it's a weird thought that Brits even *have* a "cuisine") at *both* Thanksgiving and Christmas. Everyone's happy. Except the turkeys. Our traditions were adopted by the other and therefore were transformed into something new and greater by the changes. The first year was a little jarring (not least for my belt!), but now that we've gotten into the routine of it, we love our somewhat unique traditional family meals.

It's this idea of traditions having to transform that is the focus of this chapter. Jesus had already positioned himself as the greater Adam by defeating Satan in the wilderness temptations. We will see that he also positioned himself as the greater Moses by presenting the miracles of the Old Testament Israel for the Gentiles. In doing so, he provides the mandate that access to his kingdom comes solely through himself as the true Messiah and suffering servant. The formation of this new people and nation occurs by the bringing about of the New Covenant. Jesus will do this by taking the traditions of the Mosaic covenant, such as the Passover Sedar, and updating them by making them his own. The symbols of the Old Covenant deliverance during and in response to the Exodus will be utilized by Christ to introduce the New Covenant's deliverance from sin, death, disease, and even the serpent himself.

And it all coalesced around those words, made glorious by his utterance: "Take and eat."

Context

Having bested Satan in the wilderness, Jesus embarked upon the ministry for which he was commissioned at his baptism. He called his disciples, he amassed large crowds, and proceeded to teach them, heal them, feed them, and correctly interpret scripture for them. The nature of his ministry was as an itinerant preacher and rabbi; this inevitably brought him into conflict with the various groups of religious elites. The Pharisees grew to hate him because he rejected their extra biblical teachings as not only wrong but antithetical to Torah. The Sadducees hated him because he posed a political and existential threat to their grasp on power. He disagreed with the Pharisees (who added to the books of Moses and the Old Testament in general) as well as the Sadducees (who only accepted the books of Moses) concerning what constituted scripture. His Messianic populism (even though it was often misunderstood because of contemporary misinterpretations of the Old Testament) threatened the delicate balance of political power between Jews and Romans as well as the fragile relationship between Pharisees and Sadducees. Coming together, they decided that, for the "greater good," this northern upstart must be stopped by any means possible. They frequently sent ambassadors from the Sanhedrin to challenge him in hopes he would give them cause to publicly denounce him. When that failed, they resorted to deception and, eventually, political murder.

Making things worse, Jesus had been known to meet and interact with Gentiles. Those who were outside the Mosaic covenant could not be considered "God's people" by the religious elites. Rather, they were ceremonially unclean. Although some Gentiles, seeking to worship the God of Israel, could enter the temple courtyard up to the Court of the Gentiles, they were restricted from truly incorporating into the community. For this reason, it was verging on blasphemous for Jesus to present the Messianic kingdom, with all its material and spiritual blessings, to Gentiles as well as to Jews.

Dining in the Desert

The unusual dichotomy of interacting with Jews and Gentiles on a similar basis begins with the miraculous feeding of the 5000.[1] In that miracle, Jesus led a large crowd of 5000 men into the wilderness where he taught them about the kingdom and then provided food from the kitchens of heaven despite the meagre offering of five loaves and two fishes that he had on hand. For the disciples, this was exactly what they had been hoping for; the Messiah's arrival at a time of great national distress with Israel verging on religious apostasy (at least amongst the upper echelons of the Romanizing Jewish elite and a quarter-Jewish king). Immediately thereafter, Jesus walked on the water, proving that he could do what God alone can do (Psalm 77:19; Job 9:8). In Mark's account, Jesus even used the divine name as he walked towards the boat in a scene reminiscent of God passing by Moses.

What is intriguing is that Jesus then entered a confrontation with the Pharisees and scribes about ritual defilement. In Matthew 15:1-9, Jesus rebuked the Pharisees for their bastardization of the Law. They *claimed* to be holy, but through the exploitation of rabbinical traditions such as *Korban*, they actually created loopholes to *avoid* obeying God. Jesus challenged them that true spiritual defilement isn't caused by ingested food, but by what resides in the heart. Following from this public argument, Jesus began to deliberately teach this lesson to his disciples through lived out meta-

---

[1] Although there is some debate as to the purpose of the famous feeding miracles in the synoptic Gospels, it seems clear that, when taken as a composite whole, from Matthew 12 where Jesus declares himself to be Lord of the Sabbath, through to the Transfiguration in Matthew 17, the author is trying to demonstrate that Jesus' ministry was like that of Moses, but also superior to Moses; it will culminate not in the crossing of a Jordan river, but an entirely new type of Exodus, founded upon the cross and resurrection. This argument culminates in 1 Peter 2:9-10 and is one of the major thrusts of the sermons in the book of Hebrews.

phors. After stating that one is not defiled by external things, Jesus provocatively entered Gentile territory and healed a Canaanite woman's demon-possessed daughter. His point was that *she* didn't defile *him*; rather, *he* was providing the blessings of the Messianic kingdom to *her* even though she was not a Jew. Then, to prove the point with greater clarity, he taught a large Gentile crowd over the course of three days, and healed their many sick, tormented, and possessed. The kingdom's blessings were spilling out, away from the arrogant Israelite religious elite and towards the humble, believing, Gentiles.

In a dramatic twist, Jesus then told the disciples to feed this large crowd of Gentiles. Up until this point, they may have grasped some aspects about holiness and inclusivity. But with the dramatic and miraculous feeding of the 4000 Gentiles, Jesus was very intentionally planting his flag that his kingdom would be open to any and all who would enter it. He, and he alone, is the door to the kingdom of eternal life (John 10:9-16). Thus, the disciples watched as Jesus did the Mosaic miracle of feeding a people in the wilderness from the kitchens of heaven *but for Gentiles*. The leftovers from this heavenly feast were seven baskets. In a numerological reflection, the twelve baskets from the feeding of the 5000 likely referred to the tribes of Israel; but the seven baskets in this second feeding miracle implied that the fullness of the kingdom involves citizenry from beyond Israel.[2] And, vitally, the means of entrance into Christ's kingdom comes solely through faith in him. Heritage accounts for little at the personal level; either one is "in Christ" through faith, or one is not.

Jesus, in this crescendoing series of dramatic miracles, was effectively presenting the manifesto of his kingdom. What was most perplexing of all for the religious elite was that Jesus claimed to be bringing not merely a holier Israel but some kind of new commu-

---

2 A.E.J. Rawlinson, *The Gospel According to St. Mark*, 5th edition (London: Methuen, 1942), p. 87 makes a convincing case that the Greek word for the basket used in the two miracles are different, implying (or strongly suggesting) that the feeding of the 5000 was for Jews and the feeding of the 4000 was for Gentiles.

nity of faith that would be born *from* Moses but claims superiority *to* Moses. He was not merely *another* Moses; he was claiming to be the *greater* Moses who would produce a larger, grander, and more glorious kingdom comprised of citizens from *beyond* Mosaic Israel.

This claim of superiority can be seen most vibrantly at his transfiguration. Atop the mountain with Peter, James, and John, Jesus presented to them something of the beauty of his holy form as God the Son. In that moment, all the Old Testament narratives and histories where the glory of God was shown to men would have rushed into the amazed minds of the three mesmerized disciples. But to their amazement, when they looked at Jesus, he was standing between two men. It soon became apparent to them that Jesus was conversing with Moses and Elijah. Together, Moses and Elijah form the human foundation of the Law and the Prophets, which is a shorthand way of saying the Hebrew Bible.

In that moment, the disciples may have been tempted to believe that they were witnessing the arrival of Jesus' generals. This era of Jewish history had cultivated a belief that the Messiah, when he arrived, would be a warlord who would resurrect the resplendent empire of David and Solomon. This would entail raising a rebellion against the Romans. After thrashing the juggernaut of Rome's legions, they expected Messiah to introduce an Elysian era of peace and prosperity for the whole world, centered around Zion. With Elijah and Moses at his side, Jesus would be unstoppable. But if those thoughts were going through their minds, then they were soon to be disabused of that notion.

In another dramatic moment in the ministry of Jesus, the *bat kol* from heaven boomed again. God the Father spoke with an epoch defining statement: "This is my beloved Son, with whom I am well pleased; listen to him" (Matthew 18:5). The startling implication of this for a Jew in the first century is hard to grasp today. In Deuteronomy 18:15, God promised that a day would come when he would "raise up for you a prophet like me [i.e., Moses] from among you, from your brothers–it is to him you shall listen."

What God was saying was that Jesus was the promised prophet who would supersede Moses. At the Transfiguration, the entirety of the Hebrew Bible found the heart of its prophetic fulfillment. Like giant signposts, every typological prediction finds its source, fulfilment, or meaning in or through Jesus of Nazareth: It's always been all about Jesus. This is made clear from the gospel of Luke: "Beginning with Moses and all the Prophets, he interpreted to them in *all the scriptures* the things concerning himself" (Luke 24:27). God's point at the Transfiguration was that the Law and the Prophets give way to Jesus. He is the greater Moses and the greater prophet. He is the promised Messiah. And he was introducing the greater covenant to build a greater nation than ethnic, corporate Israel. He, the true and faithful Israelite would create a new Israel, one not bound by the strictures of the Mosaic Law or sacrificial system, but implemented by his own, once-for-all sacrifice. This new household of faith transcends ethnic boundaries, consisting of faithful men and women from every tribe, tongue, and nation, united by faith in the work of the Jewish Messiah. In this new kingdom, there will be no distinction between Jew or Gentile, no hierarchy of free or slave, nor rejection of inherent equality between male or female (Galatians 3:28); rather, all will be united to one Lord, in one faith, through one baptism (Ephesians 4:5-6).

Immediately after the Transfiguration, Jesus explained that he would go to Jerusalem where he would be betrayed and crucified before coming back to life. God had just told Peter, James, and John to listen to Jesus, the greater Mosaic prophet. He was now teaching them that he was not going to be the earthly warrior who would take on Rome; rather, he was the suffering servant. Thereafter, he continued his journey towards Jerusalem and the cross.

The Upper Room

The final week of Jesus' life began with his triumphal march into Jerusalem. He was seated on a colt rather than a white steed to highlight that, although the king had indeed come to Jerusalem, he was not instigating an earthy revolution against the might of Rome. His ministry was of a different nature. Despite the jarring juxtaposition of what they expected and what he presented, the people nevertheless waved palm branches before him, shouting "Hosanna to the Son of David" (Matthew 21:9). This was followed the next day by an attack on the greed of the religious elite. He cleansed the temple by overturning the tables where the moneychangers gleefully counted their profits (Matthew 21:12-13). In contrast to their exploitative behavior for which the Jewish religious elite had long been excoriated (Ezekiel 34:1-10), Jesus proved himself the good shepherd by caring for those who came to him (Ezekiel 34:11-15). As the Messiah, he exhibited the blessings of the kingdom by healing the blind and lame in fulfilment of Isaiah 35:5-6. The drama of his temple visit led to a temper tantrum from the chief priests and the scribes.

The following day, Jesus proclaimed that the Scribes and Pharisees and priests were "blind guides" who were like "whitewashed tombs, which outwardly appear beautiful, but within are full of dead people's bones" and were "snakes" (Matthew 23:24-33). These antics did not endear him to the already murderously hostile religious elite. After this outburst, he ascended the Mount of Olives beyond the city limits and prophesied the fall and destruction of Jerusalem. We know little about what happened the next day, but most likely the disciples and their families were preparing for the upcoming Passover.

Thus, we come to the final Passover meal that Jesus observed. We've already considered the first Passover, prior to the Exodus. Jesus, as a faithful, Law-abiding, covenant-observing Jew, was diligent to honor the required rituals of the Torah. Because of this, on the Thursday of his final week, he sent Peter and John ahead to the Upper Room to make the preparations for their entire group to celebrate the meal together. As this was the Passover festival, the city of Jerusalem would be filled with devoted worshippers on their pilgrimage to the temple. Some estimates suggest that the city could swell to as many as one million worshippers during this period. For the religious elite, passions were already running high; the last thing they needed was a rabble-rousing supposed Messiah disturbing the peace.

Jesus, not oblivious to the pernicious plans being concocted by the arch-traitor and the chief priests, went to the Upper Room with his disciples and reclined with them (Matthew 26:20). At the table, now with a heavy heart, he informed the disciples that treachery would come from within their own band of merry men. In sorrowful shock, they each in turn asked if it would be they who'd betray him. Jesus responded that it was one with whom he had dipped his hand into the dish. As was custom, however, the Passover meal was a communal meal, and each person would take their bread and dip it into a common bowl of sauce or oil or spice. In other words, he didn't narrow it down. But he then condemned the traitor, saying: "Woe to that man by whom the Son of Man is betrayed! It would have been better for that man if he had not been born" (Matthew 26:24). In a moment of extreme pathos, we read that after Jesus had given a morsel of bread to Judas, Satan returned. Remember that he'd left the humiliation of the wilderness with anger burning in his breast; bruised, but not beaten, he'd sought another opportunity to derail the Messianic mission. Now, in Judas he had his mark. John records that "after he [Judas] had taken the morsel, Satan entered into him. Jesus said to him, 'What you are going to do, do quickly'" (John 13:27). The disciples were confused what Jesus meant, but Judas presumably realized his treacherous jig was up, took the opportunity to leave and fled into the night to prepare the ambush that would ultimately lead to the killing of the king.

In the Upper Room, the Passover Sedar continued. Passover is punctuated by four moments of drinking red wine, each signifying different aspects of the history of the Hebrews. There's a general pattern for the celebration (though there can be variation). The red wine represents the blood of the Passover lamb. The first "cup" is the cup of sanctification, taken after the bread is broken, beginning the Sedar meal which will be interspersed with readings from the Torah, prayers, and hymns. The second cup is the cup of plagues. The third cup, which Jesus interrupts, is the cup of redemption.

As the Sedar was being observed, the voice of the master broke through their holy reverie with a scintillating echo: Moses was giving way to Jesus. The celebration of an Exodus from Pharaoh was giving way to an Exodus from the serpent. Passover was giving way to the Eucharist. Jesus, in a moment that would reverberate throughout the corridors of time, overturned the serpent's invitation to "take and eat" with one of his own. As his disciples looked at him, expectantly, he took one of the loaves of bread in his hands.

"Take and Eat"

In that candlelit Upper Room, filled with delightful odors and melodious hymnody, Jesus "took bread, and when he had given thanks, he broke it and gave it to them, saying, 'This is my body which is given for you. Do this in remembrance of me'" (Luke 22:19). The disciples were invited to "take and eat" the bread after this pronouncement, scarcely able to recognize the vast theological implications of Jesus' words. Under the Mosaic covenant, a lamb was to be sacrificed as a means of expressing the forgiveness of sins by "placing" the sins of the people onto the sacrificed animal: Jesus was proclaiming that *he* would become that sacrificial lamb. The disciples were to understand that the suffering servant would become a sacrificially-offered servant. Jesus had already taught that he was to die as part of his Messianic mission; now, he made the same point, by using the symbolism of the Passover. By drawing upon that historical and theological symbolism, Jesus was revealing more about the nature of his sacrifice. As the sacrificial lamb, *he* would bear the judgement of God for the punishment of any and all who would repent and believe the gospel. The breaking of his body, symbolized by the breaking of the bread, would provide an atonement for the rebellious humanity; God would indeed "pass over" the sins of his people who believe in the work of the Messiah.

In Genesis 15, God made a covenant with Abram.[3] God had already made grandiose promises with Abram in Genesis 12, but time had passed and still those promises still seemed very far away. Thus, in Genesis 15, Abram asks God, "How will I know that I am to possess the land?" In response, God commanded Abram to bring animals before him. Having brought the required animals, he "cut them in half, and laid each half over against the other. But he did not cut the birds in half" (Genesis 15:10). This created a channel or a pathway between the severed carcasses. This was a bloody, stinking, messy, gruesome sight. The pungent aroma of death would sit in the back of your throat. Despite its unpleasant character, it was not an entirely uncommon event in the ancient world. Abram understood that this was preparation for a covenant ceremony.

The ceremony would traditionally involve the king and the vassal walking through the bloody pathway together. If either partner broke the covenant, the implications were all around for everyone to see and smell. The unfaithful covenant partner would be torn apart, just like the animals—broken in a bloody mess. In this covenant ceremony, God made a promise to Abram that his promises *would* come to pass. If they didn't, God would pay the ultimate punishment. Likewise, Abram was making a promise to God, both on his own behalf as well as that of his descendants, that he would obey the terms and conditions of the covenantal agreements and accepted the consequences if they failed. This was what Abram expected. But in verse 17, we read that "when the sun had gone down and it was dark, behold, a smoking firepot and a

---

[3] Understanding the theme of *covenant* is vital in seeking to grasp how the work of Christ fulfils the Old Testament. See Gentry and Wellum, *Kingdom Through Covenant* and Scott W. Hahn, *Kinship by Covenant: A Canonical Approach to the Fulfillment of God's Saving Promises* (New Haven, CT: Yale University Press, 2009), for excellent introductions to covenants, covenant oaths, and how the covenants form the skeletal structure of the Biblical witness.

flaming torch passed between these pieces." The incredible reality is that God *took upon himself all* the responsibilities of the covenant punishment. Even though God alone was the sole faithful covenant partner, it would fall to *God* to pay the penalty for the faithlessness of humanity. Ray Vander Laan expresses the depth of this covenant thus:

> Think of it. Almighty God walking barefoot through a pool of blood! The thought of a human doing that is, to say the least, unpleasant. Yet, God, in all his power and majesty, expressed his love that personally. By participating in that traditional, Near Eastern covenant-making ceremony, he made it unavoidably clear to the people of that time, place and culture what he intended to do.
>
> "I love you so much, Abraham," God was saying, "and I promise that this covenant will come true for you and your children. I will never break My covenant with you. I'm willing to put My life on the line to make you understand." Picturing God passing through that gory path between the carcasses of animals, imagining the blood splashing as he walked, helps us recognize the faithfulness of God's commitment. He was willing to express, in terms his chosen people could understand, that he would never fail to do what he promised. And he ultimately fulfilled his promise by giving his own life, his own blood, on the cross.
>
> Because we look at God's dealings with Abraham as some remote piece of history in a far-off land, we often fail to realize that we, too, are part of the long line of people with whom God made a covenant on that rocky plain near Herbon. And like those who came before us, we have broken that covenant. When he walked in the dust of the desert and through the blood of the animals Abraham had slaughtered, God was making a promise to all the descendants of Abraham—to everyone in the household of faith. When God splashed through the blood, he did it for us...
>
> But there's more. When God made covenant with his people, he did something no human being would have ever considered doing...When God made covenant with Abra-

"Take and Eat"

ham, however, he promised to keep both sides of the agreement. "If this covenant is broken, Abraham, for whatever reason—for my faithlessness or yours—I will pay the price," said God. 'If you or your descendants, for whom you are making this covenant, fail to keep it, I will pay the price in blood."

And at that moment, Almighty God pronounced the death sentence on his Son Jesus.[4]

When Jesus told his disciples that his body would be broken for them, during the Passover Sedar, he was telling them that the time was drawing near when the covenant promise made with Abraham was to be fulfilled. He, God-made-flesh, was preparing himself to be torn apart. Despite having lived a sinless life and having succeeded where every other covenant partner had failed, he was nevertheless going to bear the covenant punishment. The statement hung over the gathering, pregnant with poignancy. But Jesus wasn't finished.

He continued to speak to them, after they had eaten their meal. This would be at the moment of the third cup of the Sedar. He said: "This cup that is poured out for you is the New Covenant in my blood" (Luke 22:20). This statement is also filled with theological significance. The Mosaic covenant between God and the Israelites included the spilling of blood. Although the sacrificial system, in and of itself, had no real power to forgive sin by mere ritual (Romans 3:25; Hebrews 10:1-10), it was predicated upon faith that God would not hold the sins of the faithful against them if they observed the covenantal agreement until the serpent was crushed by the promised Messianic king. Jesus, by stating that his blood was the blood of the New Covenant was declaring that this moment had arrived. His blood would be the true vicarious and effective means for the forgiveness of humanity's cosmic treachery and rebellion through his once-for-all sacrifice. His broken body,

---

[4] Ray Vander Laan with Judith Markham, *Echoes of His Presence: Stories of the Messiah from the People of His Day* (Colorado Springs: Focus on the Family, 1996), pp. 8-9, as recorded in Gentry and Wellum, *Kingdom Through Covenant*, pp. 257-258. Emphasis in original.

in fulfilment of Genesis 15, and his spilt blood, in mirroring Exodus 24, would make him the true Passover lamb, overseeing a greater Exodus.

Jesus' death and resurrection was foretold in his invitation to "take and eat" of his body and "take and drink" of his blood. The theological significance of this offer hearkens back to Genesis 3 and the invitation from the serpent. There, Satan taunted Eve to "take and eat" and *be like* God; here, Jesus invites his followers to "take and eat" and be *restored to* God. This blood is the seal of a new covenant agreement between God and the citizens of the kingdom of God, who place their faith in the completed and satisfactory work of Jesus on the cross. The pouring out of Jesus' blood speaks not only of his immanent death, but also the nature of his work on the cross. He isn't paying Satan nor buying him off; rather, he would endure the wrath of God which was poured out onto Jesus "for many for the forgiveness of sins" (Matthew 26:28).

But Jesus was also pointing *towards* a new covenant. This new covenant had been promised in the Old Testament because the covenant between Israel and God had ruptured. In Jeremiah 31:31-32, God promised that new days would come when he would make a new covenant that would be different to the covenant he made with the fathers of Israel. This new covenant would not rely on outward observance but would begin with inward change and be built around a personal communion with God (Jeremiah 31:34). In this covenant, the sins of the covenant partners would be truly forgiven such that they will never be remembered ever again. Likewise, in Ezekiel 36 and 37, we see implications of the power of this new covenant; it will result in a new heart in each believer, providing immediate spiritual life and the promise of resurrection life. This heart will not be one of stony rebellion but will be transformed into flesh. The Spirit of God will be given to each believer so that they will know God and obey his rules with a joyful and willing heart (Ezekiel 36:26-27).

With his invitation, Jesus told his disciples that he would pay the penalty that would *propitiate* the wrath of God, *atone* for the sins of humanity, and *inaugurate* the New Covenant that would be greater and grander than the old covenant. The symbolism of the Passover meal would now reflect an even greater deliverance by an even greater founder of an even greater nation.

Despite this great work, however, the immediate implications of his words, although perhaps not totally clear to the disciples, were very evident to Jesus. After the meal had finished, Jesus took his disciples beyond the cramped and bustling streets of Jerusalem towards the Mount of Olives. There, after begging his disciples to keep watch and to pray (Mark 14:34), he went a little further and prayed earnestly. In this bittersweet communion between divine Father and incarnate Son, we hear a whisper of the agonies of Jesus' soul. The imminent violence was indeed something to be feared: "My Father, if it be possible, let this cup pass from me; nevertheless, not as I will, but as you will" (Matthew 26:39).

Jesus understood the full weight of his upcoming suffering. As God the Son, he would bear the eternal wrath of the Godhead for the infinite sinfulness of humanity. On the cross, in the earthly hours of his suffering, God would pour out upon him the eternal fullness of the judgement our sin deserves. As the Son of God, he would hang in our place to receive the punishment that we deserve. This is *penal substitutionary atonement*. Simply put, Jesus willingly received the *penalty* of sin as the *substitute* for sinners to make *atonement* for our rebellion. At the cross, all the human violence was outdone by the righteous wrath of God, poured onto Jesus for you and for me. But both aspects of his suffering were real. The wrath of God that is meted out on unrepentant rebels for eternity in hell was experienced by Jesus on the cross for all who would be his followers and disciples. On the cross of Calvary, Jesus experienced the hell of Hell.

The violence of his earthly suffering was not negligible, however. The fierce whipping of his flesh, the beatings, the humiliation and indignity of being spat upon, being forced to drag the implement of his own execution through the riotous streets, the nails hammered through his flesh, and the thorns pushed into his scalp caused real pain and debilitating biological reactions. Blood loss, deep lacerations, dehydration, and hunger would have weakened him to the point of complete and utter exhaustion and begin the process of systemic collapse. Then, at the moment of his defeat (yet, simultaneously, his hour of triumph), a spear pierced his side and sliced through his heart. All the while, that serpent of old watched on, savoring every lash, celebrating every punch, relishing every barbarous act, licking his lips in uncontained glee at the ghastly horror of the murder of the king. Unbeknownst to him, however, the moment of *his* victory, the killing of God, was also the moment of his vanquishing.

This other dimension of the sacrificial work of Christ was that the serpent was crushed. The rebellion he had fomented all the way back in Genesis 3 had come to a terminus. By the cross, the power of sin was broken because the debt had been paid. By the resurrection, a new life, a redeemed humanity, and a new creation was produced. Jesus, the greater Moses, by fulfilling the Old Covenant's stipulations through his sinless life, and by fulfilling the Old Covenant's prophecies in his vicarious and propitiatory death, had forged yet another re-creation event from the midst of the ashes of the Fall. The new creation kingdom life was born when Christ, the firstborn of the new creation, was delivered from the womb of the tomb! And, because of his work on the cross, all who now find refuge in the Messiah will be freed from the judgement of a holy God and liberated from the tyrannical violence of the serpent.

The point of the Lord's Supper is that we're invited to "take and eat" in a very real way in remembrance of the work of Christ that has redeemed us. We've been brought into the New Covenant by the pouring out of his atoning blood. His sacrificial death was the propitiation of God's righteous wrath at our sinful rebellion and treachery. Because Jesus was God, he was able to fulfil Genesis 15's death sentence. Because he is God, he was able to bear the eternal punishment for every individual who would repent and believe the gospel. Because he is God, death couldn't hold him. On the other side of the equation, because he is human, a son of Adam, he was able to stand as a representative of humanity. Because he is human, he was able to be the new head of the new creational community. And, vitally, because he was sinless to the very end, he was able to be a substitute for sinners, by his own willed choice. Because he is both God and man, he is the faithful covenantal partner for the fulfilment of the Law, its abrogation through his death and resurrection, and for the inauguration of the New Covenant, brought through his blood.

The Promise of the Lord's Supper

When we observe communion in our churches, we ought to consider that the Lord's Supper has three dimensions to it. The first dimension calls us to remember the past. The command Christ gave was to repeatedly take communion "in remembrance of him." Thus, when we take the bread and wine, we are invited to meditate on the death of Christ. His body was beaten into a bloody pulp, whipped by a vicious Roman *flagrum* (a type of cat-o-nine-tails) that was designed to rip flesh off the bone. He was spat upon and verbally insulted. Nailed to the wooden cross, his lungs struggled for air when he rested his feet on the lower block; when he needed to breathe, he would raise himself up by his feet (causing excruciating pain). Over time, this would wear the victim out so that they would slowly suffocate. Occasionally this could be hastened if the legionary broke the prisoner's legs so that they couldn't raise themselves to breathe. For Jesus, however, his punishment was infinitely worse than the two men on the neighboring crosses. Whilst he was suffering the physical trauma of the pain of the cross, God the Father poured out his wrath on Jesus the suffering servant (Isaiah 53: 4), his sword striking the good shepherd (Zechariah 13:4). His eternal wrath towards the millennia of sinful treachery and rebellion against his holy and righteous rule was poured out on the only begotten Son. So deep and brutal was this spiritual trauma that Jesus cried out "my God, my God, why have you forsaken me" (Psalm 22:1). His agony was in the experience of the eternal judgment for the sin of every believer who would find refuge in his redeeming work. On the cross, Christ bore the infinite wrath of God for every single soul who would come to the good shepherd to find spiritual rest. He provided the blood that would protect every individual housed inside his kingdom.[5] The cross was the exquisite desecration of God the Son.

The second dimension of communion moves from remembering the past to reverence in the present. When we take communion, we do so as a community of believers corporately professing our faith in the work of Christ and our union with him by faith. This act binds us to one another as a family, but it also provides a unique moment of spiritual union with Christ where, by his Spirit, we spiritually feast on Christ and are nourished by him. This is why, prior to eating and drinking, we take the time to ensure that we're in right relationship with our brothers and sisters in Christ, lest we eat and drink in an unworthy manner and subsequently bring judgement upon ourselves (1 Corinthains 11:27-30). The Lord's Supper is a corporate, family meal for the household of faith.[6] When we participate in communion, we're uniting ourselves to Christ and declaring that we believe in the same sacrifice as the generations of believers who likewise trusted in the work of Christ by taking and eating.

The third and final dimension of communion is that it points us forward to the future. Jesus made clear that the celebration of

---

5   This is penal substitutionary atonement. There are numerous other views of how Christ's work on the cross atones for sin and reconciles man to God. It is highly probable that the work of the cross is like a diamond through which the light of redemption is beautifully refracted. That being the case, however, it is my position that penal substitutionary atonement is the dominant action; the victory over evil powers, the ransom, and the satisfaction theories are all true and helpful to reflect upon, but the vicarious work of Christ's death *in my place* ought to be central.

6   This is why unbelievers should not be permitted to take the Lord's Supper; it's a family meal with very specific connotations and implications for the believer. To eat and drink it in an unworthy manner would be, in the first place, conceited, and in the second place, to eat and drink judgment upon yourself.

the Lord's Supper was to be consistently repeated by the household of faith as an expression of faith in his work, a means of receiving sanctifying grace, and a declaration of unity and community. But it would not be repeated *forever*. The Lord's Supper is but a shimmering portrait of the great feast we will celebrate at the wedding of the Lamb to the church. It therefore points us forward to his glorious return. We see this promise in Matthew 26:29: "I tell you I will not drink again of the fruit of the vine until that day when I drink it new with you in my Father's kingdom."

By holding these three dimensions in our mind every time we "take and eat" the body of Christ and "take and drink" the blood of Christ, we remember the cost of our redemption. This will encourage us to live for Christ through the enabling and empowering of the same Spirit who raised Christ from the dead and who now indwells us.

A Tale of Two Gardens

The Upper Room gave way to the garden of Gethsemane. As Jesus prayed that this cup might be passed from him, he nevertheless willingly submitted to the will of his father and endured the cross. Thereafter, his body was removed and buried in a stranger's tomb. On Sunday morning, however, Mary Magdalene, Mary the mother of James, and Salome brought spices to anoint his body and say their final goodbyes. When they arrived at the tomb, they were shocked that it lay open. With trepidation they walked into the tomb. As their eyes adjusted to the darkness of the chamber, they noticed a young man wearing a white robe. They were scared. He turned his face to them and opened his mouth to speak. The moment would have felt like an eternity. His voice pierced the silence: "You seek Jesus of Nazareth, who was crucified. He has risen; he is not here" (Mark 16:6). In their fear, they fled and kept it to themselves (Mark 16:8). After all, if we place ourselves in their sandals for a moment, we'd consider that the body of a political prisoner, executed for treason against Rome and blasphemy against Israel, is missing, and a stranger in the tomb accuses them of seeking this rebel. It's a recipe for disaster. When they do eventually tell the disciples, they weren't initially believed (Luke 24:10-11). Finally, Peter and John raced to the tomb and corroborated the words of the terrified women: The tomb was empty.

All this drama takes place under the shadow of dread. If Jesus, the Messiah, had been murdered for challenging the status quo, what would befall his most intimate followers? Would the religious elite be content with simply executing the head of the supposed political revolution? Or would they continue to bay for blood? These panicked thoughts were no doubt bouncing around the minds and conversations of the disciples as they continued to grieve the loss of their friend, their rabbi, and their "failed" Messiah: Had they been duped?

But there was another figure caught up in the torrents of tearfulness: Mary Magdalene. In her sadness, she didn't return to her home, unlike Peter and John (John 20:10). Rather, she stayed near the tomb and mourned. Eventually, she reentered the tomb to find two angels in white raiment seated on the funerary plinth where Jesus' body had once lain. They looked at her and asked her: "Why are you weeping?" She responded that "they have taken away my Lord, and I do not know where they have laid him" (John 20:13). She turned from them back towards the door, perhaps to exit, or perhaps a noise caught her attention. The contrast of light probably temporarily limited her vision such that, although she saw a figure standing there, she couldn't identify him. This figure also asked why she was weeping and for whom she was looking. Mary, still discombobulated by the events of the last few days, and caught up in her grief, guessed that this was the gardener. She said to him: "Sir, if you have carried him away, tell me where you have laid him, and I will take him away" (John 20:15). Another interminable silence hung inside the cool chamber. Eventually a single word reverberated throughout the stony atrium and would echo throughout the corridors of time and space: "Mary." At that word, Mary's heart erupted with euphoria for this was not the gardener. A single, shocked, disbelieving word burst from her lips:

"Rabboni!" Suddenly, for Mary, and for every human being, everything changed.

The impact of this scene is one of poetic juxtaposition and anticipation. Mary's grief so swiftly turns to radiant joy. But beyond the immediate context of the narrative lies something larger and more poetical than Mary's experience. In the garden a reenactment or recapitulation was taking place. Mary's confusion about the gardener is not entirely incorrect; Jesus was not *the* gardener, but as the Final Adam he is certainly *a* gardener. Jesus being found in a garden and being confused for a gardener is a throwback to the First Adam, the gardener and overseer of creation. There are many other parallels between the garden of Eden and the garden of Golgotha. In Eden, Adam walked with God; here Jesus walked as God. In Eden, Adam had chosen to sin and brought death's dominion over creation; here, Jesus had remained sinless and was "made to be sin" (2 Corinthians 5:21), thereby defeating death and introducing the resurrection life. In Eden, Adam's sin had attempted to dethrone God by rejecting God's rule and authority; here, Jesus had lived out absolute obedience saying, "Not my will, but yours, be done" (Luke 22:42). In Eden, Adam had sought to protect Eve by adding to the words of God; here, Jesus is the presence of the Word of God. In Eden, Adam had failed to protect Eve when Satan tempted her; here, Jesus comforted Mary with his words, his presence, and the completion of his redemptive work. In Eden, Satan had upended the creational order by speaking to Eve and ignoring Adam; now Mary, another woman, was the first to hear the voice of the Second Adam. In Eden, the serpent had connivingly scurried into the garden to wreak havoc and condemn creation to damnation; now, the resurrected Christ has inaugurated the new creation, having crushed the head of the serpent with his victory and vanquished death with his resurrection. In Eden, Adam failed and brought about the corruption of the image of God, the enslavement of humanity, and the rise of the triumph of death; but now, standing in the garden of Golgotha, the Final Adam was the actual imprint of the invisible God who has redeemed humanity by the death of death itself. The true and Second Adam is the true image of God, the true Israel, and the truly obedient Son. He, too, now walked in the garden in the cool of the day. He too, faced the temptation of a tree (though for Jesus, it was to avoid the tree altogether); unlike Adam, he remained obedient. Paul says of this tale of two gardens in Romans 5:18-19: "Therefore, as one trespass led to condemnation for all men, so one act of righteousness leads to justification and life for all men. For as by the one man's disobedience [Adam] the many [humanity] were made sinners, so by the one man's obedience [Jesus] the many will be made righteous." The tale of two gardens reveals that Jesus has been victorious in every way: *Christus victor*.

Another oft-overlooked parallel comes slightly after Adam's fall and judgement. There's something powerful in the symbolism of God's provision of animal skins to cover Adam and Eve's earthly nakedness and shame. God provided for them the means by which they could somewhat remain in his presence without the fear of their nakedness. That covering, however, was through a bloody death. Likewise, in the Mosaic covenant, the sacrificial system was required to allow the Israelites to remain in covenantal relationship with God. At Calvary, Christ provided his blood-stained body as a covering for humanity. We can enter the presence of God because we wear the righteousness of Christ. Just as Adam and Eve were covered by garments not their own, we're covered by a righteousness not our own.

Application

The are a plethora of applications that flow from the Lord's Supper through to the death and resurrection of Christ. Perhaps the one that is most pertinent to this book is that the work of Christ is the culmination and climax of scripture. The entire Old Testament converges around the singular person of Jesus of Nazareth, God-made-flesh, and his victory (Luke 24:26-27). From the very first mention of creation, scripture is directing us inexorably to the arrival and exaltation of Jesus, the creator. He is the "radiance of the glory of God and the exact imprint of his nature, and he upholds the universe by the word of his power" (Hebrews 1:3). He is the faithful Adam. He is the promised serpent crusher. He provides the robes of righteousness that covers our sin and permits us to enter the presence of God. He is the ark of the New Covenant, protecting us from the storms of rebellion and the tempests of judgement. He is the promised seed of Abraham. He is the scapegoat who carried the sins of the people. He is the heart and soul and power of the entire sacrificial system. He is the greater prophet, priest, and prince. He is the true mediator between God and man. He is the good shepherd. He is the obedient covenant partner. He is the greater David and the fulfillment of the Davidic promise for an eternal reign. Every spiritual promise given by God throughout the entirety of scripture finds its ultimate fulfillment in, and by, and through Jesus of Nazareth because of his faithful, sinless, obedience to the Father.

A second application concerns our communion with Christ. Because of his death and resurrection, the New Covenant was finally inaugurated. Unlike the old covenants, this one is the final covenant, and it also fulfils and abrogates the requirements of the Mosaic covenant. We're united to Christ because of what he has achieved. This is our adoption into Christ and into the heavenly family. When we partake of communion, we're expressing our faith in the success of his death and resurrection. By faith in Christ, we're united to the *resurrected* Christ and therefore we're *in* Christ, which gives us access to all the spiritual blessings that God has promised. This resurrection power, brought to bear on our lives by the Holy Spirit, changes how we think and act and worship. Because of Christ's invitation to "take and eat" of his body, we're being invited into a dynamic, eternal, relationship with him that brings us into the family of God and the household of faith. By our communion with Christ, we have access to the rights, the power, the promises, and the privileges of being sons and daughters of God.

A third application flows naturally from the second; if we are, *individually*, united to Christ by faith, we are *corporately* united to one another by each one being in Christ. When the Marys went to the tomb, they were going to pay their respects to their friend. Yes, they were passionate about him. Yes, they were loyal to him. Yes, they were going to provide Jesus with the appropriate homage and respect he deserved. But they were fully aware that they were going to anoint a corpse. But when believers gather, we don't come to remember a dead king; we come to worship the resurrected king! When we gather, we sing Christ-exalting songs to remind one another of the glorious gospel of Christ because it's all about him (Colossians 3:16; Ephesians 5:19). We pray for one another because we believe Christ is *alive* to hear our prayers and *powerful* enough to answer them. We read scripture publicly and sit under the proclamation of scripture to equip us to be ambassadors of the gospel. Why? Because he's alive, and his resurrection is the only hope for a struggling brother or sister. By gathering with the saints, we're publicly declaring our belief in the power and purpose of the resurrection.

In terms of the larger narrative of redemption, of course, Jesus' offer to "take and eat" is a direct repudiation of Satan's seductive invitation in Genesis 3. The breaking of Jesus' body and the spilling of his blood at Calvary is how the curse is undone and salvation is assured. Because of the resurrection, sin was subjected to him, the fall was repealed, shame is ruined, suffering is sweetened, disease is destroyed, demons are conquered, death was defeated, God's wrath was satisfied, justice was delivered, creation is renewed, salvation was achieved, atonement was completed, regeneration was brought, propitiation was made, reconciliation was attained, justification was declared, adoption was completed, union with God is provided, sanctification is possible, forgiveness is given, our resurrection is promised, his return is guaranteed, and eternity is granted by him. Because Jesus is the anointed of God who crushed the serpent, routed the rebellion, and inaugurated the kingdom of God, everything has changed. The battle has been won and his authority is established forever more. The greater Adam is ruler of a new nation, a new people, from every tribe and tongue and nation. His throne is an eternal throne, and his reign is marked with righteousness and justice.

But we must be wary of taking the hell of Calvary too lightly. The cost of our redemption was that Christ suffered the ignominy of our eternal punishment. We dare not use the fact of our salvation to cheapen the grace that God has provided through the sacrificial death of the Son. The suffering of Christ was the most despicable and pernicious event in all cosmic history. At Calvary, the creature sought not only to dethrone God, but to destroy God. Our sinful rebellion was willing to kill God. Jesus, the king of kings, was forced to stand before petty rulers. Jesus, the great high priest, was interrogated by crooked priests. Jesus, the healer who had touched the sick, who brought relief to the leprous and the lame, who loved the unlovable, who mingled with the unclean, and who raised the dead, was given nothing to succor his own suffering, bar a dribble of soured wine. He went to the cross and suffered the ignominy, the shame, and the humiliation therein. He experienced the rejection of his own people. He faced the castigation of the Gentiles who crucified him. He heard the mockery of the serpent as blood gushed from his wounds. He listened as Satan whispered to him on the cross that this could *all* have been avoided had Jesus simply knelt to him in the wilderness. But worst of all, Jesus understood the wrath of God the Father as God's sword was thrust at him and his righteous wrath poured over him. And he died. For us. So that all our sin would be covered by his righteous sacrifice. All our anger, bitterness, hatred, rebelliousness, jealousy, lust, slander, gossip, envy, murder, greed, bullying, faithlessness, oppressiveness, violence, addictions were placed upon him on the cross. He who had never known the taste of sin now drained the bitter gall from sin's chalice and was suddenly and entirely plunged into the infinite ocean of its corrosive corruption. And all so that his precious blood would be the elixir that brings us life. As we think about the applications of Christ's work, we must never forget the *reason* for his work nor the *experience* of his suffering on our behalf. It should always drive us to our knees in gratitude and worship. A healthy theology always leads to doxology.

It's worth considering the most obvious application also: grief. Every person has had cause to grieve. The suffocating darkness of grief's lonely tunnel is something every human knows and yet it is also something that is unique to every person. We do not deal with grief like a band-aid, sticking well-meaning, but meaningless, clichés over the raw and gaping wound. The scars of grief remain with us our entire lives. And, at our own passing, we will be the cause of scars to our nearest and dearest. Such is the implication of the Fall. As Mary grieved the loss of her friend, she was facing the horrible reality of the ugliness of death. Death is cruel and disgusting and wicked. We must acknowledge this truth and "weep with those who weep and mourn with those who mourn" (Romans 12:15), gathering our beloved brother or sister in our arms. We must let them grieve because grief is important.

To grieve is to acknowledge the loss, to accept the pain of the loss, to express our anger at the Fall which made that loss both possible and inevitable. Many of us who aren't grieving a deep loss often tend to treat grief like a medical issue. The worst part is the beginning; then medication helps diminish the pain of the symptoms, so that, in time, it goes away. Grief is not like this. Grief is like the ocean. It washes overs us in waves. There's the initial crashing wave as we acknowledge the loss. But almost immediately after that initial wave we're busily distracted with funeral arrangements, all the paperwork, getting everything in order. We push the grieving process aside and away. But grief will be with us until our own deaths. Some days we will experience it as the waves lap up to our feet; other days, the tide will be further out, and we feel like we're doing better. Still other days, it will feel like we're splashing helplessly. This is because grief is a reminder that the love was real and the loss is difficult. There will be moments when grief will flood our souls and catch us off guard: A scent of his cologne, a flitting memory pops into view, driving past her favorite restaurant, hearing their voice in your son or daughter. There will never be a day when it's all better, but there will be a progression to where we are *doing* better. Nevertheless, grief can be a debilitating, isolating, and terrifying place. But although we permit grief, and although we share in grief, we do not succumb to grief. Because death is *not* the end.

Because of the work of Jesus, everything has changed. Even as we watch our loved ones die, and our loved ones grieve, we mourn differently. We *do* mourn, but we mourn with hope and with confidence. Because Christ did not remain dead, a failed political revolutionary. No, he is risen, and the sting of death is dead. It's not vapidity to point to the resurrection; it's the *only* certainty because it points us to the promises of the only person in the entire history of the world who faced death and bested that old nefarious enemy. When we encounter grief, therefore, we acknowledge its reality, and we accept the breadth and depths of the seas of sorrow; but we refuse to drown in them. The gospel of the resurrected Christ points us, ultimately, away from our loss to the grave and towards the Lord over the grave. When death and sorrow come our way, the gospel tells us to acknowledge it but lead our grief back to the Lord of life. This world is fleeting; even the wounds of sadness and sorrow, although they last until our own dying day, will come to an end. Christ has promised, by his resurrection, that a time will come when our tears will be forever wiped away.

This brings us to our final application. The communion in the Upper Room and the resurrection of Christ both inexorably point to the future. Christ will return in might and majesty because he is alive. Not only is Christ the fulfilment of the Old Testament's hopes and prophecies, but he is also the reigning king having been exalted and seated at the right hand of the Father. Because of this truth, we can be confident that all our injustice, pain, persecution, heartache, sickness, grief, will be dealt with by Christ. All the secret or forgotten crimes will be brought to justice. Jesus is not a genie in a lamp to make us rich. He is not a therapist who impotently listens to our problems. He is not an SOS call when times are tough. He is more than simply a prayer prayed for a get-out-of-hell-free card. He is the *resurrected* king. And therefore he is the *returning* king.

When we come face to face with the reality of the work of Jesus, we're left with a very distinct choice. Jesus has crushed the serpent and has inaugurated the kingdom of God. Even now, he's ruling over creation in anticipation of his glorious return. Satan, like a cornered rat, is lashing out with ever greater violence as the noose of his ultimate condemnation tightens around him. But until that day, the children of Adam and Eve have a choice to make. Are we going to remain as servants of the serpent or will be "take and eat" of the fruit of redemption and become servants of the Savior?

Conclusion

The ministry of Jesus began with his baptism and rejection of Satan's temptations. It culminated on the cross and was validated by the resurrection. In between, Jesus taught many sermons to thousands of people. He presented the mandate for the kingdom of God and demonstrated the power of the kingdom by exorcising demons, defeating disease, disarming death, and fulfilling prophecies. During the Upper Room celebration of the traditional Passover, Jesus introduced the New Covenant. This covenant was the fulfilment of the predictions and promises found throughout the entire Old Testament corpus, and yet, despite its *familiarity*, it's a unique covenant based on the shedding of his own blood. This both fulfilled the consequences of Genesis 15 and initiated a new epoch of redemptive history. There would be no future need for any more sacrifices, because Christ's once-for-all sacrifice was sufficient. There would be no need for a distinct and separated caste of priests because, in Christ, we are to minister each to one another, submitting to one another in the household of faith.

The New Covenant was not another iteration of ethnic, corporate Israel but would expand the covenantal blessings to all the peoples of the earth with no salvific distinctions made concerning ethnicity, gender, power, wealth, or social status. When Jesus invites us to "take and eat" of his body, he's doing more than merely providing an alternative to Satan's offer; he's proclaiming the death of Satan's regime, a return to the righteous rule of God, and a restoration of the image of God through our union to Christ. By that union, any repentant person can enter the kingdom of God, provided they enter it through faith in the work of Christ alone.

Despite the excitement concerning the inbreaking of heaven through the resurrection, there remained much confusion amongst the disciples as to what this new world might look like. When two followers of Jesus were on the road to a nearby village from Jerusalem, Jesus surreptitiously joined them. Like Mary, they didn't recognize him. They were attempting to parse through the events of the last few days, seeking to understand what had happened, what would happen, and what it all meant. As they continued their journey to Emmaus, Jesus began to explain to them that everything that had happened, from Messiah's betrayal to his resurrection, was all part of God's plan to fulfil the scriptures. Scripture was, he said, all about the Messiah and his mission. As they reclined at dinner together, Jesus "took the bread and blessed it and broke it and gave it to them" (Luke 24:30). It was at that moment that they realized that this was no normal rabbi; this was the resurrected Jesus.

It's interesting that Cleopas and his companion first recognized the Lord by yet another offering to "take and eat." Because of this, they immediately returned to Jerusalem, found the eleven disciples (Judas having already committed suicide) and excitedly told them that Jesus had indeed risen from the dead. Not only that, but they told the disciples that they had only identified him in the breaking of the bread. The likelihood is that they were starting to put the dots together. The broken bread in the hands of the living Lord could only mean one thing: His sacrifice had been sufficient. From this point onwards, the full weight of the implications of the work of Christ would become clearer in the minds of the disciples. Though not without a few hurdles.

8

"Take and Eat": A New Creation Mandate

And Jesus came and said to them, "All authority in heaven and on earth has been given to me. Go therefore and make disciples of all nations, baptizing them in the name of the Father and of the Son and of the Holy Spirit, teaching them to observe all that I have commanded you. And behold, I am with you always, to the end of the age." (Matthew 28:18-20)

Introduction

Wherever you go on God's green earth you can be sure of two things: Taxes, and an Irish pub. When I travelled to Germany for research for a book on Martin Luther, I was tickled to get fish and chips in an Irish pub deep in the heart of Wittenberg. I'm quite certain that Luther would have approved. When I was on a mission trip to South Africa, I thoroughly enjoyed bangers and mash from a local Irish pub. There are countless Irish bars throughout America. No matter where you go, it seems, the Irish have expanded across the face of the earth with the two things for which we are known: Booze and community. But in each place, although the *menu* remains the same, the *ingredients* are contextual. The fish in Wittenberg was not the cod or haddock of Ireland. The bangers in South Africa were not sourced from McAtamney's but were traditional boerewors. This unique smorgasbord of cultural sharing was not insulting to the "original intent" of the meal; rather, it was delightful because it suggested a local ownership of the meals.

In this chapter, we're going to see something similar. The singular gospel of Christ was won through his death and resurrection as a one-time event. But it would travel throughout the world, into local communities of every tribe, tongue, and nation. They would each experience Christ's rule in ways that make sense to their culture and community without compromising the central message of his redemptive kingship. The new creation community he is building will be founded upon his own status as the greater Adam. His kingdom will be comprised of kingdom citizens from all over the world who submit to his lordship and obey his constitution. This diverse inclusivity will be presented through a dramatic vision in the book of Acts; before that, however, we will explore how Christ appropriates the Great Commission and adapts it to present his New Creation Mandate for his kingdom. When Peter is commanded to "take and eat" of things hitherto considered unclean, therefore, the implications are clear: Christ's kingdom is not Eden simply restored, it is Eden sublimely reimagined!

A New Creation Mandate

The Creation Mandate was the command given to Adam and Eve as creation's regents to procreate as a species, spread the image of God throughout the earth, and thence to exercise dominion over that creation. But after their treachery, they were exiled from the garden, their tasks became difficult, and their relationship experienced division. Throughout the duration of human history, therefore, although humanity has managed to *procreate*, the implementation of our rule has been little short of depraved, while our human expression of marital fidelity and sexual morality has been compromised in a myriad of ways. The exercise of our delegated authority would be better understood as narcissistic and suicidal tyranny.

The work of Christ is the unwinding of human failure and the inaugurating of a restored humanity. Not only did the resurrection introduce the new creation paradigm, but Jesus is the firstborn of a *new humanity*. This humanity resides within him as the Final Adam and is situated under his authority as the Messianic king. As he is the head of this new humanity and the king over this newly inaugurated nation, his commands to his citizenry are of the utmost importance. This brings us to what has been dubbed the Great Commission. I'm going to argue that the Great Commission is an update to the Creation Mandate that brings God's original command to Adam and Eve under the authority of Christ for his kingdom. The first step in this argument is to see how Jesus is the greater Adam; he himself is present throughout the world by his Spirit and he has a dominion over creation superior to anything Adam and Eve had experienced. Only after this is established can disciples of Jesus apply his authority as he has commanded. This does not *nullify* the original command but advances its application to be consistent to this new epochal reality post-resurrection. Thus, we can say that *humanity* remains under the Creation Mandate (to some degree), but only the *new humanity* (those who are in Christ's kingdom) are responsible to fulfil the Great Commission. In other words, from within the dying husk of the old creation world, the new creation is blossoming throughout every tribe, tongue, and nation of the world. The New Testament witness shows how Christ is the recapitulation of the Old Testament. Yet, we are to go further; because we're united to Christ, believers are also to recapitulate the Old Testament through and in Christ. This can be seen in many ways, but the primary ways are the recapitulations of Adam and Israel.

Expansion from Genesis

Jesus the Greater Adam

In Matthew 28:18-20, Jesus gives his disciples two commands which are buttressed between two promises. In verse 18 we read the first promise. Jesus told the disciples that "all authority in heaven and on earth has been given to [him]." This promise is a statement that encapsulates his divinity, his exaltation, and his sovereignty over all things. As with the First Adam, this authority is delivered to the resurrected Christ by the Father (Ephesians 1:10; Philippians 2:9-11). However, unlike the First Adam, this delegated authority has been earned *through* obedience, even unto death. Jesus is not merely another Adam, he is the greater, the successful, and thus the Final Adam.

Exercise Dominion

As king, he's been given all authority in heaven and on earth. Jesus is the incarnate Second Person of the Triune God. By dent of his divinity, God the Son is all powerful in his own right. But as the incarnate Son, who has taken upon himself the frailty and limitations of human flesh, he stands as the king over humanity *as one of us*. His two natures are hypostatically united in the one individual Jesus of Nazareth. His ascension means that Jesus is in the heavens as the *heir apparent*, but he is God's anointed Lord over the material world. It needs to be understood that Jesus is not *replacing* the Father on the throne but is co-ruling in his incarnate nature. This fulfils numerous Old Testament passages such as Psalm 2:8-12, Psalm 110:1, Isaiah 6:13, with Isaiah 11:1-10, and Daniel 7:13-14. Jesus, therefore, has been given the authority of God as the Messianic king over all things; he is co-ruler in the heavens, seated by the Father, and he is princeps over the kingdom of God. This earthly authority is what Adam had originally enjoyed in the holy sanctuary of Eden. In the New Creation Mandate, Jesus is the one to exercise this authority correctly and eternally.

Jesus' power is also limitless: "*All* authority *in heaven and on earth* has been given to me" (Matthew 28:18); in the Old Testament passages mentioned above, we see that the Son of Man in his exaltation will govern the nations with a righteous authority that will uphold and bless the godly (Psalm 2:12) but will hold the wicked and rebellious to justice: He will "break them with a rod of iron and dash them in pieces like a potter's vessel" (Psalm 2:9). The enemies of this king will perform *proskynesis* before him as he ceremonially rests his feet upon them (Psalm 110:1). His reign will be in the midst of his enemies for a season (a debated concept, but I take to mean the era of his ascension where his authority is executed through his people), but on the "day of his wrath" he will "execute judgement among the nations" (Psalm 110:5-6) exercising dominion throughout the world and cultivating the thorny thrones by deflowering their wicked heads with the sheers of holy justice. In Daniel 7:14, we read that he's given a "dominion [that] is an everlasting dominion, which shall not pass away, and his kingdom one that shall not be destroyed." Unlike the First Adam, Jesus' throne will never diminish, nor his reign terminate. He's the eternal king with an everlasting reign over an indestructible kingdom.

The language of "dominion" is instructive because it reminds us of Genesis 1:26. Here, however, the dominion is expanded from being "over the fish of the sea and over the birds of the heavens and over the livestock and over the all the earth and over every creeping thing that creeps on the earth" to including "all peoples, nations, and languages [who] should serve him" (Daniel 7:14). Jesus' authority is larger than Adam's because his exaltation is greater. Where Adam failed, Christ succeeded; and what Adam wrought Christ has bought with his blood sacrifice. Thus, Christ's kingship not only includes Adam's *domain* but also Adam's *descendants*. Christ, as the resurrected Jesus, God-made-flesh, is sovereign even over Adam himself and is given dominion over all the children of the First Adam. This dominion includes providing both justice and grace; those who enter his kingdom through faith will be given a further delegated authority as well as adoption into the heavenly family, with all the rights of inheritance that such adoption guarantees (Ephesians 1:11-12), whilst those who remain outside his kingdom will ultimately be exiled in judgement. Thus, Jesus is in his own way adopting and adapting the Creation Mandate's command to exercise dominion by reigning alongside God the Father and being positioned as the judge and Messiah over creation and the nations of the world. Further, as ruler of the kingdom of God, he has *sole* dominion over the new creation.

Spread the Reign of God by His Presence

The second promise in the Great Commission concerns the presence of Jesus. As God the Son, he shares the divine attribute of omnipresence. But as Jesus of Nazareth, he shares the human limitations that means he is located in one place at a single time. This apparent contradiction appears to be a problem for Christ's promise that he is with us to the end of the age. However, a little systematic theology can help clarify what he means by this. In this current interregnum, where Christ is absent in person, he is present through the ministry of his Holy Spirit. In John 14:15-17, Jesus tells his disciples that he will ask the Father to send the advocate to them after his own departure. This advocate is the Holy Spirit who will help the disciples and be with them forever. But in John 16:7, Jesus promises that he, himself, will send the Spirit to the disciples *as a consequence of Jesus' absence.* In other words, the Spirit of Christ who indwells both Church and believers is the Spirit who will "guide the disciples into all the truth" (John 16:13) and will "teach you all things and bring to your remembrance all that I have said to you" (John 14:26). The presence of Christ in the era of Christ's heavenly interregnum is one in which geographical proximity to the king is not *spatial* but *spiritual.* Access to him is not predicated upon entrance to an earthly palace or throne room, nor is it limited through a hierarchy of nobles and aristocrats (dare we say popes and prelates?); rather, "where two or three are gathered in my name, I am there among them" (Matthew 18:20) because Christ *is* present through the ministry of his Spirit. Every believer, in every hidden recess of the globe, is equally as present to Christ as any other because of the Holy Spirit. Thus, we can see that Jesus, the Final Adam, is in his own way adopting and adapting the Creation Mandate's command to spread throughout the world through the provision of the Spirit who makes him everywhere spiritually present.

Because Jesus has been given all authority in heaven and earth as the successful Adam, he has the power to build his kingdom amidst the ruins of the old creation. He is the king over a greater creation who will inherit the new earth and new Jerusalem upon his glorious return. The local expressions of his kingdom, until then, will continually expand and assault the strongholds of the serpent throughout this realm with an inexorable might such that "the gates of hell will not prevail against it" (Matthew 16:18). Jesus adopts the two old Creation Mandate commands (to spread throughout the world and exercise dominion) through his promises in the Great Commission. It's only after we understand *this* aspect of his being the Final Adam that we can appreciate how his followers can subsequently obey *in his name*. He has chosen to use his followers to be the agents of the advancement of his kingdom; this is why he has promised his presence with them, even to the end of the age. It's by his power that his kingdom *will* expand, and it's by his presence that his faithful followers can be used to bring about that expansion. This will inevitably have significant implications for the composition and organization of the outposts of Christ's kingdom here on earth: The church.[1]

We have assessed the two *promises* of the Great Commission, noting that Jesus adopted the concepts of the Creation Mandate but modified them for his kingdom. Before we can assess the two *commands* of the Great Commission, we must first consider the new humanity that populates Christ's new creation kingdom.

Inclusion of the Gentiles

Because Jesus is the Final Adam over a new creation paradigm, his kingdom has a different composition than an exclusively Israelite community. As Adam was regent over *all* creation, Jesus is king over *all* who enter his kingdom. Access to his kingdom is not predicated on inherited rights of lineage but through a personal and genuine faith in the work of Jesus. This means that anyone, Jew or Gentile, can enter Christ's kingdom as a bona fide child in

---

1 The church is not synonymous with the kingdom of God. Christ's kingdom is larger than the church and includes the church; but it stands over and beyond it. His reign is not limited to the churches of the world; he is king over all kings, seated upon a throne over all thrones, given a name above all names.

the household of faith. Where the Mosaic covenant with God limited access to those who entered God's household through union with ethnic, corporate Israel, Jesus has blown the turnstile wide open for the whole world.

"Take and Eat"

Scripture makes this point about the openness of the kingdom to Peter in a vision recounted in the book of Acts. In Acts 10, we encounter Peter's initial experience of his vision; in Acts 11, we hear Peter repeat his vision to the church. Why is this vision included twice? The most plausible reason is that the content was so incredibly difficult to grasp from a first century perspective. The church in Jerusalem had been dividing into two factions. The first faction contains the "Judaizers" or the "party of the circumcision." They argued that to be a follower of Jesus one must first become a Jew. The second faction disagreed, for reasons that were becoming clearer throughout the book of Acts. In Acts 11:2-3, we read that after news of Peter's vision spread to Jerusalem, the party of the circumcision criticized him, saying, "You went to uncircumcised men and ate with them." The implication was that Peter had become ritually unclean as per the typical standards of the Jews of his day.

In response, Peter provided the second telling of his vision. In doing so, he was arguing for the rejection of the Jewish ritual purity laws. This was to be a vital moment for the early church. This vision forced the church to answer the question: "Did the death and resurrection of Jesus achieve something *different* from the Law of Moses or was Jesus *under* the Law of Moses?" In other words, is Jesus or Moses superior?

Peter explained that while he was praying in the city of Joppa, he experienced a vision in which a great sheet from heaven descended towards him. On the sheet were animals of various kinds: beasts of prey, reptiles, and birds of the air. Importantly, these animals were the types that were declared unclean and off-limits by the terms and conditions of the Mosaic Law.[2] Peter, as a faithful Jew, was disgusted by these unclean animals. He was shocked that a voice from heaven ordered him to "take and eat" the animals from the sheet. Peter, however, was a good and faithful Jew. He declined: "By no means, Lord; for nothing common or unclean has ever entered my mouth" (Acts 10:14; 11:8). The voice from heaven was unimpressed; it boomed out to him again, saying: "What God has made clean, do not call common" (Acts 10:15; 11:9). This experience happened three times.[3] After the third admonition, Peter watched as the sheet was taken up into heaven. At this point the vision ended, and he pondered the meaning and significance of the vision. He didn't have long to reflect, however, for at that moment some men arrived at the house.

Cornelius was a Gentile. He was *more* than merely a Gentile, however; he was a Roman centurion from the Latin cohort. As a centurion, he was the equivalent of a junior officer. In other words, he was a man with a degree of wealth, significant respect, and military authority. He was quite literally one of the oppressors of the Jewish people and of the same citizenship as the murderers of the Messiah. Despite his ethnic background, Cornelius appears to have been a convert. Acts records that he was a devout man whose entire household feared God, gave alms to the poor, and prayed continually to God (Acts 10:2). It was because of his genuine faith in God that God sent an angel to him with instructions to call Peter to his house to explain the gospel.

Thus, we arrive at the interpretation of the vision. The men who had been sent by Cornelius to find Peter arrived at the house

---

[2] Leviticus 11 contains a thorough list of animals that were to be declared unclean by the Israelites under the Mosaic Law. Remember that Israel was to stand apart from their neighbors by "making a distinction between the unclean and the clean" (Leviticus 11:47).

[3] It's curious that Peter's walk with Jesus had numerous "threes": he was in the inner circle of three disciples (Matthew 17:1); he denied Jesus three times (Luke 22:54-62); the Lord was raised on the third day; Peter was restored by three poignant questions concerning Jesus' sheep (John 21:15-25); and this vision's dialogue was repeated thrice.

and sought Peter. Simultaneously, the Holy Spirit explained to Peter that three men were seeking him and commanded him to go with them. Peter obeyed immediately, met his guests, and enquired about their purpose. After being informed that the local God-fearing and respected centurion desired his presence, Peter followed them to Cornelius the next morning.

Arriving at Cornelius' house in Caesarea, Peter met this gruff, authoritative, and accomplished soldier, and was horrified to see Cornelius prostrate himself at his feet in worship. He told Cornelius to get up and reserve his worship for God, not man. Entering the house, he was surprised to see that Cornelius had gathered his family and close friends together to hear what Peter had to say. This was a gathering of Gentiles who had profited from war and violence against the Jewish people. And now in their midst was a leading disciple of a man crucified by Rome for treason. Every ounce of common sense told Peter that this gathering was unwise and perhaps even dangerous.

And yet when Peter started speaking, his calm voice conveyed a deeper truth and a grander reality that had, until this moment, eluded so many people in the post-resurrection world, including Peter himself. His words were to shake the foundation of Jewish cultural norms and Roman sensibilities. His words would begin the restructuring of global society in a way that had barely been considered plausible since the Tower of Babel. For, with his opening statement to the assembled Gentiles, Peter taught that the old distinctions of the Mosaic covenant and various boundaries that sin had erected were no more. The work of Christ was the great leveler; all who enter Christ's kingdom would be considered equal in value, worth, and dignity. All would have equal access to God. Just as the old creation paradigm of the First Adam had given way to the new creation realm of Christ, so too had the old covenant of Moses given way to the New Covenant of Jesus.

Peter began by acknowledging the tradition of the Jews: "You yourselves know how unlawful it is for a Jew to associate with or to visit anyone of another nation" (Acts 10:28). At this, one could imagine the pride of the victorious Romans raising its heckles. But Peter was speaking the truth. The Mosaic Law forbade the eating of unclean animals. Later Jewish traditions developed by various rabbis and religious leaders endeavored to protect the Jews from unknowingly touching or associating with unclean people, foodstuffs, or implements. Through these later traditions, it became almost impossible to interact with a Gentile without being considered ceremonially unclean. But Peter did not stop with the Jewish dividing lines. He continued, saying: "God has shown me that I should not call any person common or unclean" (Acts 10:28). With these words, Peter repudiated centuries of Jewish thought and ritual.

Cornelius then explained his own part in this dramatic experience; his interaction with the angel, and his obedience to the command of the angel to send for Peter. In the full view of his family and intimates, Cornelius commanded Peter to share "all that you have been commanded by the Lord" (Acts 10:33). This language is fascinating because it bears a remarkable likeness to Matthew 28:20 where the Great Commission demands discipleship: "Teach[ing] them to observe all that I have commanded you." Cornelius, perhaps unwittingly, was exhorting Peter to *fulfil the Great Commission* by discipling him. Peter, having just been forced to learn that the gospel is larger than ethnic, corporate Israel, was given an opportunity for evangelism and discipleship that would reshape the praxis of worship for the early church.

With this revelation in mind, Peter grasped the magnitude of the moment: "Truly, I understand that God shows no partiality, but in every nation anyone who fears him and does what is right is acceptable to him" (Acts 10:34-35). Jesus' kingdom was to expand beyond the confines of Palestine or the ethnic, corporate community of the Jews. It was *through* the Jewish covenant community that the gospel would come, but it would be presented and offered *to* the world. At this moment, Peter evangelized this gathering of Gentiles in fulfilment of the promise in Acts 1:8 that the disciples would be a witness of Christ's work to the ends of the earth. It turns out, Peter did not necessarily need to go to the ends of the earth to reach them. As had been God's plan from the days of Abraham, the geographic location of Israel was critical. People from all over the world traveled through Judea for purposes of war, trade, and diplomacy. People just like Cornelius.

After Peter's proclamation of the good news of Jesus to this gathering of Gentiles, and his comments that "all the prophets [of the Jewish scriptures] bear witness that everyone who believes in him receives forgiveness of sins through his name" (Acts 10:43), we read that "the Holy Spirit fell on all who heard the word" (Acts 10:44). This is a second Pentecost event, but, as Luke records for us in Acts 10:45: "The believers from among the circumcised who had come with Peter were amazed, because the gift of the Holy Spirit was poured out *even on the Gentiles.*" The means of receiving the gift of the Holy Spirit was not tied to ethnicity, nor was it tied to Moses, but to faith in the work of Jesus for the forgiveness of sins. After receiving the Holy Spirit, Peter's theological revelation was complete. He had understood the message of the vision of the food on the sheet and God's command to "take and eat." Discerning the validity of their conversion to faith in Christ, Peter commanded that each believer present was to be baptized in compliance with the Great Commission.

The Jerusalem Council discussed in Acts 15 affirmed Peter's interpretation of his vision from Acts 10, even if the need for a formal declaration was necessitated by Peter's failure to stand up for what he himself had been so dramatically shown. The decision affirmed that the historic divisions were no longer to be used to separate Jew from Gentile; rather, it sought to highlight a truly humble sensitivity to those still under the Law without adding an unnecessary burden to those who knew that they were not under it. Paul's rebuke of Peter in Galatians 2 served to remind Peter of his primary duty, which was to be an ambassador for the New Covenant reality of kingdom of God. He had to remember that Moses and Elijah had given way to Jesus. The lesson would be well learned; according to tradition, Peter would be martyred in Rome for his faith. His lack of courage on the night of Christ's betrayal, fearing his own arrest, and his cowardice in Jerusalem, fearing the Judaizers, would be replaced with a stalwart confidence and strength of will that would echo through the ages as an example of what the Almighty Lord can do with a braggadocious, cowardly, fisherman.

The importance of Peter's vision in Acts 10 is difficult to express. By being commanded to "take and eat" of previously "unclean" specimens, Peter was forced to reckon with his personal distaste and dislike for uncircumcised Gentiles. God was using a visual aid to highlight the transition in redemptive history from exclusive Jewish religious expression to an expanded kingdom citizenry. Further, the means of access to Christ's kingdom, and therefore to God the Father, was through the once-for-all sacrifice of God the Son. Being a Jew no longer bore significant eternal salvific importance. The paradigm of salvation had changed. Now, to be in the New Israel of God, one had to be united to the single True Israelite by faith. Once again, God used the motif of "take and eat" to advance the narrative arc of redemptive history. But there are to be no isolated Christians. Christ is not producing a network of individual castles; he's building a single, unified, kingdom of saints. From the ashes of the old creation, Christ is producing a new creation. With a new Exodus from an even more diabolically nefarious Pharaoh, Christ is forming a new people, constituting a new nation, bound by a new covenant loyalty, and which rejects the restrictions of the Mosaic covenant.

A New Nation

With Peter's comprehension of the kingdom's composition solidified, we can follow his maturing theology through to his first epistle. In 1 Peter 2, Peter speaks about the new birth into the new creation as something achieved by God and given as a gift of grace to those who trust in the work of Christ. After a section in chapter one calling for all believers to be holy as God is holy, he explains how believers are being built up into a "spiritual house, to be a holy priesthood, to offer spiritual sacrifices acceptable to God through Jesus Christ" (1 Peter 2:5).[4] This temple is comprised of those who come to faith in Christ because the Spirit of God indwells them; thus, just as the temple in the Old Testament was the "house of God" where he dwelt in the midst of his people, now, in fulfilment of Jeremiah 31 and Ezekiel 36, he will dwell *in* his people. God's people are a temple for God himself.

Further, Peter's point is that every believer is a living stone through faith in Christ and therefore every follower of Christ is part of a holy priesthood. The priesthood of all believers is in view here; every Christian functions as a priest to one another, preaching the gospel to one another (1 Thessalonians 5:11), singing psalms, hymns, and spiritual songs to one another for edification (Ephesians 5:19; Colossians 3:16), confessing our sins one to another (James 5:16), and providing hospitality and benevolence for those in need (1 Timothy 5:3-14). All of these are acts of spiritual service to one another *in the name of Christ*. As the church faithfully lives out these privileged obligations as priests for one another, the temple itself will expand; through evangelism the church will grow as more and more people become enchanted with the message of Christ that cultivates a genuine love for neighbor.

Peter is taking Old Testament imagery and demonstrating how it's beautifully and poetically fulfilled by Christ and understood in light of his work. The Old Testament imagery is giving way to the New Testament realities; the temple of stone is replaced with a living temple. The priesthood of Levi has given way to a priesthood of all believers. The food laws of Moses are no longer obligations (though we ought to show restraint and exercise wisdom with what we consume; we aren't to be mastered by food, or drink, or drugs). Christ's work has reshaped the religious community. Peter continues this idea in verse 9: "But you are a chosen

---

4   This motif is a *temple* motif; the third temple is the household of faith, which is built upon the cornerstone of Christ, but is itself comprised of his people. To build this temple, we must be about the work of the Great Commission; evangelism leads to conversion of the lost who are raised to life to be living stones in Christ's temple.

race, a royal priesthood, a holy nation, a people for his own possession, that you may proclaim the excellencies of him who called you out of darkness into his marvelous light. Once you were not a people, but now you are God's people" (1 Peter 2:9-10a). To understand what Peter is saying, it must be understood that the language he uses is extraordinarily Jewish.

In Exodus 19, Israel entered their covenant with God. In verses 5-6, God says to the Israelites: "If you will indeed obey my voice and keep my covenant, you shall be my treasured possession among all peoples, for all the earth is mine; and you shall be to me a kingdom of priests and a holy nation." Through their newfound covenantal relationship with Yahweh, the Israelites were transformed from a tribal people into a treasured possession. Although God is Lord over all creation, he chose to bestow a genuinely unique relationship with the children of Israel. They were to be a kingdom of priests, meaning that they were to consistently serve God and be a light to the nations, mediating the heart and words of God to the nations. They were to be a holy nation, meaning that they were to be obedient to the terms and conditions of the covenant, loving God as their sovereign, and being set apart by observing his regulations.

In 1 Peter, however, these titles are no longer spoken of as belonging to ethnic, corporate, Mosaic Israel. Peter adopts them for followers of Jesus, irrespective of historic ethnicity. Peter sees the church as a new Israel, a new temple, and a new priesthood. Crucially, this is because the church is united to Christ who is the true Israel, the true temple, and the great High Priest. This is vital: Christ's kingdom is a *new nation*. Citizenship in his kingdom is based upon the new birth not old familial ties. A Christian is not someone who has been circumcised in the flesh but rather one who has had their heart circumcised by faith (Romans 2:29; cf. Jeremiah 31:33). Peter is telling his readers that they're a chosen race because God the Father chose them from before the foundation of the world to be in the kingdom of his Son (Ephesians 1:4). This reveals to us that the work of salvation is ultimately a work of

God. It's not the will of men that they should be saved; children of God (by adoption through faith in Christ) are born by God's sovereignty (John 1:12-13). Believers are from every tribe, tongue, and nation (Daniel 7:14; Revelation 7:9), having been brought into faith through a spiritual rebirth (John 3:3) and adoption into the heavenly family (Ephesians 1:5).

As a chosen race, and as the living stones in the ever-expanding house of God, believers are a royal priesthood whose duties are to serve one another with the same humility as Christ exhibited when he served the church by dying for her (Ephesians 5:25-27). In Eden, the tasks of the very first priesthood were to work and keep Eden; these were the same duties given to the Levitical priests in the tabernacle and temple. To cultivate the rule of God in the midst of the people of God was the duty of every generation of priest; to achieve this today, the royal priesthood must proclaim the constitution of the king, which is to say, "teach them to obey all that I have commanded you" (Matthew 28:20). Christians therefore should be seeking to establish the reign of Christ in our lives and in the lives of our churches.

As adopted children in the family of God, we are *royal* priests; just as Christ is the Great High Priest, he is also the greater Davidic king, combining into a single office the three Hebrew offices of prophet, priest, and king. Every single Christian bears a resemblance to Christ as princes under his kingship, priests to one another, and prophets who proclaim his word. This is why we can intercede for one another as priests before the throne of God through the preaching and teaching and application of scripture.

To be a holy nation now is to be like Israel was then: A people set apart in the midst of a sinful realm. Israel failed to be covenantally obedient (Exodus 19:5). Peter reminded the Judaizers of this important fact at the Jerusalem Council. Thus, Christ's citizens are not expected to be sinless (because we are weak), but, instead, to abide and rest in Christ's sinlessness. It's only by being united to Christ by faith and adoption that we can be God's holy nation and a people set apart for his own possession. Each human being has been fearfully and wonderfully woven together in their mother's womb by an immanent and loving God; likewise, each believer has been intentionally and lovingly called out of darkness into his glorious light. Everyone who has entered the kingdom was sought by God and bought by the blood of Christ. This reveals the powerful breadth of God's love for his own people. Every single believer is a cherished individual, lovingly brought into the kingdom as such a cost, and given a family of brothers and sisters from across every region and family of the earth.

This is why Peter can say to his readers that "once you were not a people, but now you are God's people" (1 Peter 2:10a). There was nothing at all that unified Peter and Cornelius. They were from different corners of the world. They had different social circles. They followed very different career paths. They would have been raised to worship different gods, wear different attire, submit to different governments, subscribe to different ethical systems, and exhibit very different moral values. Nevertheless, Peter and Cornelius were *made* to be a new people, siblings in a chosen race, servants of a single priesthood, citizens of a single holy nation. Their old barriers and divisions were torn down as they were united into a single entity through the majestic work of redemption. Now Cornelius was just as much a child of God as Peter. This fulfils Christ's command to accept the little ones (by which he meant true followers of his, not biological children) whom he came to seek and to save (Matthew 18:10-14).

The removal of *division* does not mean the erasure of *diversity*. The kingdom of God spans time and space; a Christian at the Jerusalem Council would most certainly look and sound different to a Christian in the mountains of Tibet or the islands of Hawaii. That being said, there will be a uniformity of *doctrine* that unites believers across history and geography. We may look, sound, speak, and even think differently than many other believers on an almost infinite range of subjects. But we will all be united by the single fact that we are redeemed by the death and resurrection of Christ. When we sit together to eat the holy meal of communion, our earthly diversity may well be in full display even as our spiritual unity is joyously celebrated.

Jesus is the greater Adam and the greater Moses. He has inaugurated a new creation through his resurrection and is populating it with his expanding temple of faithful followers. The gates of hell and the rebellion of the old creation will not stand against the march of his kingdom citizens as they live out the Great Commission. By properly understanding Peter's vision in Acts 10, the early church was enabled to conceive of a kingdom that was larger, greater, and more diverse than they could ever have imagined. Christ has burst the doors of the kingdom wide open for any and all who would repent and believe the gospel. No more would there be separate temple courts for Gentiles, women, and men, and a completely separated Holy Sanctuary with access limited to the High Priest on a single day of the year. Rather, with the temple curtain torn in two at the moment of Christ's death, the message was clear: The kingdom of God was open to all.

Kingdom Citizenship

Above, it was argued that the two *promises* in the Great Commission highlight how Jesus has adopted the Creation Mandate. It was then explained that Christ's kingdom is meant to include Gentiles and Jews indiscriminately, as seen through Peter's experiences. Next, we will explore how the two *commands* of the Great Commission explain how Christ's new humanity is expected to live under his kingship. His Adamic dominion and presence enables the people of Christ, his kingdom citizens, to both expand the kingdom and exercise dominion within it.

Spreading the Image of God

In the first command, Christ updates the Creation Mandate's demand to procreate by telling his people to evangelize. This is the thrust of verse 19: "Go therefore and make disciples of all nations, baptizing them in the name of the Father and of the Son and of the Holy Spirit." Whereas the Creation Mandate anticipated biological progeny, the New Creation Mandate bears Christ's commission to evangelize rebels from the old creation with the message of his gospel so that they can be "born again" into his spiritual life (cf. John 3:3). These converts will be those who hear the good news of the serpent's vanquishment by Christ, turn towards Christ in faith that his grace (alone) is sufficient for their redemption, and who will take up their cross and follow him (Matthew 16:24). This is the process we call "repentance." Through the process of repentance, an individual dies to his old self and is born into the kingdom as a babe in the household of faith. Upon the profession of faith (for those who are Baptists, at any rate), conversion and repentance is followed by baptism.[5] The point is that the Creation Mandate's command to procreate has been advanced into the New Creation Mandate of evangelizing and baptizing in the name of the Triune God. In this way, the kingdom of God expands with each new believer. The souls of the lost are brought into resurrection life through faith in the work of Christ. This baptism is a passport that identifies the individuals as citizens in the kingdom. It's an identification process that belongs to the church but is performed on individuals. These kingdom citizens are brought into the kingdom and, simultaneously, begin to worship with a local church body where they can experience the second command of the Great Commission.

Exercising Dominion by Teaching His Commands

In this second command, Christ updates the Creation Mandate's demand to exercise dominion by telling his people to disciple one another. Thus, in the first part of verse 20 he tells his disciples to "teach them to observe all that I have commanded you." I call this the constitution of the kingdom. When someone

---

5   This is the difference between paedobaptism and credobaptism. Credobaptism argues baptism must come after a profession of faith. Paedobaptism argues that baptism ought to be given to infants in anticipation of their conversion later in life, at which point their baptism can be "confirmed." There are various technical and systematic arguments for both sides that are beyond our scope.

migrates to a new country, and becomes a citizen of that nation, they're expected to integrate into their new homeland. They ought to learn the language, observe the laws, and experience life as if they belong there. Sometimes, that experience can be very jarring. Nevertheless, a citizen is expected to represent the nation. As converts to Christ, we're brought into his kingdom (identified by the passport of baptism) and now we must know what is expected of us (learning the constitution). Just as Adam was expected to bring creation under his rule as a microcosmic expression of God's rule, followers of Christ are to teach new believers what Christ commands. This is the process we call "discipleship." The work is ongoing, intercultural, intergenerational, and requires a genuine humble vulnerability. Mature believers can still learn from newer believers. Indeed, I would argue this is essential. Mature believers may have wisdom, but can often grow complacent; conversely, new believers are often zealous, but lack spiritual wisdom. By deliberately engaging intergenerationally, wisdom is shared while zeal becomes contagious. This is how we, in the new creation, are to exercise dominion. As in Eden, this is not about being dictatorial, but providing a genuinely Christ-centered discipleship.

The household of faith has a duty to hold one another to account. This is not, of course, an excuse to implement a kind of spiritual police state or introduce a churchwide *Stasi* spy network. Rather, it's how we protect one another from the ongoing violence of the serpent. Believers who are passionate about obeying Christ will find themselves attacked and pressured by Satan. He desires to discredit their witness and disarm their effectiveness. A critical tool to withstand his cunning machinations is to be intentional in seeking the fellowship of the saints. By being present in the household of faith (Hebrews 10:25), individual members are blessing one another and being fed a healthy diet of the words of Christ. When believers "confess their sins, one to another" (James 5:16), we're allowing our brothers and sisters to apply the balm of the gospel to the recent wounds of sinful behavior. By "addressing one another in psalms, hymns, and spiritual songs" (Ephesians 5:19),

Christians teach one another the truths of the gospel that deepen devotion and increase our desire to honor the Lord. By being vulnerable, we're letting others be the hands and feet of Jesus to us whilst simultaneously teaching (and being taught) how to be more Christlike. Fundamentally, the purpose is to develop a deeper understanding of what Christ demands of us as citizens so that we can "be holy as I am holy" (1 Peter 1:15-16).

A comment ought to be made about the Great Commission's first word: "Go." The Greek command is perhaps better understood to be something like "as you are going" rather than a direct imperative "go." During the Protestant missionary boom of the 17th and 18th centuries, the Great Commission was transformed into a call to global missions. This movement was a good thing for the church and for the globe, ultimately, but it did have the negative effect of turning the Great Commission into something primarily (and, in some cases, exclusively) for overseas missionaries. This interpretation is not the point of the Great Commission. Whilst it can (and assuredly does) *contain* global missional efforts, the Great Commission is so much larger than merely that. It's a call, a commission, and a command for *every* believer, in *every* location, and in *every* era, to *be* making disciples *where they are*. For some, that may mean crossing the seas; for most of us, it means crossing the street. For every Christian, it means preaching and proclaiming Jesus in our lives and in our communities. This also, incidentally, means that the primary work of evangelizing your friends and family and social circle is *you*. There are many people who, for various reasons, will not voluntarily enter a church building or listen to your pastor's sermons. But they will enter your home or spend time with you. Every citizen in the kingdom of God is commanded (and, vitally, *empowered*) with the authority of Christ to fulfil the Great Commission. Likewise, the work of discipling belongs to every believer, not just the "professional" cadre. Discipleship is something that everyone needs to do and receive. It's also something in which every Christian must be involved. There's no mechanism in the Great Commission that permits any of us to be absent from our duty. Christian history is replete with Christians evangelizing even on their deathbed and discipling through their faithfulness to Christ. We have no excuse.

Although we're called to be obedient in evangelizing and discipleship, it's not something that we do on our own. At the immediate level, we have the household of faith to share with us, teach us, help us, and walk with us as we endeavor to be faithful to Christ's calling. At the larger level, however, we have the promises of Christ in Matthew 28:18 and 28:20 to inspire and empower us. *All* authority is given to Christ. If that is true, and it is, then we need not fear the nations who rage against the Lord's anointed; we know that their time is limited. Even if they're given temporary power over us, it is nevertheless *temporary*. Christ *is* reigning in the heavens and he *is* going to return to exercise justice. This reality means that we don't need to be afraid of what the world might say about us, or even what it might do to us. Christians throughout history have listened to this promise of Christ's ultimate power and, by trusting in it, have been able to live through the most vitriolic, violent, and horrific persecution imaginable. And, incredibly, come through it with love.[6] Indeed, the very act of being obedient (amid opposition) brings us almost full circle; by the power of the indwelling Holy Spirit, we're able to be faithful to the commands of Christ that hearkens back to Eden. The image of God is restored in those who are in Christ because we wear his perfect righteousness, and he is the actual visible imprint of the invisible God. The New Creation Mandate points us forward to the restoration, indeed the advancement, of the *imago Dei* in the redeemed.

Restoration of the Imago Dei

Having returned to Christ's adoption and adaptation of the Creation Mandate, we must consider what it means to be citizens in Christ's kingdom. Fundamentally, this begins with his provision of his image as the prototype for his people. In essence, just as

---

[6] For a recent example of such bold faith during horrific persecution, see Wurmbrand: *Tortured for Christ* (Voice of the Martyrs Books, 2023).

Adam was made in the image and likeness of God (Genesis 1:26) and Christ is the visible image of the invisible God (Colossians 1:15), those who are united to Christ by faith are to be conformed to the likeness and image of Christ (Romans 8:29; 2 Corinthians 3:18; Ephesian 4:11-15).

A New Imago Dei in Christ

When Adam and Eve sinned, their ability to reflect God was marred by corruption. They were given punishments by God that reflected their two tasks in the Creation Mandate: Disharmonious relationships and difficulties in work. With the New Creation Mandate in Christ, Christians have new relationships and new purpose. Our purpose is to spread out across the world through evangelism and to disciple new believers into the kingdom. Our new relationships are grounded in an equal kingdom citizenship; all are welcome in the kingdom and all will be equal in the kingdom. A critical reason why these relationships can work is because of a restoration of the *imago Dei* by Christ.

We must remind ourselves that the image of God combines two aspects: kingship and sonship. These two aspects were damaged by sin; our rule became tyrannical as we were subjected to the arch-tyrants of sin and Satan whilst our sonship was reduced to rebelliousness. We faced judgement because we were cosmic traitors against our loving and holy God. That would ultimately lead to Adam's expulsion from Eden (and from the presence of God). In time, after his toiling came to an end, he would die. But, in mercy, God permitted Adam and Eve to continue to procreate, leading to the birth of sinful sons, who bore the *imago Dei* in the corrupted form. The primary work of humanity became self-worship whilst the primary relationships within creation concerned kinship rather than a holy kingship over creation.

Family Resemblances

With the work of Christ and his inauguration of the kingdom of God, however, that paradigm of sinful humanity's interaction with creation has shifted once again. Those who are united to Christ by faith in his atoning work are brought into the heavenly family through adoption (Galatians 3:24-27; Ephesians 1:5). Throughout Paul's letters he appeals to the familial implications of salvation. According to Paul, to be a redeemed believer is more than to be saved from sin and the avoidance of hell; it's to be restored into right relationship with God and made to be children of God. Consequentially, the nature of our image bearing rebellion is transformed and given a holy purpose. The larger catechism of the Westminster Confession of Faith memorably phrases this purpose thus: "Man's chief end is to glorify God and enjoy him forever."[7] What had been Adam's privilege, lost through rebellion, has been restored through the Final Adam's redemption.

As adopted children of God and heirs with Christ, we're now to take on the family resemblance. A practical and pastoral implication of being a believer in Christ is that we're adopted for *more* than the mere task of obedient Great Commissioning; we're restored to the dignity of Edenic image bearing. Granted, we continue to be tainted by sin and sinfulness in this fallen realm; but we're no longer citizens of a dying realm. Rather, we're sojourners in this world because our citizenship belongs to a kingdom not of this world (Philippians 3:20-21). Thus, even though we remain in temples infected by the disease of sin, we're nevertheless anticipating the transformation from these fallen carcasses into mansions specially prepared for us by the Lord Jesus (John 14:2-3). Whilst Jesus is in heaven, preparing the mansions of glory and the incorruptible flesh that will be ours because of the resurrection (1 Corinthians 15:52), our responsibility is to reflect the family appropriately. This means that we must begin to look and sound and think and act like Jesus, who is our elder brother and the prototype of the new creation. As the only truly sinless man, and the ruler of the kingdom of God, we're dutybound to consider his example so that we know what a member of God's family looks like.

---

[7] https://westminsterstandards.org/westminster-larger-catechism/, accessed 5/27/2024.

We're to emulate Christ, our elder brother, and thus live as befits a member in God's family (1 John 2:6; 1 Peter 2:21; Ephesians 4:22-24; Ephesians 5:1-2).

Learning from Jesus is a lifelong pursuit. He was the perfect, innocent, and holy Son. We, in contrast, have spent years and decades in sinful rebellion. Unlike Christ, we have not mastered temptation nor become perfectly holy as God is holy. Thus, for us to look *like* Jesus we must be able to look *at* Jesus with humility and obedience. We're to follow in his footsteps. When we submit ourselves to an analysis of his biographies, we see someone who was passionate about respecting God's authority and loving God's image bearers. Throughout the New Testament accounts, we read of his repeated assaults on the corrupted spiritual shepherds of his day juxtaposed alongside his tender compassion for those who were in need of the Good Shepherd. He knew the words of God intimately and lived them out perfectly. He sat with sinners but didn't leave them wallowing in the sinking sands of their shame. The Jesus of the gospels is not the "meek and mild" pushover so often portrayed in modern media; this was a revolutionary who was inaugurating a topsy-turvy kingdom of holiness, justice, grace, and glory.

When we consider Jesus thus, we're forced to think about how our *imago Dei* has been restored. Where once our minds were enslaved to sinful thoughts and desires, our nature has been freed from sin's snares. This is why Paul commands believers to "present your bodies as a living sacrifice, holy and acceptable to God, which is your spiritual worship" (Romans 12:1). This speaks of our actions. Our lives are no longer to be sacrificed on the altars of self-worship and selfish desire but are to be poured out as an offering to God just as Christ was poured out as an acceptable offering. Our actions must reflect the humble devotion to God's holiness that Christ has modelled for us. When we face temptation, our desire should be to say "not my will, but yours, because you are my God, and my father." The means of working towards this practical experience is found in the next verse: "Do not be conformed to this world, but be transformed by the renewal of your mind, that by testing you may discern what is the will of God, what is good and acceptable and perfect" (Romans 12:2). The will of the believer has been renewed through our redemption. Where once our wills were enslaved to sin, now we're freed to serve the kingdom as adopted children of God. Therefore, our purpose has been transformed from advancing my kingdom to advancing Christ's kingdom. With the renewal of our minds by the work of Jesus, it's as if we've been woken from a sinful haziness; our slumber shaken off, we now see clearly how we're to live. The words we say should be Christ-honoring and Christ-exalting. The things we look at should be holy and righteous. The way we deal with people should be ethical, with integrity, and respectfully.

The more we resemble Jesus, the more our lives will mature in sanctification and holiness. As we mature, the old nature will struggle to breathe whilst the new nature will thrive. It is one who seeks to be Christlike who can begin to joyously follow the many commands of Paul in the rest of Romans 12: "Bless those who persecute you…live in harmony with one another…do not be haughty, but associate with the lowly…repay no one evil for evil, but give thought to do what is honorable in the sight of all…never avenge yourselves…if your enemy is hungry, feed him; if he is thirsty, give him something to drink" (Romans 12:14-21). Such actions are not natural to the sinful man; they're only possible because they have been taught to obey the Lord by the indwelling Spirit (Ezekiel 36:26-27; Jeremiah 31:34). Our family resemblance goes even beyond merely looking and living like Jesus; it speaks to what he has achieved by his resurrection. We're not simply made to be "better" human beings; we're created into something "new" in Christ Jesus: A new creation. We're still *humans* and therefore still *image bearers*; but the image we reflect is no longer that of the Fallen Adam but that of the Final Adam.

A Restored Likeness and Image

The restoration of the likeness and image of God in redeemed human beings brings us back to the garden of Eden. The paradox of the Fall was such that, although the image bearing nature of mankind was not lost, *humanity itself* was lost in the salvific sense. Through the redemptive work of Christ, however, both the corrupted image and the captive likeness of God is redeemed and restored. Adam was God's regent as well as *a* son of God. Because Adam failed, we needed a successful serpent crusher, a victorious king, and a true son of God. In the dramatic incarnational event, *the* Son of God entered the material realm. At the cross he suffered as our vicarious substitute to victoriously bring about atonement for our sin. By the resurrection, he established his rule and crushed the head of the serpent. Jesus's obedience in the work of redemption enables humanity to once more stand in the presence of God as children of God. When, in faith, we enter his kingdom, we're adopted into his family and given a restored image. Cullman speaks of Jesus "remaking men" which is an action that only God can do; but because of the incarnation, Jesus, the Son, is both God and man, and therefore he is able to make a new creation from within the old creation by being both *of* creation and *beyond* it.[8] In an appropriate way, we are restored to our original nature by being made anew in Christ; we're not lesser because of the restoration, however, such as a restored monument or artefact is less than the original. Rather, we're made to be something *greater* in the new creation because we're made into the image of a greater Adam. To be made in *his* image is to reflect a sharper imprint of God. Adam, despite being made "very good," was not *the* Son of God. He was made sinless and his likeness was unique, though it was so *only for the duration of his sinlessness*. In contrast, Jesus was, and remains, the sinless Son of God and the exact imprint of the invisible God (Hebrews 1:3; Colossians 1:15). Yet, through the

---

[8] Oscar Cullman, *The Christology of the New Testament*, Revised Edition (Philadelphia, PA: Westminster John Knox Press, 1959), p. 104-106. I am indebted to Scott Stine for this reference.

resurrection, he is also the firstborn of the new creation. We, who are united to Christ by faith, are not only adopted into God's family but are being revivified into the likeness and image *of Christ*.

For believers, our restoration is experienced in part in this life as we are being conformed into the likeness and image of the *prototype* of the new creation, the Lord Jesus. The true and full transformation will occur at death when we experience glorification and stand before our God at the beatific vision. Nevertheless, the pleasure of having a spiritual likeness to God as sons and daughters is a real experience that we're meant to enjoy in our spiritual maturation. Our joy is found in growing into our family resemblance as adopted children. Likewise, in our spiritual context of the Great Commission, we're to enjoy the holy and spiritual task of exercising our renewed and restored regency by teaching one another to obey all that Christ has commanded us. It is Eden revisited. The task at hand, for believers, is to "put on the *new* self, created in the likeness of God in true righteousness and holiness" (Ephesians 4:24). This can be comprehended, despite our residence in the fallen world, because we have received "the mind of Christ" through our union with him (1 Corinthians 2:14). Together, discipleship and obedience, constitutes a renewed holy labor. It *is* spiritual "work" (not in a salvific sense, for works do not save) in a sanctificational sense because we're to put fleshly desires to death. Paul highlights that this work is not to be undertaken in isolation; rather, it's achieved in the midst, and with the aid, of our renewed *community* (Ephesians 4:25-32). Christ's work in us is an individual work that ripples beyond us into the community *through* us. We are each to be Adamic in that we're all priests to one another in the kingdom, under the Great High Priest; we're to "work and keep" our fellowship of faith in unity and order (cf. Matthew 18).

The new image that is created and to be cultivated is not a return to Adam and Eve in the garden, but rather is a new identity of Christlikeness. The corruption of the *imago Dei* is restored, but the finished product will not be a return to Eden; we're made for something more. A perfect illustration is the Japanese art form of kintsugi. When a valuable piece of pottery breaks, the various shards are carefully pieced back together with gold lacquer with the result that the piece is of greater value *because* of its journey and history. Perhaps this explains the mysteriousness of the gospel to the angels who long to understand it (1 Peter 1:12). It's for believers alone to truly understand and experience the incredible mercy of redemption; we're not monuments of a failed project any more than we're artefacts of the fallen empire of Adam. Rather, the wounds of our current clay bodies have been bound by the golden bandages of the gospel so that we're more beautiful, more vibrant, more dynamic than even Adam had been on the day of his creation. This is not to say that the breaking was not painful; sin is always destructive. But the art of Christ's restoration takes our brokenness and makes it beautiful, not because of the severity of our damage, but because of the tenderness and patience of his workmanship in us. The beauty of our restoration is in the work of the master craftsman; he lifted us out of the old Adamic paradigm and brought us into a whole new world so that we shine with a luster that reflects his autobiographical portrait. Where once we shared the wearied wrinkles of a fallen father, now we are being formed into the likeness of an eternally youthful and sinless elder brother.

Application

Although there are almost innumerable applications that could be drawn from this New Creation Mandate, the main application will be that Christ's victory as the Last Adam unwinds the curse and punishments of Genesis 3. Almost like the beginning and end of a book, the parallels are deliberately, indeed divinely, intentional. Adam's failures are reconstituted in and by Christ's victory such that all that was enslaved to Satan under Adam is redeemed to God by Christ (though not all will be redeemed *to salvation*).

Unwinding the Curse(s)

The devastating consequences of the Fall were detailed in Genesis 3: The serpent was reduced to slithering and eating dust whilst the archserpent himself will eventually be crushed; Eve was to experience relational turmoil at the hands of Adam and biological pain in childbearing; Adam would find work to be toilsome and troublesome, and death would come to him and all his descendants. By the work of Christ, we see that these consequences are being unwound. From within the ruinous echoes of creation's cathedral, we hear the crescendoing melodies of a resurrected host singing a new song of praise. Although this fallen world will come to an end in judgement, a new realm is dawning, and will come with the return of the king. On that day, as C.S. Lewis magisterially portrayed: "Wrong will be right, when Aslan comes in sight / At the sound of his roar, sorrows will be no more / When he bears his teeth, winter will meet its death / And when he shakes his mane, we shall have spring again."[9] The image in Narnia was one in which the reign of evil was "always winter, never Christmas." It was a world devoid of hope, of joy, and of life. But wherever the power of the good and righteous king, Aslan, was to be found? Snow melted, grass grew, flowers blossomed, and hope abounded. Although we have yet to reach the fullest and final expression of the new creation, we're able to experience the inbreaking of the blessings of the kingdom of Christ in this age. The snow of sin is melting, and the life of Christ is blossoming around us everywhere his word is faithfully proclaimed and observed. Sin's dark tyranny is in retreat as Christ's gospel advances. For all their vitriolic violence, the generals of the gates of Hell are unable to halt the campaign of the Church Triumphant, marching under the banner and to the beat of the King's drum. The curse has been conclusively defeated at the cross and the shockwaves of that celestial earthquake are being felt as the new creation tastes and sees that the Lord is good.

---

9   C.S. Lewis, *A Year With Aslan: Daily Reflections from the Chronicles of Narnia* (Harper Collins, 2010), p. 4.

Adam and Toil

Because of Adam's sin in eating from the tree in contravention of God's command, God cursed the ground so that thorns and thistles would invade the fields of his harvest. The work of sustenance was to be toilsome, painful, and challenging. The pain of his harvesting would be the cause of his eating bread in the midst of rivulets of sweat flowing down his exhausted face. This punishment concerns work and the sense of vacuous vapidity that so often makes our labor seem menial, unrewarding, unfulfilling, and draining.

By his redemption, Jesus' has restored us to a godly and holy work. This work involves his adoption and adaptation of the Creation Mandate such that we're now engaged in the labor of expanding God's reign over creation through evangelism and cultivating his rule through discipleship. Beyond these "higher purposes" of a redeemed labor, however, is the renewal of the mundanity of work by giving it new purpose. Even when we're flipping burgers or making copies or drafting contracts or planting seeds, our work is redeemed by our attitude and our purpose. Where once toil was exerted simply to put bread in our tired mouths, our labor becomes dignified by being part of the kingdom's effort. Most people won't have evangelistic and discipling conversations all day every day; but through financial support we can establish workers who are especially gifted in those areas. The idea is to use our earthly labor to invest in heavenly dividends, namely, souls impacted by our earthly investment. We don't *buy* salvation; but our earthly investments can be the means by which an individual has access to a Bible in their own language or comes into contact by a missionary who otherwise would not be available.

To see our work in this way is not to give a backdoor loophole to avoid *being* evangelists ourselves, but rather to identify our strengths and use them for the kingdom. Some of us aren't gifted writers, speakers, songwriters, videographers; but we can be grafters. By working diligently with our mind set on serving the kingdom, we no longer consider our work laborious and pointless but essential to our role in the advancement of the gospel. We do this by seeing our *bodies* as living sacrifices so that we recognize that time and effort is not wasted but will be impactful for the kingdom. This is the restoration Paul speaks about in Colossians where Christ's work recapitulates the original emphasis in Eden such that "whatever you do, work at it with all your heart…[for] it is the Lord Christ that you are serving" (Colossians 3:24-25). The curse on work is unwound from slavish boredom to sanctifying doxology.

Because of Jesus, the punishment of Adam to toil with a pointless exertion and to tire with a painful exhaustion is transformed into a blessing of purposeful labor that has an eternal reward.

Adam and Death

Directly related to this is the unwinding of the largest earthly consequence of the Fall: Death. Being made for holy worship in the sanctuary of the sovereign Lord, Adam instead would taste death and return to dust. However, the work of Jesus means that the sting of death is defeated (1 Corinthians 15:55-57). The great attacking dragon, crouching at the door seeking whom it may devour (Genesis 4:7), is itself defeated by the cross and resurrection of Christ and will one day face its own termination (Revelation 20:14). This is why Paul can speak of the dead in Christ as being "asleep" (1 Thessalonians 4:13). Paul is not the proverbial ostrich burying his head in the sand; rather, he's expressly arguing that death itself has been defeated and is being unwound.

For Adam and all subsequent human descendants, the corruption of the flesh is an inevitability. But from Christ, the tent we now inhabit will pass away and return to dust; the new creation, will not pass away. The paradigm of 1 Corinthians 15 lays this out. Paul says that the fleshly bodies of believers in this life are like seeds; in death we are "sown" into the ground because we bear the marks of the Fall and of our rebellion. But that seed of death will germinate and blossom into glory: "The body that is sown is perishable, it is raised imperishable; it is sown in dishonor, it is raised in glory; it is sown in weakness, it is raised in power; it is sown a natural body, it is raised a spiritual body" (1 Corinthians 15:42-44, NIV). Because of our union with Christ by faith, we are more than merely Adam; we are also in Christ the Final Adam. This means that when we die in Adam, we are raised in Christ, bearing the image of both Adam and Christ (1 Corinthians 15:49). But because Jesus is God the Son incarnate, when we are united to him, we are also like him through our adoption. And, as he is the first born of the new creation (Colossians 1:15) having been sown in death (Colossians 1:18), we are his harvest, sown in sin but raised in righteousness to enjoy our heavenly Father forever. This is why Paul rejoices that the perishable will be raised imperishable in the future resurrection when the dead in Christ are roused from our "sleep." This is also why Paul concludes the triumphant section on the future resurrection and transformation with a reminder that our spiritual labor is no longer in vain (1 Corinthians 15:58). This is because death is defeated and we can even now experience victory in the Lord Jesus Christ despite knowing most of us will die so that we will be raised to eternal life.

This can be seen in the many promises throughout the Old and New Testaments concerning life in the presence of God and eternal life in the future. By the death of death, Christians will experience a life that is eternal in duration and in the presence of God himself, where he will dwell in our midst and we will be his people even as he is our God (Revelation 21:3). This promise is larger than can ever be expressed this side of our experience of it. Suffice it to say, this Beatific Vision is when we are enabled to be in the presence of God such that we can see his face and experience him as he is (1 John 3:2). When we're in this full presence of God, we will be in the presence of the essence of life itself. God alone is eternal in his nature and essence; he is completely and utterly self-sufficient. He needs nothing in order to be who he is. This means that, when we are in his presence, we will enjoy the fullness of life because we will be basking in the source of *all* life and all goodness. Adam's sin *separated* him from God; Christ's obedience brings us into God's presence *as children* in a larger and grander sense than even Adam had enjoyed. And it will be an eternal present; in the presence of God time itself is not needed because he is not bound by, or constrained by, time. Time is a tool he uses for creation, but he is beyond and above it. At that point, our eternal presence with God will be superhistorical and unconstrained by any evil, wickedness, temporariness, or limitation.

Eve and Relational Disharmony

As Adam was restored by Christ, so too, was Eve. Her work has also experienced the renewal of the gospel and a restored spiritual purpose. The Creation Mandate was given in Eden but neither Adam nor Eve could accomplish it without the other.[10] The entirety of the Fall has been overruled by the cross, and thus the entirety of the consequences of the Fall are being unwound, not just those that pertain to Adam as the figurehead of humanity. Thus, Eve's guilt, shame, and sin are redeemed just as Adam's sin, failure, and blame-shifting are forgiven.

God's pronouncement of judgement fell on Eve by solidifying the relational disharmony her sinful encouragement caused. This division became palpable throughout the entire book of Genesis, going so far as to directly impact the marriages of the Patriarchs. Relational disunity and disharmony brought about dysfunctional families, visible even in the line of faith.

In Christ, this dysfunction is also unwound. Eve's desire was to be "for" her husband. Regardless of whether that means her desire is turned into an unhealthy idolatrous obsession (such that she would worship him) or that her desire is to dominate and control him, the redemption restores the semblance of the pre-Fall marital life. Paul explains that the Christian wife is to submit to her husband (Ephesians 5:22). Because of our progress through the redemptive arc of scripture, we know that "submission" carries the connotation of "respect" (Ephesians 5:33). It's instructive that Paul uses this submission language for the entire household

---

10 Rebekah Merkle, *Eve in Exile and the Restoration of Femininity* (Moscow, ID: Canon Press, 2016), p. 26.

of faith (Ephesians 5:21); if everyone is submitting to one another, then it follows that a wife's submission to her husband will follow a spiritual restoration of communion and community within the godly marriage. The pattern for submission is that of the church to Christ. As Christians demonstrate loyalty to Christ by submitting to his loving and sacrificial leadership, so should daughters of Eve submit to their husbands. Again, this is not a submission to tyranny, but to her husband who, in turn, ought to be Christlike in his loving treatment of his bride.

The relational disharmony had two components. The first was Eve's compunction "for" her husband, which was redeemed by Christ and brought to submission and respect "of" her husband. The second component of the punishment in Genesis was that the husband would "rule over her" (Genesis 3:16). In contrast, through the work of Christ, a godly husband ought to be the hands and feet of Jesus to her. Rather than having an aggressive domination of her, he's to love her as Christ loved the church (Ephesians 5:25-30). The Fall brought competition and violence into the marital chamber; redemption brings selfless self-sacrifice. A husband is to so love his wife that his own desires and preferences are sublimated to her well-being. This, of course, does not mean that a wife gets whatever she wants; rather, it means that a man's selfish desire and preference will be put to death on her behalf. If we return to our illustration from 1 Corinthians 7 above, men tend to have a stronger libido; rather than bludgeoning his bride with a verse that he can manipulate to mean sex should be always available, a godly husband will instead honor his wife through selfless sacrifice of his own desires in that moment.

In essence, relational disharmony is replaced with a playful, godly competition to be the most respectful and sacrificial. The overarching purpose of a Christian marriage is to reflect the grand vision of Christ's own marriage to the church. If Christ did not consider his own divine rights as something to be grasped (Philippians 2:6), then husbands and wives ought to be willing to give up their "rights" as individuals because they're now one flesh. Likewise, if God the Son was willing to take on the form of a servant, and submit himself to the will of the Father to the point even of death on the cross so that he could redeem his bride the church (Philippians 2:7-8), how much more ought husbands sacrifice their rights and preferences for their brides who are, simultaneously, sisters in Christ?

When our marriages are brought into the relational harmony envisaged by Paul in Ephesians five, we present to the world a portrait of the gospel itself. Granted, our marriages are still marred by the bodies and wills of sinful flesh (submitting and sacrificing are not *easy* things to do), but they are nevertheless portraying a kingdom love that hearkens back to Eden and throws our vision forward to the great wedding and marriage of the Lamb and his bride. This is the mystery that Paul says has now been revealed because of Christ. Consequently, redeemed marriages become intimate battlegrounds, not between husband and wife, but between the couple and Satan concerning the children born from that union. These children have the blessing of being raised in a Chrisitan home but still need to be evangelized.

Eve and the Pain of Childbearing

The pain of childbearing has been felt by mothers across the ages. This punishment was larger than merely the pains of labor and deliver; it included the monthly agonies of the menstrual cycle, the anguish of still births and miscarriages, and the anxiety of infertility. Yet, specific to Eve, was the simultaneous promise that the head of the serpent would be crushed by the offspring/seed of the woman. The reversal of the consequence of death has already been addressed above, but it's worth explicitly stating that miscarriages and still births are also recapitulated by the resurrection life of Christ. Eve's tears will be turned to rejoicing (Jeremiah 31:13).

The most poignant fulfilment and recapitulation of this punishment is the fact that the sole offspring in view is ultimately the Lord Jesus Christ. By his victory on the cross, the might of the serpent has been conquered, the breadth of his domain has been curtailed, and the end of his empire is in view. It's a completed act. The cross is the event at which the head of Satan was crushed. When Christ returns in might and majesty, he will finally and fully put that old dragon into the fiery pit where he belongs. Eve's pain in childbearing *has been* redeemed because she and her daughters led to the arrival of the serpent crusher. Additionally, Eve's pain in childbearing *will experience further redemption* because of the many sons and daughters who will be with Christ for eternity.

Creation Groaning

An often-overlooked aspect of the punishment is that creation itself experiences the Fall. We see this in numerous places throughout scripture. Perhaps most poignant are Genesis 3:18 where thorns and thistles begin to grow, and the cosmic grief when Christ was killed (Matthew 27:45 and 27:51). Creation itself eagerly anticipates the final restoration of all things. Even now, as creation continues to groan under the weight of the penalty of the Fall, Paul says that there are contractions of the new creation that tells us the arrival of the consummation of the kingdom is at hand (Matthew 24:8; Romans 8:22-23). This new creation will be a recapitulation of the old creation because it will be a return to paradise. Once more, "the wolf shall dwell with the lamb, and the leopard shall lie down with the young goat" (Isaiah 11:6) as in Eden. There will be no fear of predators because "the wolf and the lamb shall graze together; the lion shall eat straw like the ox" (Isaiah 65:25). Creation, from the smallest atom to the largest constellation, will be restored to declare the majesty of our creator God. It, too, will experience salvation from Satan's despotism and sin's slavery. Under the leadership of the king, the new creation will burst forth with prosperity and vitality. These blessings have not fully arrived yet, but they are arriving as surely as a woman's contractions predict with certainty the arrival of a child.

Conclusion

This chapter considered how Jesus adopted, adapted, and updated the Creation Mandate through his provision of the Great Commission. This transformed the Adamic expansion through human descent to a redeemed duty of evangelism as well as changing the work of exercising domination over creation to a redeemed work of discipling new believers. This expansion brought the gospel hope of the new creation to people from every tribe, tongue, and nation as demonstrated by Peter's vision in Acts. Through the command to "take and eat" previously forbidden foodstuffs, Jesus taught Peter that the gospel was offered to the world. The gospel was not to be restricted to a Jewish population nor even a Jewish remnant; rather, it was to explode and spread throughout the world via the proclamation of Christ crucified and resurrected. This invitation to repent and believe the gospel was made to be open to the entire world because Jesus is the obedient covenant partner, the Final Adam, the greater Moses, and the true Israelite who unwound the curse that had bound Adam. As the Final Adam, he recapitulates human beings as well as the community of faith. Through his work, he is remaking and recreating the fallen realm into a new creation with a New Creation Mandate. Once again, a critical moment in redemptive history is symbolically presented through a command to "take and eat."

The new reality of Christ's reign is a dynamic kingdom where heaven is in-breaking into the present world. The power of the gospel is manifest in the renewal of creation and the redemption of humanity by the work of Jesus. Although this is currently experienced in part, this is not something that is yet enjoyed in fullness. The truest and greatest blessings of the kingdom are still to come in the consummation. Jesus is preparing us for the future when we will be in his presence forevermore. Our current duty as heirs with Christ is to be about the master's work, observing the king's constitution, and spreading the king's message so that his rule expands across the world as more and more are saved and conformed into his filial likeness and glorious image. This is a work of the church, but it is empowered by the Spirit of Christ. Just as Jesus called his disciples to be fishers of men, he is now cultivating a new garden of believers, not to return to Eden, but to prepare for the New Jerusalem and the glorious feast that awaits all who are members of his bride.

Last Course: Dessert

9

"Take and Eat": A Wedding Feast

> *"I tell you I will not drink again of this fruit of the vine until that day when I drink it new with you in my Father's Kingdom."*
> (Matthew 26:29)

> *Then I heard what seemed to be the voice of a great multitude, like the roar of many waters and like the sound of might peals of thunder, crying out, "Hallelujah! For the Lord our God the Almighty reigns. Let us rejoice and exult and give him the glory, for the marriage of the Lamb has come, and his Bride has made herself ready; it was granted her to clothe herself with fine linen, bright and pure"* – *for the fine linen is the righteous deeds of the saints.* (Revelation 19:6-8)

Introduction

Weddings are usually wonderful events. People from various communities and families get to come together, witness a young man and young woman proclaim their undying devotion to one another, make solemn oaths and vows of love, fidelity, service, sacrifice, and perseverance. The guests, for the joy of attending the wedding, get to hear beautiful music, gawp at beautifully attired friends and family of the couple, and themselves get to dress up in the most glamorous of their Sunday best. By the middle of the afternoon, however, everyone's ready for the next event. We've chatted awkwardly to people we think we remember from a single meeting months or years prior. We've seen the glorious procession of the bridesmaids. We've listened to the dulcet tones of the violins playing *Pachelbel's Canon in D*. We've wiped a solitary tear from our eye as the groom just about manages to hold it together whilst his beloved slowly walks towards him. We've heard the charge of faith to the couple, and we've witnessed their first kiss as husband and wife. We've stood for the recessional and made more awkward conversation with Kevin "you remember me from earlier, right?" But now? Now we will make our way to the next venue; let the couple and their wedding party take their pretty pictures. We'll go and get ourselves situated for the *feast*.

When I attended my first wedding in the US, I was surprised at how different everything was to weddings in Ireland. In America, the entire ceremony can last *perhaps* twenty minutes from processional to recessional; British weddings are much longer. The wedding ceremony may begin around eleven in the morning (the bride's arrival depending, of course!), and the whole celebration can go on until the wee hours of the morning. Not so in America; after the reception feast, you could be home in time for dinner. That's not to imply, of course, that American weddings are any less celebratory.

I make this contrast for a specific reason; for a Brit in America, weddings feel short. I suspect for an American in Britain, weddings would feel interminably long. It's this second feeling that this penultimate chapter will dwell upon. As we turn our thoughts to the wedding celebration of the Lamb, we ought to have this sense of *duration* in our minds. At this wedding feast, we're once more invited to "take and eat," but this invitation is the final one. This is because the wedding feast of the Lamb is not a short meal with a few speeches. Rather, it's the dawning of eternity. The wedding feast is the recapitulation, fulfilment, expansion, and final development of the grand narrative that began in Eden. It's the point where heaven most directly joins with earth, where time becomes eternity, and where history bleeds into superhistory. This is the moment when the "not yet" becomes the "yes, amen" of redemption. And the feast we're enjoined to enjoy is an eternal buffet in the presence of the king.

As a caveat, I want to acknowledge that the book of Revelation is perhaps the most debated book in the entire canon of scripture. The point that I want to make is a simple one: Adam and Eve's utopia has become Christ's utopia. Many of the symbols in Eden are present in the New Jerusalem (a tree, fruit, water, a marriage, angels, the presence of God etc.) and the main idea is that, finally, the new humanity in Christ will live with Christ forevermore as a bride resides with her husband. God will be present, peace will triumph, sin will be destroyed, and the enemies of God will be no more. This is the *reason* for the celebration, irrespective of the various interpretations of the *chronology* or *timing* of the feast. And it is the reason that we will focus on. For clarity, I am taking the position that the wedding feast of the Lamb is the event that bridges history and superhistory, or eternity. Although there are other views as to the placement of the feast concerning the end of the old creational age, and even if you hold to a different chronology, we can all agree with the central theme that, at the wedding feast, peace reigns because of the presence of the king.

I also want to highlight that the book of Revelation is largely a book of symbols and images. Much of what John speaks about in his vision is so heavily couched in symbolic terms that it's difficult to penetrate the reality of what the *eschaton* will look like. One suspects that is both deliberate and an inevitability. The fact that the book draws heavily on symbolism and imagery is in no way suggestive that the reality is merely symbolic or even fictional. When we speak of, for example, the twelve fruits from the tree of life, for example, we don't need to presume that to be a solely literal harvest. The symbolism of twelve, for example, is replete throughout the book, and the fruit is a recapitulation of Genesis. It seems highly implausible that the guests at the wedding feast are only to eat from this one tree, when Adam and Eve had the freedom to feast on all *but* one tree in Eden. By this caveat, I want to explicitly state that the imagery in Revelation is given by John to point to larger biblical themes and concepts. The wedding feast of the Lamb teaches us that our eternity is sure: Christ's bride will be protected by the conquering king, be fully provided for, and will be able to prosper in the presence of God. John uses a multiplicity of symbolism to make these truths as evident as possible.

Context

There are some key concepts that need to be understood about marriage in a Jewish context in the ancient world. This context will help explore the implications of the wedding feast of the Lamb. Jewish marriages typically comprised three steps. The first is what is termed *betrothal*. This is proximate to our engagement, though betrothal was a weightier commitment. Typically, to terminate a betrothal, one would seek a *divorce* because the betrothal was seen as the beginning of a covenant relationship (though not sealed by consummation). The second step occurred on the day of the wedding. The groom and his entourage of celebrating groomsmen and family members would leave his house with boisterous noise and celebration. This noise would, as they approached the house of the bride, alert her to his immanent arrival. In the house, the final adornments and preparations would take place, beautifying the bride as she eagerly anticipated his presence. It's this second step that Jesus references in his parable in Matthew 25:1-13.

The third step was the wedding feast. This was the celebration of the marriage by the groom and the bride; all their family and friends were invited to share in the joy of their new relationship. We know from John 2 that the wedding feasts in Jesus' day could last for quite some time, as seen by the fact the guests had outdrank the provided booze. They'd put even British weddings to shame! Typically, weddings in ancient Israel lasted around a week and were designed to showcase the couple's new life together. The fact that, in Cana, the family ran out of wine would have been a humiliation because it suggested either poverty or poor planning; either way, an inauspicious start for the new couple. Of more significance, however, is that we have already encountered a promise made by Jesus to his disciples. He promised that, after the institution of the Eucharist, he would not drink the fruit of the vine until he drinks it with his disciples in the kingdom. This promise points us towards the wedding feast in Revelation.

For our purposes, although the timing and chronology of the wedding feast is hotly debated, I'm going to contend that the events of the previous chapter comprise the second step of the betrothal between Christ and the church. This is our current era when the bride of Christ (the church) prepares herself with the washing of the word and good works that will be like beautiful garments. These good works will, in fact, be seen to be the wedding dress for the bride who, though wearing the tattered rags of the Fall, is given beautiful linen cloth by God the Father for the special day (Revelation19:8). The wedding feast will be the inauguration of the eternal joy of union between heaven and earth, where God will once more dwell with man.

Another point of context is that in the book of Revelation itself, the author, John, provides a vivid picture of the Fall of the empire of evil as the destruction of the city of Babylon. In my view, the tone and timbre of the imagery is a symbolic means of presenting a literal reality. Babylon is the opposite of Jerusalem throughout scripture. From the tower of Babel, Babylon has been the epitome of human rebellion against God's rule. In contrast, also from Genesis, God used Melchizedek, the righteous king of Salem, to introduce his city where, at the height of Israel's obedience, the presence of God dwelt in the Holy of Holies in the temple. Thus, to truly grasp the implications of the wedding feast of the Lamb and the bride, we need to first understand what John records before the celebration; this contrast sets up the reason for the sheer joy experienced at the wedding feast.

A Contrast: Babylon and the Bride

The seven bowls of God's wrath in Revelation 16 give way to the vision of Babylon the whore. Babylon is the archetypal nemesis of the people of God; consistently, she's presented unfavorably in contrast with Jerusalem. John takes the imagery further and shows the opulent, decadent, and arrogant city to be little more than a prostitute who sells herself for prestige, power, and position. In the ancient world, there was a hierarchical system for almost everything. Prostitution was no different. Ancient kings had access to harems of beautiful, or powerful, women whose sole duty was to respond to his beck and call. But in the marketplace, women would offer their services to any passerby. If a harem was restricted, the dockyards and brothels of ancient cities, such as in Corinth, were accessible cesspits of lewd and sexual depravity. So sexually compromised was Corinth that the city was used as a slur: to *corinthianize* was to be involved in the basest of debauchery! There was a third class of prostitute, however, that is probably the image John has in mind here: A courtesan. In ancient Greece, we know of *hetairai* who were educated prostitutes. They would conduct long-term relationships with powerful men without the legal provision or protection of marriage. Many would indeed act like wives for a season, but there was a clear distinction between a *wife* who was a citizen (and therefore produced citizens) and a *hetaira* who produced illegitimate children. This tradition of courtesanship was also present in Rome, though perhaps not identical in nature. It's likely that the whore of Babylon is in this form of prostitute: Wealthy, boastful, powerful, and alluring.

John gives us quite the description of the Babylonian prostitute: She's seated on a scarlet beast which is, itself, covered in blasphemous names (Revelation 17:3). This beast evokes both Daniel's earlier vision as well as that of prior images in Revelation. Babylon herself is "arrayed in purple and scarlet, and adorned with gold and jewels and pearls, holding in her hand a golden cup full of abominations and the impurities of her sexual immorality" (Revelation 17:4). The image is an imperial image; she's presenting herself as an empress of Rome (whose purple dyes were jealously guarded by the imperial family). Her linen is provocative because she is *not* an empress but a prostitute. The entire image is a façade. Babylon projects power and wealth and status but in reality is like the emperor with new clothes. The image only persists because the kings of the earth have bought into the illusion (Revelation 17:2).

For temporary pleasure and power, they've sold their souls to sup at her table.

This image is not neutral. These kings are wicked and rebellious. They've given themselves entirely to the illusion and to the wicked plans of the prostitute. This is seen in Psalm 2:1-2 where David asks: "Why do the nations rage and the peoples plot in vain? The kings of the earth set themselves, and the rulers take counsel together, against the LORD and his anointed..." John's answer to David's question is that these kings are plotting *because* they're part of the sedition that had been hatched by the serpent millennia in the past: The dethroning of God. By their leadership, the kings led the inhabitants of the earth to drink at Babylon's table also. It's as if a goblet of wine has fallen from her drunken hand and a cascading waterfall of wickedness has plunged over the whole earth. The rebellion of Eden has found a willing human counterpart in this most cruel and despotic of cities.

Suddenly, John jolts us out of our comfortable position because we see just exactly what this harlot has been drinking: "I saw the woman, drunk with the blood of the saints, the blood of the martyrs of Jesus Christ" (Revelation 17:6). Our blood freezes when we realize she's not merely a persecuting harlot; a significant portion of her perverse pleasure is derived from her sadistic persecution of the people of God. It is, in fact, her twisted joy to attack *God* by attacking God's *children*. So successful has she been throughout the ages that she's inebriated. And the kings of the earth, and the dwellers of the earth who clammer for her disinterested approval, are the cause of her intoxication. As if in a romantic competition, these kings have sought to impress her by their own bloodthirsty persecution of the saints of Christ. This factoid explains that the criminal acts of the harlot are not primarily sexual but spiritual. Her image is that of wanton impurity, arrogant haughtiness, and the pretense of power; but her wickedness is rooted in the fact that she's an idolatress. She has seduced the sons and daughters of Adam from their devotion to God such that they have instead worshipped her wealth, her lust, her supposed power, and her vain promises of yet more to come.

Because of her sinful rebellion, John promises that she will be destroyed. This destruction is described in 18:1-3. As she's being destroyed, there's another *bat kol* in which the voice of heaven calls the faithful to come out of Babylon, lest they be caught in the turmoil. This hearkens back to Lot and the city of Sodom: "Come out," God says, "and do not look back." Her boast that she sits as a queen will be upended when she is condemned as the rebel she is. Disappointingly, her condemnation is not sufficient to cause her admirers to repent; rather, they lament her fate, unaware that their own is intimately tied to hers. The kings who supped at her table and committed adultery and idolatry with her wail in grief, and terror, at her fate (Revelation 18:9-10). Even as they cry in terror, the merchants who had grown fat from her markets weep because the consumers for their sinful products have vanished (Revelation 18:11-17). Finally, the sea captains and sailors who fostered and profited from the global trade that fed the idolatrous brothels of the city and kept the various ne'er-do-wells drunk on their evil victuals also mourn her collapse (Revelation 18:18-20).

The next section presents her doom. In fulfilment of Jesus' warning in Matthew 18:5-6 that anyone who leads one of his little, faithful, sheep astray will have a millstone tied to their neck and thrown into the sea, an angel evocatively throws a stone into the sea and declares: "So will Babylon the great city be thrown down with violence, and will be found no more" (Revelation 18:21). Thereafter, in a mirror of the three laments, there is a threefold roar of praise and rejoicing from the angelic and human faithful. The first is from a great multitude in the heavens, praising God for his salvation and the justness of his judgements on Babylon (Revelation 19:1-3). The second is from the twenty-four elders and the four living creatures who declare "hallelujah" to the majesty of God (Revelation 19:4). The third is once again from the multitude (both earthly and heavenly beings), declaring praise to God for his reign (Revelation 19:6-7a).

It's during this third triumphant call that we're introduced to the wedding feast of the Lamb. John records the song of praise: "For the marriage of the Lamb has come, and his Bride has made herself ready; it was granted her to clothe herself with fine linen, bright and pure" (Revelation 19:7b-8). The contrast between the harlot of Babylon and the faithful bride is as sharp as possible. John spent more time detailing Babylon than the bride because he wanted to convey the utter depths of her depravity. In contrast, the bride is given respectful modesty. When we consider the contrast, we see that Babylon was provocatively dressed as an empress, whereas the bride is dressed in fine linen, bright and clean; Babylon was drunk on violence, but the bride has prepared herself for her groom; Babylon was perverse and adulterous, but the bride is chaste and anticipates the embrace of her husband; Babylon took sadistic pleasure in the persecution of the saints, but the bride has performed works that honor her bridegroom.

The sharpest contrast is, of course, between the clothing of the harlot and the bride: The bride is wearing fine linen. John's explanatory comment is that the linen "is the righteousness of the saints" (Revelation 19:8b). These are the good works and deeds that God has graciously given believers to perform (Ephesians 2:10) so that we can be conformed into the likeness of Jesus. This is evidenced by the fact that the bride "was granted her to clothe herself" with this linen (Revelation 19:8b). By the accomplishment of these good deeds (including, but not restricted to, the Great Commission), the bride is declared "beautiful." It's the doing of these deeds that has made her beautiful in the sight of Christ. The bright linen is pure and clean, in contrast with the blood-splashed purple of the pretentious pretend-empress. Unlike the harlot, the bride is certain of the enduring affection of her groom who has sought her, bought her, and brought her to this glorious feast. The bride of the Lamb reflects the wise woman of Proverbs, not the silky-tongued seductress whose promises of life last only as long as the gold in the purse.

It's at this point in Revelation 19 that we're convinced that the bride is the covenant community of Christ. The saints, it must be understood, have not *earned* their salvation by their good deeds; rather, having already *been* betrothed to the Lamb by faith, they *prepare* for the wedding feast. The context of this image is important. John is describing the third step of the marital ceremonial ritual: The prince has arrived to bring his bride to the wedding feast. This means that this occurs *post-conversion* in redemptive history.[1] We see echoes of this in Ephesians 1:13-14, where the Holy Spirit is given to believers as a downpayment, guaranteeing our salvation. The imagery is different, but the point is the same: Our salvation is by faith and experienced in the present as a promise of what will be received in full. The good deeds are expressions of our preparation for the consummation; they're our efforts at reflecting the family of God, demonstrating our honor for our heavenly Father, and preparing for our eternity in his presence. Those who are invited to the wedding feast, to *be* the bride of Christ no less, are there *because they have been saved by faith in the bridegroom*. She is not saved *by* her works; rather, her works were provided by God to *prepare* her for the wedding day. And as the angel speaks to John, we hear one of the seven "blessed" moments in Revelation: "Blessed are those who are invited to the marriage supper of the Lamb" (Revelation 19:9). The celebration is about to begin.

A Marriage Celebration

I want to recall that Eden witnessed a wedding. Adam was tasked with naming the animals and I suggested that his doing so functioned much like our ceremonial procession of the bridesmaids. Despite the many variations within the animal kingdom, none had been fit for Adam until Eve. In like manner, we come to the wedding feast of the Lamb and realize that the parallel is present and the narratival arc has, in a sense, come full circle. This time, however, the bride is not guilty of leading Adam astray; rath-

---

[1] Incidentally, I am rejecting the Dispensational chronology and interpretation.

er, the Final Adam has paid the debt to redeem *her* (cf. Hosea 3:1-3), prepared a place *for her*, and has come for *her*. Meanwhile, she has prepared herself by accomplishing the deeds set for her by God, so that she has been washed by the word and is made presentable to her bridegroom as a radiantly holy and blameless bride (Ephesians 5:26-27). Thus, we see that the parallelism is meant to portray the restoration to an Edenlike state of purity and renewal (though not to *Eden* itself).

We see in Revelation 19:7 three calls for praise: We are to rejoice, exult, and give glory to God. The preceding verse is the foundation for this praise: "The Lord our God, the Almighty reigns." However, the direct *cause* for this praise is the wedding feast. This is seen in the rhythm of the stanza and the use of the word "for" that connects 19:7a and 19:7b: "*For* the marriage of the Lamb has come." Of further interest is the fact that the wedding "*has come.*" The grammar of this word is suggestive that there is an overlap between the present and the future; this is the conception that Christ's kingdom has come and is coming. In Revelation, the "is coming" is now at hand. The "already, not yet" is giving way to the ever after. The celebration is present in the imagery of a wedding feast, and it stands in marked contrast with the destruction of the prostitute of Babylon. Indeed, the joy of the bride is not only in contrast to, but as a consequence of, Babylon's destruction. Because the bride of Christ is the church of Christ, believers are finally free from the persecution of the whore. The prince's destruction of the ugly and cruel stepmother allows the Cinderella of scripture to finally embrace her beloved and see him as he is. The wedding "signals the consummation of God's plans for his people, the church of Jesus Christ...[but] the wedding itself doesn't commence until the resurrection, the dawn of the new creation (21:1-22:5)."[2]

The recapitulation theme in Revelation is visible in the celebrations of Revelation 19. Schreiner notes that the bride is the

---

2 Thomas R. Schreiner, *Revelation: Baker Exegetical Commentary on the New Testament* (Grand Rapids, MI: Baker Academic, 2023), p. 634.

corporate image whilst the invitees are the individual image.³ Both images refer to the same group: Believers in Christ. Celebration is given from every individual mouth who declares Christ as Lord (Philippians 2:9-11). In this, we agree with Schreiner and the weight of church history; this is not a picture of *only* the church, as apart from Israel, as if there are two destinies for two separate entities. As this book has argued, *all* are either in Christ the Final Adam, or remain enslaved with the Fallen Adam. The wedding feast of the Lamb is a celebration for every follower of the serpent crusher, from Genesis through to Revelation. All are invited to the celebration *as the bride of Christ*. When this image is fully grasped, we realize that we will be seated at the heavenly venue of the reception meal with saints from all of history. Corporately, as one bride, the wife of Christ is comprised of every individual saint. It's because of Jesus, who recapitulates and fulfills the Old Testament, that the saints of old are invited to dine. Likewise, it's because of Jesus, who forged the New Covenant and brought about the new creation paradigm that we're invited to the feast.

When all are seated, the wine will be poured, and the festivities will begin. For the first time since the Passover in the Upper Room, Jesus will taste the fruit of the vine as a symbolic gesture that the war has ended, and the celebration of peace and the dawn of prosperity has arrived. Unlike the First Adam, the Final Adam was not tempted by the fruit. Unlike Noah, the greater Noah was not intoxicated by the fruit of the vine. This is a celebration, a moment of triumphant "hurrahs" and "hallelujahs" from every mouth in heaven and from the earth! The Lord almighty reigns and he has enthroned his anointed on Mount Zion; and with his marriage the kingdom is established and the future is secure.

What is it that the bride is celebrating? There are many things. The most important cause for rejoicing is that the Lord's reign has brought an end to the rebellion. Babylon has fallen and with her demise the threat and danger to the redeemed is removed. Regardless of your specific chronology of the end times, the point is that

---

3   Schreiner, *Revelation*, p. 635.

the serpent is cast into hell along with death, Babylon, sin, evil, and wickedness. With the reign of the Lord manifest over every square inch of the universe, the redeemed rejoice and celebrate the arrival of the eschatological peace that had for so long seemed so far away. With the defeat and eradication of evil, the bride celebrates the even greater reality that finally she can see her Lord and Savior face to face. This is the Beatific Vision and it speaks of eternity. Where once Moses alone had beheld the glory of God from the cleft of a rock, then every eye shall see him as he is. All the righteous holiness and majestic beauty of the mighty God will be visible.

The joy of the saints who will inhabit eternity with no fear of decay, disease, or death is palpable in the thunderous songs of praise throughout Revelation 19. To know that never again will there be a threat of evil or a tempting voice urging sinful behavior is the yearning of every weary believer. Death's defeat will be witnessed. Satan's demise will be public. And God's judgement will be final. The feast is a celebration of the certainty of the end of all ends and promise of the finality of redemption.

A Promise of the Finality of Redemption

The greatest reason for celebration, however, stems from the fact that God will dwell with his people. This is perhaps the shadow that has loomed over this entire book. Behind every moment, we've been desperately seeking an audience with God. From the moment of Adam's expulsion from Eden, humanity has sought a return to the fold of God. At each epochal moment, we got glimpses of what that might look like, but they remained frustratingly hazy and unclear. After Eden, God spoke with people, but only infrequently. In Israel, when he dwelt in the Holy of Holies in the temple, access to his presence was restricted. Even when Christ tabernacled amongst men (John 1:14), his presence was limited to the person of Jesus, and for a short period of time. During the current church era, the Spirit of God indwells the church, but so often we're deaf to his voice and blind to his activity. At the wedding feast of the Lamb, however, that changes.

The greatest means of our redemption is God residing with his people. We're saved by Christ *for* Christ. No more will believers have to squint to see his present activity, but we will be his people in his presence forevermore. There can be no surer guarantee of our salvation and redemption and protection than the presence of the conquering king who has subdued the serpent, defeated death, and reduced the rebellion. The New Jerusalem is not safe because of the height or strength of its walls (though that is what they symbolize); the city is safe because the king will be there. And thus, the bride can rest, knowing that the king who protects her is reigning and his reign is an everlasting reign. Our redemption is final because he has secured it at the cross and accomplished it at the consummation. His presence, as our temple, is our greatest hope. Our redemption is best visualized in the reality that we will dwell with our redeemer and he shall be in our midst.

After the initial mention of the wedding feast of the Lamb, John's Revelation once again retells the destruction of Babylon. This time, however, the vantage point is not that of her clients but of her conqueror, arrayed in the armor of heaven, draped in a robe dipped in blood, and crowned with many crowns. These crowns represent his superior kingship over every opponent. Like his bride, the armies of heaven wear white linen, and rejoice to hear the words of God flow from his mouth in judgement against the nations. He is the King of Kings and Lord of Lords (Revelation 19:16), the word of God made flesh (John 1:1). This is our king who has achieved our victory. The image of Christ on the steed is in marked contrast to the suffering servant on the cross; but in both images he is conquering. He is no less majestic or powerful when he hangs in death than when he rides to war.

There is then an angelic voice delivering to creation yet another call to "take and eat." This call is to the carrion, inviting them to come and glut themselves on the flesh of the fallen enemies of God. The wicked who had arrayed against him are destroyed, with no respect for status, or wealth, or power. The promises of the prostitute are finally exposed as empty and vapid. She provided no safety from the righteous warrior on the steed of heaven. The very beast upon which the harlot had ridden is captured and condemned to hell (Revelation 19:20). With the judgement of Satan (Revelation 20:7-10) and the dead (Revelation 20:11-15), we see the end of *history* and the movement into eternity.

The judgement of the dead provides us a glimpse into the finality of our redemption. Every human being will stand before the great white throne of heaven and the one seated on it. In contrast to the harlot, who had sat in the midst of the waters in gross indecent mockery of God's throne, when God's throne is visible the "earth and sky fled away," seeking refuge from his justice (Revelation 20:11). But there's nowhere to hide; everything committed in the dark will be brought into the light with the penetrating brightness of God's holiness (Luke 12:3; 1 Corinthians 4:5; Ephesians 5:11). At the throne of God, every single soul will stand in judgement. No matter the earthly glory they once enjoyed, all will stand as equals before God and in the public gathering of all the created realm, sins long hidden and forgotten will finally receive their judgement. Think of it: Every murder, rape, act of violence and abuse, finally brought to justice. Every act of hatred. Every wicked thought and every deed that betrayed the goodness and holiness of God finally dealt with. The yearning of every victim finally quenched. What inexpressible relief to know that "these are the true words of God" (Revelation 19:9b).

Yet although there is judgement and justice, and the wicked cast into the darkness, this is not the fate of every human (though it ought to be). This is because the names on guest list for the wedding feast are written in the Lamb's book of life. All those whose names were found written then are identified as belonging to the Lamb. They're his bride, redeemed by his blood. This does not mean that the bride is sinless; rather, all the sins of the bride have been forgiven by Christ's sacrificial blood. He paid the bride price, and, by that payment, he took upon himself the covenantal obligations for her. This included the penalty that she deserved.

My favorite illustration for the salvation of the bride comes from Martin Luther, the reformer. He speaks of a prince who marries a prostitute.[4] When they get married, the prostitute becomes a princess. Through no right of her own, she leaves behind the life of shame, grime, dirt, humiliation, and sorrow. In its place, she's clothed with the rights and privileges of her new office, none of which she earned; all however are freely bestowed upon her by the love of her husband. In contrast, however, his honor is impugned. He, a noble prince of high birth and goodly social status, takes upon himself her scorn, her past, her disreputable history. He wears her shame even as she wears his righteousness. This is the pattern of redemption visible at the judgement. No man or woman will be welcomed to the wedding feast because of his or her greatness or goodness. Yet every single guest will be welcomed because of Jesus.[5] At that moment, the redemption that had been secured by the crushing of the serpent at Calvary will be consummated. We will receive in full what had been promised on earth and guaranteed by the Holy Spirit. No more will we have to contend with sin; we will be content with the Savior. As with Thomas,

---

[4] This illustration also works with the Emperor Justinian who put this into practice, marrying a notorious prostitute, Theodora.

[5] Consider Jesus' parable of Matthew 22. There the hypocrites refuse to come to the feast and instead oppose the king for his invitation, up to and including violence. In contrast, the king sends his servants out to invite a multitude to come to the feast with language very similar to that of the Great Commission. The interloper, only found in Matthew's account of the parable, is kicked out for his garments. Despite some claims this was to do with cultural norms of hosts providing wedding garments, it's much more likely (through the context of Matthew's account) that the interloper was a pretender. If we take John's comments in Revelation about the bride being adorned in righteous garments which were good deeds prepared for her (Revelation 19:8; cf. Ephesians 2:10), then it seems likely that this interloper was exiled because he was a devil in disguise or a wolf in sheep's clothing. He could confuse and deceive the servants and his fellow guests, but the king sees through the charade.

we shall see the wounds on his hands and feet, and rejoice that we have, finally, arrived at home. And that is a moment worthy of celebration.

A Future Meal in the Kingdom

Considering our theme of "take and eat," the Messianic banquet of Revelation must be considered alongside Isaiah 25, where Isaiah foretells the great destruction of the enemy cities and the humbling of wicked rulers. Thereafter, God will put on a banquet for all peoples. The oppressed and weak, the abused and broken, the sick and the distressed will emerge from their subjugation and from their hiding places at the heavenly invitation to "take and eat" a feast of "rich food" and "well-aged wine" (Isaiah 25:6). Combining Isaiah's prophecy with John's, we get the sense of a plenteous, overflowing, buffet of culinary delights. This brings us back, not only to Eden, but also to the wilderness wanderings of Israel and the feeding miracles of Jesus.

Those miraculous meals, as well as the Lord's Supper, were each different foretastes of what the bride will experience at the wedding feast. The manna and quail of the wilderness taught the Israelites dependence on God for his faithful provision. At the wedding feast, we will eat and remember the goodness of God's faithfulness throughout all human history. Every wilderness moment will finally be comprehended in light of the finality of our redemption. The sufferings and challenges of this life will adorn us for all eternity as good deeds undertaken for Christ. The bread and fish of Jesus' miracles taught the crowds to look to Jesus as the greater Moses. At the wedding feast, we will eat and remember how Jesus fulfilled all that God had promised. The bread and wine of the Last Supper taught the disciples that Jesus would bring about the New Covenant that had been promised centuries before. At the wedding feast, we will eat and drink in acknowledgment of the completion of that work. The vision of Peter taught him that the gospel was available for all people. At the wedding feast of the lamb, we will look around, our mouths filled with foods of all kinds, and be amazed at the diversity of the bride. Men and women from every tribe, tongue, and nation, and from every era and epoch of human history, will be there, eating and drinking and celebrating together in perfect harmony. No dissension or division will arise between us, because we will be enraptured by our king. We will "take and eat" and rejoice that God's word has triumphed.

Banquet imagery is common throughout scripture as a way of describing celebration, victory, peace, and prosperity. Unlike the gluttony of the prostitute of Babylon, the language surrounding the wedding feast does not convey the idea of greed but of satisfaction. This can be seen from the fact that, although heavenly wine is present, drunkenness is not (unlike the prostitute). The river of life flows from the singular throne that belongs to God and the Lamb (reiterating for us that the Lamb is God, yet distinct from the Father). The water of life is cool and refreshing to all who take and drink it. This river also reminds us of Eden where a river flowed throughout the garden, watering it and bringing life to the vegetation (Genesis 2:10). Here, the water flows throughout the city and is greater than the river of Eden because this is the river that gives life (Ezekiel 47:1). No doubt this is an allusion to Jesus' claim to provide living water, and the fact that this river flows from his throne demonstrates the proof of his claim (John 4:10-14).

Likewise, the food at the wedding feast comes from the tree of life, rather than the fields of exploitation. In a marvelous parallel with the tree of life in Eden, from which Adam was restricted after the Fall (Genesis 3:22), Christ here invites us to "take and eat" the fruit from the tree (Revelation 22:2). This tree yields fruit every month and, coupled with the river that flows through the city streets, provides all the nourishment that we will need: "The river and water of life for John, then, symbolize eschatological life in the new creation – life that is vivifying, invigorating, and refreshing."[6] If the river of life quenches our thirst, the tree "signifies that one has eternal life...and the twelve fruits describe the enjoy-

---

6   Schreiner, *Revelation*, p. 747.

ment of that life."[7] Because the tree provides fruit every month, we see the fullness of God's provision. Unlike Adam, who had to toil for food from the ground in a seasonal cycle as part of the curse, in the future kingdom, there will always be nourishment available. There will be no season for planting and sowing and another for harvesting. In a reversal of the curse made memorable by the Narnian cry "Always winter, never Christmas," in the kingdom, it will be "always harvest, never fallow!" We return to an Edenic sense of abundance. This reminds us that the fruit of the tree that we will eat in eternity will be sufficient for all our needs; there will be no malnourishment, neither will there be a need to store foodstuffs for a rainy day. The feast will be unending because the river will flow forever, and the tree will produce perpetually.

An Eternal New Creation

The nature of the various elements of this feast indicates the eternality of the new creation. Having the river of life continually flow from the throne on which the God of life and the resurrected Lord of life reign teaches us that the new creation is greater than the old creation. The tree of life gives fruit for every month, implying that the harvest is not only consistent but unending. Further evidence for the eternality of the new creation stems from the imagery of the New Jerusalem provided by John. Comments about a new topography are debated; what is clear is that there is a discernible difference between the old natural realm and the new. Humanity is not taken upward to dwell on clouds, but a new heaven and a new earth descends. This strongly suggests that we will continue to be material beings, even in eternity. What this means is that the old creation is transformed into the new (some prefer to think of the entire old creation as being destroyed and a new creation coming separately; I think this goes too far). What Revelation most clearly teaches is that the entirety of evil, of wickedness, of rebellion is destroyed. We have seen that there are significant re-creation moments in the Old Testament which

---

7   Schreiner, *Revelation*, p. 748.

were unique developments in the narrative, yet also contained significant overlap with the previous era. It seems most likely that the new creation will be likewise a place with some continuity and some discontinuity.

Nevertheless, the new creation is visualized by John as the descent of the New Jerusalem (as well as the bride). Significantly, we have to remind ourselves that the New Jerusalem is not to be equivocated with the Jerusalem of old, nor, indeed, the Jerusalem of the present. The reasons for this are many, but the most obvious reason is that the city in both Ezekiel and Revelation is not in any material way similar to Jerusalem as we know it. Rather, John contrasts the New Jerusalem with the Babylon of old. Whereas the harlot was the epitome of evil, violence, rebellion, lust, and horror, the city of God comes from the purest of heavens. It has no blemish or stain of sin, and therefore is the opposite of Babylon. As the New Jerusalem descends, this is the moment when we can say the bridegroom receives the bride. We see this in Revelation 21:2, where John returns to wedding imagery.

This city is presented as the bride of Christ both in Revelation 21 and in Ezekiel 40 (although Ezekiel wouldn't have conceived of the city in his vision in those terms). The New Jerusalem descends and John hears a voice saying: "Behold, I am making all things new" (Revelation 21:5). The renewal of creation stems from the fact that God will make creation fit for *himself* to dwell with his creation: "Behold, the dwelling place of God is with man. He will dwell with them, and they will be his people, and God himself with be with them as their God" (Revelation 21:3). This new creation will bear many of the traits and characteristics of Eden, but, as typology demands, with a heightened escalation. As we have seen, the river of life is greater than the river of Eden, and the tree of life bears greater fruit than in Eden; now, we see that the city is greater than the garden.

John describes the city in vast terms. He's trying to explain that the city will provide prosperity and security and culture and blessing *because* God is present. When John talks about the scale of the walls and the presence of angelic guards, he's not suggesting that beyond the city danger still looms. To suggest that is to miss the point entirely; the fact is that the inhabitants are secure and safe. Nothing can threaten the bride because the king is reigning and the city is secure. This is epitomized by the fact that the twelve gates are always opened during the day. Because there's no night, there's never a time when the gates are closed. Thus, there's never a time when the bride is at risk.

The twelve gates of the city are therefore not for protection, but to symbolize the ease of access to citizens. In accordance with Ezekiel's vision, John teaches that there are three gates on each wall (north, south, east, and west). One should be able to surmise the significance of this. With Peter's vision and the expansion of the Creation Mandate to include the Great Commission, the city is open and accessible to citizens from every corner of the map. As Schreiner explains:

> John teaches his readers that the gates of entrance into the people of God are the tribes of Israel. The church of Jesus Christ consists of the sons and daughters of Abraham…, and those who trust in Jesus are the true Israel…and the true circumcision…The gates facing east, north, south, and west signify that the nations of the world are invited to belong to the people of God…The promise made to Jacob was that his offspring would come from the west, south, north, and south, and that all nations would be blessed through him.[8]

Beyond his description of the gates, however, John describes the size of the city. Remember that the city is symbolic for the people of God. Thus, the description of the city as a cube hearkens back to the Holy of Holies in the temple (cf. 1 Kings 6:20). The symbolism of the Holy of Holies then returns us to Eden; there, it was argued that Eden served as a holy sanctuary for the presence of God. From that sanctuary, Adam and Eve were to expand the reign of God by cultivating creation and creating new Adams and Eves to share their duties. In the New Jerusalem we have the fulfil-

8   Schreiner, *Revelation*, p. 731.

ment of Adam's task through the Final Adam. The city is measured to be incalculably large; this symbolic size is meant to convey that the whole earth is in view. Rather than a single city at the center of the world, John is explaining that the New Jerusalem *is* the new creation world. As this is the case, the city is sufficient to house the innumerable inhabitants that have been saved by and for Christ. None whom the Father has given the Son will be rejected: No visa will be denied. Never again will any Mary or Joseph be told there's no room in the inn because the new creation is large enough for every citizen of the kingdom.

If we consider our marriage illustration for a moment, it's perhaps fitting to consider that the distinction between heaven and earth is brought into the image of "one fleshness." With the descent of the New Jerusalem, the holy city joins to the material realm, renewing creation, and bringing God to reside with man. In a sense, not only has the old become new, but heaven and earth are now one.[9] This idea makes sense of the wedding imagery up to this point as well as the recapitulation of Genesis 1 and 2. The First Adam was given a bride specially made and prepared for him. Likewise, the Final Adam will receive a bride, chosen by God from eternity past, and adorned in garments prepared for her by God. With the third step of the Jewish marital ritual, the groom and the bride come together and reside as husband and wife. In this manner, John's imagery of the union of heaven and earth is fitting (though, again, to be clear, not literal).

As we are contrasting Eden with the New Jerusalem, it's worthwhile recognizing that there's no temple in the New Jerusalem. This is because we will be in God's presence forever. If we must, we can say that God *is* the temple in that he is *there,* and we are *with* him. This reinforces the idea that humanity in the New Jerusalem will not bring sacrifices to a temple complex as in the days of old; rather, we will worship God directly at the foot of his throne (Revelation 22:3). If the contention is correct that Adam and Eve were to function as priests in Eden, then it's quite suit-

---

9   Cf. Schreiner, *Revelation*, p. 733.

able that redeemed humanity would likewise worship God in the New Jerusalem. The *form* of our worship will be different (indeed, perfected); but the *fact* of our worship is reminiscent of Eden's original command (and every era since, for God is always worthy of worship). In fact, this commission to be priests is explicitly stated in Revelation 20:6, where we witness both God and Christ receiving worship from the redeemed.

Not only were Adam and Eve tasked with priestly worship in the garden, but they were to be regents, conveying God's reign to the world as they expanded across the face of the earth. Although they failed in their priestly and kingly task, we nevertheless see that in the New Jerusalem believers will "rule forever and ever" (Revelation 22:5). The Creation Mandate will, in a sense, return to its original form. There are differences, of course, most importantly that there will be no failure. There will also be no marriage in eternity (Matthew 22:30) and therefore the command to procreate will cease. Nevertheless, the *pattern* of priest-kings is reestablished and renewed in the new creation. Just as God's reign will never end, neither will the worship of God terminate. Thus, we who have been raised to Christ in the imperishable resurrection will enjoy the eternal state of ruling over the new creation in all its peaceful prosperity and purposeful worship. There will be no division or death, even amongst the animal kingdom, for the "wolf shall dwell with the lamb, and the leopard shall lie down with the young goat" (Isaiah 11:6). Our eternal rule as subkings under the true king will not be lazy; we will have royal duties, as Adam had in Eden. But because of the perfection of our king, we have no fear that the peacefulness of his utopia will ever be jeopardized.

The new creation is more than something new; it's grander than a renewal and more poignant than a re-creation event: It's a recapitulation. Jesus is the Final Adam, the obedient Adam, and the true covenant partner. It's his reign in the new creation that solidifies everything that is promised for the new order. Without him, there's nothing. But with his reign, the new creation is bursting with life. The river will flow, providing all creation with the water of life. The feasting will continue forever as the Lord's provision will never end. There will never again be a command given to test our allegiance because by our union with Christ our loyalty will be assured. Rather, as the reign of Christ continues into eternity future, we will be able to continually "take and eat" of his bounteous provision and learn anew that we can "taste and see that the Lord is good" (Psalm 34:8).

Application

Anyone who has every stood by the gaping hole and watched as lifeless remains are lowered into the belly of the earth knows the futile anger at death. The wedding feast of Christ reminds us that death does not have the last word. When we consider the invitation to "take and eat" at the marriage supper, we remember that Christ's victory at the cross has real, tangible, implications. The resurrection is not a fairy tale to make the loss of death more palatable; it's a cry of victory that death, for all its awesome power, will one day spit up its innumerable victims. Death itself will die when Christ condemns it to Hades. Believers can find comfort that, even though we will each make that frightening journey through the doorway of death, we are not lost to an empty chasm. Death is the entrance to glory. We need not fear death (though, of course, the manner of our death may be frightening). The wedding feast of the Lamb encourages us to focus on the promises that Christ has given to us so that we are bold in our faith and childlike in our trust. This life has many pitfalls and persecutions, trials and tears, but when we sit at the feast we will see with the fullest clarity the plan that God was working out. That should give us confidence in the journey. Because there is a guaranteed end to the horrific treatment of Christ's church in this world, we have the strength to carry on as sojourners through this world.

Coupled with this first application, however, is the reminder of the vicious hatred Satan has for the bride of Christ. The image John paints of the whore of Babylon is one of disgusting wickedness, vile perversity, despicable cruelty, and horrific violence. Believers need to constantly remind ourselves that we contend with an enemy much more devious, cunning, and ruthless than we could ever imagine. Babylon is portrayed as a seductress because her lies are tempting. Her words are filled with falsehoods and half-truths, and drip fed into our thoughts. Beyond the pretend empress sit the kings and merchants, nobles and commoners, who are bewitched and besotted with her. This reminds us that culture and society are not neutral; they're very much under her sway. Governments, laws, media, music, theatre, movies, universities, are all propagandized by Babylon. Even religious institutions fall sway and prey to Babylon's machinations. We must be vigilant, lest we begin to listen to her sweet lies. The best defense against her is the sword of truth: Scripture. By immersing ourselves in the words of God, we feast on the bread of life. As we do so, we're in communion with the king who will one day ride out against her and destroy her. He alone can protect us and shield us. The wedding feast of the Lamb reminds us of the *certainty* of his victory because it's grounded in the victorious work of the cross.

Flowing from these two applications is another call to respond to the Great Commission. Christ has called us to make disciples of all nations. The wickedness of the harlot explores why we need to be active; Satan's empire of evil never rests in its attempts to diminish the gospel and derail evangelism. When the church is on the march, the gates of hell will not prevail against it. Satan therefore desires to keep the church from decamping. The fact that so many are still living in darkness, embracing the rebellion, ought to inspire us to greater feats of evangelism. Lest we fall into despair at the scale of the task, however, the wedding feast reminds us that there will be a guestlist so large that it cannot be numbered and that those guests will come from every point on the compass. Although the task *is* vast, we are promised a *vast* harvest. The problem is that the workers are too few (Matthew 9:37). Let us use the promises surrounding the wedding feast of the Lamb to inspire a deeper passion and effort to be about the work of the king.

We are also reminded that God is victorious. The contrast between the harlot of Babylon and the holy bride is not merely their apparel and behavior but also their destiny. God's victory is seen in that Babylon, for all her decadent wealth, power, support, and persuasiveness, quakes in the presence of the sovereign Lord whose throne is the heavens and who makes the earth his footstool (Isaiah 66:1). Although the rebellion is fierce, convincing, and enduring, it is not eternal. It will come to an end when God's king pronounces judgement on it. The victory of God is never in doubt; throughout the Bible he has shown his absolute sovereignty over sin, Satan, and death. In the person of Jesus, as the center of the redemptive historical narratival arc, Satan met his match. Jesus refused to be tempted towards sin. Then he began the process of overwhelming Satan's hold on the created realm. After his victory at the cross and through his resurrection, he shared his power with the church who spread throughout the world, adding precious souls to the bride of Christ. At the wedding feast, the full scale of Christ's victory over Satan's domain of darkness will be fully comprehended for the first time. We will see the effects our meagre efforts will have had because of Christ's power and the work of his Spirit through his church, and it will stir us to praise God for his extravagant grace.

Finally, there is no greater application than the fact that the curse will finally be unwound in every respect. In that day, when Christ pours the fruit of the vine and brings his chalice to his lips, we will know that we're beginning an eternity in the presence of our holy God. Never again will we have to flee from his presence because of sin, or shame, or embarrassment. We will have perfect, unmitigated, unimpaired access to our heavenly Father. We will be like him and be holy as he is holy. We will see God as he is in all his Triune, transcendent glory. We will enjoy him in every conceivable way. Each and every moment of eternity will be under the glorious radiance of our loving Father's repeated refrain: You are mine.

Conclusion

With the wedding feast of the lamb, we have come full circle. All that Adam had lost Christ has restored. When the feast begins and we're invited to "take and eat" at the banquet to end all banquets, we will have witnessed the destruction of the rebellion, the judgement and incarceration of Satan, the death of death, and the arrival of the new creation. The horror of Babylon will have been reduced to dust and the virginal beauty of the New Jerusalem will transfix our gaze. We will have seen the contrast between the dragon and the Lamb; the fury of the monster will be put to shame by the fierceness of the Lamb. The traitors of the world will stand before the king to receive the justice of his righteous scepter.

The joyous celebration of the people of God will not be muted. It will be a boisterous cacophony of jubilation. The union between Christ and the church will be one that God has joined, and will never be separated, by man or beast. The new creation will dawn, and it will be perfect in every way. History will give way to eternity. The bride of Christ will reign with the Lord over the created realm. We will worship in spirit and in truth in the presence of God our salvation. His provision for us will be bountiful and we will want for nothing. In the midst of the new creation will stand the throne of God. Every eye will see His Majesty seated on the throne, worthy of our adoration and praise. And peace will permeate his realm. The kingdom of God will finally be experienced in all its supernatural wonder. Every saint who struggled to be victorious, to overcome the world, to be faithful to the Master, will find the spiritual rest they had been yearning for. We will blissfully wear the garments of praise that reflect our best efforts at faithfulness and bask in the glow that Jesus is proud of every single strip of bright linen that reflects accomplishment of a work assigned us by the Father. The New Jerusalem is not only Eden renewed but Eden recreated with fellowship restored. We will serve God as priest-kings forever with no fear of the curse of the old Adam, for the reign of the Final Adam is underway and will never end.

Tea and Coffee: A Biblical Theological Conclusion

Introduction

The story of redemption is the work of the eternal and Triune God to redeem a remnant for himself to the glory of his name. Despite superintending creation, and therefore witnessing just how deep into the filth of sin human beings would descend, he neither refused to create us, nor eradicate us as we justly deserved. Rather, in his glorious mercy, God sought to display the immensity of his grace by providing the means for reconciliation. The work of salvation was an entirely Triune act, as the New Testament frequently points out. In the book of Ephesians, Paul explains that the Father chose us to be in Christ even from before the foundation of the world so that we should be holy and blameless before him (Ephesians 1:4).

The eternal Son became flesh at the incarnation and provided the means of redemption through his substitutionary atoning work on the cross. Jesus, God-made-flesh, died in our place for the penalty of sin, experiencing the judgement we deserved, despite his perfect, covenantal sinlessness. By his death, he answered the question Satan had posed in Eden: Is God worthy of your worship? By his death, Jesus displayed the heart of a God who is loving, merciful, forgiving, compassionate, and fatherly. Through Jesus, we can see and know our heavenly Father.

The Holy Spirit was sent by Father and Son after the ascension of Jesus. The Spirit's work is not mystical or paradoxical; like a flashlight, he illuminates Jesus' work on the cross and the resurrection and applies it to those who repent and believe the gospel. By this work, believers who were dead in sin are made alive; we who were enslaved to sin are freed in Christ; we who were prisoners in the domain of darkness now bask in the kingdom of his glorious light. Further, Paul teaches us that the Spirit was given by God as a downpayment, or guarantee, so that we can know that our salvation is secure and our future certain. This guarantee is God's promise that we *shall* possess our spiritual inheritance. God has staked his entire reputation on this promise, and God is not a liar but the Father of truth. It will come to pass.

The grand narrative of redemption that this book has sought to retell is an historical account of God's deliberate, intricate, and powerful actions inside history. From the moment of creation, when Adam first inhaled the breath of life, right through to the great celebration of the Lamb, God has not been absent nor disinterested in creation. Throughout history he has provided signposts that point us back to worship him. There are few signposts quite so powerful as the tale of three trees. Through these *types*, our own retelling of the story of salvation through the "take and eat" motif is visible.

A Tale of Three Trees

In Eden, God's perfect and sinless creation was given a single command: Do not eat from the tree in the center of the garden. Beyond that, the blessing of God's munificence, his extravagant generosity, was on full display. There was nothing that Adam and Eve needed that God had not provided. Even their very nature was uniquely blessed. Adam and Eve were made in the image of God, sharing his likeness, and being enabled to pass both likeness and image down to their children as they worked to fulfil the Creation Mandate.

But that tree. Standing in the center of the garden. It was a test to demonstrate that they would *choose* to be obedient to their sovereign. When the serpent entered the garden, he brought with him all the vestiges of the rebellion that had already taken place in the heavens. And through his tactical dialogue he brought doubt into the garden, then division, then disobedience, and then dissension. When Eve took the fruit from the tree and saw that it was good, her humble heart proved fertile soil for the thorns of rebellion. "Take and eat," the serpent urged. And she did. Then, echoing her new master, she bade her husband "take and eat" and join the coup. And he did. Immediately, sin's ugly presence pounced on the hapless couple and, like a lion digging its teeth into its prey, it started to tear them apart. The first marriage was to set the pattern of so many ever after: Competition, distrust, power imbalance, abuse, and, fundamentally, distraction from their God-assigned task.

And so it was to be for millennia. As we climbed the mountain of redemptive history, we hit certain crests when we thought we had reached the summit. But, from each successive vantage point, as we looked around, all we saw was destruction. The rebellion lived on and continued through Noah and the flood. A new start, but sin remained and led another effort to overthrow God at Babel. Then, as we continued to climb, we reached the pinnacle of Abraham; yet, as we watched, his faith was mingled with faithlessness and failure. The search for the promised serpent-crusher went on; we climbed to the next pinnacle where, at the Passover, we saw the mighty hand of God deliver his people from the Pharaoh of Egypt. To no avail: Even as the covenant document was being prepared, the Israelites had already fallen into sinful idolatry. Yet God steadfastly refused to abandon his project of redemption. He would defeat the rebellion.

The arrival of Jesus on Christmas Day was the moment for which creation had been yearning. God had returned. After the beginning of his ministry, he was led into the wilderness to face the enemy. Satan threw everything at his adversary, but Jesus remained resolute. His obedience was to God alone. Defeated, the serpent slithered off into the shadows, awaiting another opportunity to attack. He didn't have long to wait. A mere three years later, he found a willing vessel residing in the Eden of the inner circle of Jesus' own followers: Judas Iscariot.

On the night in which he was betrayed, Jesus enjoyed the Passover meal with his disciples. He invited them to "take and eat" the bread but transformed the meaning into something newer and grander. This bread was to be his own body, broken for those who would follow him. He bade them "take and drink" of the wine which was to be his blood. By this, he taught them that a new covenant was dawning. This covenant sealed the fulfilment of the Mosaic covenant and answered the Abrahamic covenant. He was the perfect, obedient, covenant partner. And yet he would bear the consequences of the sinfulness of every faithless rebel. Thus, on the cursed tree at Golgotha, Jesus of Nazareth, God-made-flesh, was torn apart and judged by God the Father. His blood flowed freely down the jagged trunk as his lungs gasped for air. Fed a bitter mixture of wine and water from a sponge, he finally breathed his last and gave up his spirit; the debt of Adam's treachery had been paid. But at what a cost. Creation groaned and moaned at what it had been forced to witness and endure.

For three days, creation feared the worst. If God the Son could be killed, then the success of the rebellion was surely guaranteed. Yet fear turned to hope and mourning to rejoicing when, on the first day of a brand-new creation week, the tomb burst open, and Christ triumphantly walked out. The king had conquered; the serpent had bitten the heel of God's anointed, but the Savior had crushed the snake. With the resurrection, death had been defeated. The kingdom had been inaugurated and the king gave to his disciples a new commission: They were to become his apostles, messengers of the good news of the offer of the gospel. They were to preach this good news to any and all, irrespective of ethnicity, history, culture, location, or sinful condition. Because of the magnitude of Christ's victory, *all* were to be invited to come and worship the king.

And as the apostles spread out and brought the message to the ends of the earth, the gospel of Christ reached into the furthest depths of Satan's empire and redeemed captives. From the dungeons of addiction, lust, violence, anger, hatred, racism, murder, rape, cruelty, idolatry, murder, lying, theft, witchcraft, abortion, drunkenness, pride, covetousness, dishonor, sons and daughters were rescued, restored, renewed, and resurrected. Those who submitted to the rule of Jesus were given tasks to serve the kingdom. It will only be at the end of all ends when the true value of these tasks will be completely understood.

At the end of all ends, the third tree, the tree of life, will stand in the center of the New Jerusalem as a testimony to the completed restoration of all things. The judgement of the rebellion will be completed, the celebration of the redeemed will begin and continue forevermore. Never again will we be tempted to "take and eat" in sin. Never again will God restrict access to the tree of life. Rather, we will forever be able to reach up and pluck its ripened, luxurious fruit from its branches and "take and eat" and see that the Lord, in his majesty, residing with us forever, is good.

By the work of Christ, according to the will of the Father, and brought to completion by the Holy Spirit, we will enjoy a restoration of worship in the presence of the Triune God, once and for all. We will once again govern as regents over creation, with a restoration of our true purpose: Serving God in his holy, earthly, New Jerusalem. We will have a restoration of peace with God, and with one another, and with creation. And we will enjoy a restoration of our true humanity; being fully restored to the uncorrupted, incorruptible, imperishable, glorious, and dazzling image of God (1 Corinthians 15:42-45). In fulfillment of Psalm 133:1, we will dwell in unity with our siblings in the heavenly family because of our union with our heavenly Father. We will eat and drink with God in his presence, where evil has been forever cast away. In his new throne room, in the midst of the new heavens and the new earth, we will gather. There, in our new bodies, bought for us by the blood of the Final Adam, we will sit at our tables at the wedding feast of the Lamb, as a member of his radiant bride, and we will watch as he lifts the decanter containing the fruit of the vine. Eyes transfixed on our Lord and Savior, we will hear the wine sloshing into his magnificent cup, and we will raise our own and drink with him in celebration. Then, in a dim echo from the Upper Room all those centuries ago, we will hear the words that every child of God has yearned to hear: "Beloved, take and eat." And the feast to end all feasts will begin.

Bibliography

Alexander, T. Desmond. 2008. *From Eden to the New Jerusalem: An Introduction to Biblical Theology.* Grand Rapids, MI: Kregal Academic.

Armstrong, George D. 1867. *The Christian Doctrine of Slavery.* New York, NY: Scribner.

Augustine. 1983. *City of God.* Vol. 2. Grand Rapids, MI: William B. Eerdmans Publishing Company.

Backman, Clifford. 2015. *The Worlds of Medieval Europe.* New York: Oxford University Press.

Barrett, Matthew. 2020. *Canon, Covenant and Christology.* Edited by D.A. Carson. Downers Grove, IL: InterVarsity Press.

Beale, G. K. 2004. "The Temple and the Church's Mission: A Biblical Theology of the Dwelling Place of God." *New Studies in Biblical Theology* (Apollos) (17): 70.

Beaumont, Francis. n.d. *Key to Poetry.* Accessed February 16, 2024. https://keytopoetry.com/francis-beaumont/poems/on-the-tombs-in-westminster-abbey/.

Blackburn, W. Ross. 2012. *The God Who Makes Himself Known: The Missionary Heart of the Book of Exodus.* Edited by D. A. Carson. Downe's Grove, IL: IVP Academic.

Blocker, H. 1984. *In the Beginning.* Downers Grove, IL: InterVarsity Press.

Blomberg, Craig L. 2006. *From Pentecost to Patmos: An Introduction to Acts Through Revelation.* Nashville, TN: B&H Academic.

Carson, D. A. 1995. *The Expositor's Bible Commentary with the New International Version: Matthew 1-12.* Edited by Frank E. Gaebelein and J. D. Douglas. Grand Rapids, MI: ZondervanPublishingHouse.

—. 1995. *The Expositor's Bible Commentary with the New International Version: Matthew 13-28.* Edited by Frank E Gaebelein and J. D. Douglas. Grand Rapids, MI: ZondervanPublishingHouse.

Chrysostom, John. 1947-. "Homilies on Genesis." *Fathers of the Church: A New Translation.* Washington, D.C.: Catholic University of America.

Clark, W. M. 1969. "A Legal Background to Yahweh's Use of 'Good and Evil' in Genesis 2-3." *Journal of Biblical Literature* (88): 266-278.

Cullman, Oscar. 1959. *The Christology of the New Testament.* Revised. Philadelphia, PA: Westminster John Knox Press.

Dumbrell, William J. 1984. *Covenant and Creation: A Theology of Old Testament Covenants.* Nashvile, TN: Thomas Nelson.

Dunn, T.K. 2023. *Prophet, Priest, Prince, And the Already, Not Yet: A Theology of the Kingdom of God in Dialogue with Dispensationalism and P.T. Forsyth.* Eugene, OR: Pickwick Publications.

Emesa, Nemesius of. 1953-1966. "On the Nature of Man." *The Library of Christian Classics.* Edited by J. Baillie, John T. McNeill and Henry P. Van Dusen. Philadelphia, PA: Westminster.

Federation, World Wildlife. n.d. *Endangered Species.* Accessed March 01, 2024. https://www.worldwildlife.org/species/directory?direction=desc&sort=extinction_status.

Gentry, Peter J. 2020. ""Humanity as the Divine Image in Genesis 1:26-28." *Eikon: A Journal for Biblical Anthropology* 2 (1): 56-69.

Gentry, Peter J. 2020. ""Sexuality: On Being Human and Promoting Social Justice"." *Eikon: A Journal for Biblical Anthropology* 2 (2): 110-127.

Gentry, Peter J., and Stephen J. Wellum. 2012. *Kingdom Through Covenant: A Biblical-Theological Understanding of the Covenants.* Wheaton, IL: Crossway.

Goldsworthy, Graeme. 2000. *Preaching the Whole Bible as Christian Scripture.* Grand Rapids, MI: Wm. B. Eerdmans Publishing C.

Hahn, Scott W. 2009. *Kinship by Covenant: A Canonical Approach to the Fulfillment of God's Saving Promises.* New Haven, CT: Yale University Press.

Helm, David R. 2008. *1-2 Peter and Jude: Sharing Christ's Sufferings.* Edited by R. Kent Hughes. Wheaton, IL: Crossway.

Henley, William Ernest. N.d. *Poetry Foundation.* Accessed February 19, 2024. https://www.poetryfoundation.org/poems/51642/invictus .

Henry, Matthew. 1991. *Commentary on the Whole Bible: Complete and Unabridged.* 2nd. Peabody, MA: Hendrickson.

Herodotus. 2003. *The Histories.* Translated by Aubrey de Sélincourt. London: Penguin Books.

Hoekema, Anthony A. 2024. *Created in God's Image.* Grand Rapids, MI: William B. Eerdman's Company.

Hugenberger, Gordon. 1994. *Marriage as a Covenant: A Study of Biblical Law and Ethics Governing Marriage Developed from the Perspective of Malachi.* Leiden: Brill.

Jerome. 1995. *Question on Genesis.* Translated by C. T. R. Hayward. Oxford: Clarendon Press.

Jr, James M. Hamilton. 2012. *Revelation: The Spirit Speaks to the Churches.* Edited by R. Kent Hughes. Wheaton, IL: Crossway.

Jr., James M. Hamilton. 2014. *What is Biblical Theology.* Wheaton, IL: Crossway.

Kimble, Jeremy M., and Ched Spellman. 2020. *Invitation to Biblical Theology: Exploring the Shape, Storyline, and Themes of Scripture.* Grand Rapids, MI: Kregel Academic.

Klink III, Edward W., and Darian R. Lockett. 2012. *Understanding Biblical Theology.* Grand Rapids, MI: Zondervan.

Kreider, Glenn R. 2014. *God With Us: Exploring God's Personal Interactions With His People Throughout The Bible.* Phillipsburg, NJ: P&R Publishing.

Laan, Ray Vander, and Judith Markham. 1996. *Echoes of His Presence: Stories of the Messiah from the People of His Day.* Colorado Springs: Focus on the Family.

Ladd, G.E. 1959. *The Gospel of the Kingdom.* Grand Rapids, MI: Eerdmans Publishing Company.

—. 1974. *The Presence of the Future.* Grand Rapids, MI: Eerdmans Publishing Company.

LaVerdiere, Eugene. 2023. *Dining in the Kingdom of God: The Origins of hte Eucharist in the Gospel of Luke.* Unknown: Amazon Digital Prints.

—. 1998. *The Breaking of the Bread: The Development of the Eucharist According to Acts.* Chicago, IL: Liturgy Training Publications.

Lawrence, Michael. 2010. *Biblical Theology in the Life of the Church.* Wheaton, IL: Crossway.

Levering, Matthew. 2017. *Engaging the Doctrine of Creatin: Cosmos, Creatures, and the Wise and Good Creator.* Grand Rapids, MI: Baker Academic.

Lewis, C.S. 2010. *A Year with Aslan: Daily Reflections from the Chronicles of Narnia.* Harper Collins.

Luther, Martin. 1859. *The Epistles of St. Peter and St. Jude Preached and Explained.* New York, NY: Anson D.F. Randolph.

Martyrs, Voice of the. 2023. *Wurmbrand: Tortured for Christ.* Voice of the Martyrs.

McDowell, Catherine. 12016. ""'In the Image of God He Created Them': How Gensis 1:26-27 Defines the Divine-Human Relationship and Why It Matters"." In *The Image of God In An Image Driven Age" Explorations in Theological Anthropology*, edited by Beth Felker Jones and Jeffrey W. Barbeau. Downers Grove, IL: IVP.

—. 2015. *The "Image of God" in the Garden of Eden: The Creation of Humankind in Genesis 2:5-3:24 in Light of the mis pi pit pi and wpt-r Rituals of Mesopotamia and Ancient Egypt.* Winona Lake, IN: Eisenbrauns.

Merkle, Rebekah. 2016. *Eve in Exile adn the Restoration of Femininity.* Moscow, ID: Canon Press.

Merrill, Eugene H. 2008. *Kingdom of Priests: A History of Old Testament Israel.* 2nd. Grand Rapids, MI: BakerAcademic.

Middleton, J.R. 2005. *The Liberating Image: The Imago Dei in Genesis 1.* Grand Rapids, MI: Brazos.

NA. n.d. *rts.com*. Accessed January 11, 2024. https://www.rts.com/resources/guides/food-waste-america/.

—. 2023. *United States Environmental Protection Agency.* October 5 2023. Accessed January 11, 2024. https://www.epa.gov/facts-and-figures-about-materials-waste-and-recycling/food-material-specific-data.

Nazianzus, Gregory of. 1990. "Theological Orations." *Faith Gives Fullness to Reasoning: The Five Theological Orations of Gregory Nazianzen.* Leiden and New York: E. J. Brill.

Ortland, Gavin. 2014. ""Image of God, Son of God: Genesis 5:3 and Luke 3:38 in Intercanonical Dialogue"." *JETS* 57 (4): 673-688.

Ortland, Raymond C. 2006. "Male-Female Equality and Male Headship: Genesis 1-3." Chap. Four in *Recovering Biblical Manhood and Womanhood*, edited by John Piper and Wayne Grudem, 95-112. Wheaton, Illinois: Crossway.

Pagels, Elaine. 1989. *Adam, Eve, and the Serpent.* New York: Vintage Books.

Payne, Philip Barton. 2009. *Man and Woman, One in Christ: An Exegetical and Theological Study of Paul's Letters* . Grand Rapids: Zondervan.

Pelikan, Jaroslav Jan, Hilton C. Oswald, and Helmut T. Lehmann. 1999. *Luther's Works: Word and Sacrament.* Vol. III. Philadelphia: Fortress Press.

Pollan, Michael. 2001. *The Botany of Desire: A Plant's-Eye View of the World.* New York: Random House Trade Paperbacks.

—. 2006. *The Omnivore's Dilemma, A Natural History of Four Meals* . New York: Penguin.

Pope, Alexander. 2015. *An Essay on Criticism.* Accessed February 16, 2024. https://www.eighteenthcenturypoetry.org/works/o3675-w0010.shtml.

Quarles, Charles L. 2017. *B&H Exegetical Guide to the Greek New Testament: Matthew.* Edited by Andreas J. Köstenberger and Robert W. Yarbrough. Nashville, TN: B&H Academic.

Rawlinson, A. E. J. 1942. *The Gospel According to St. Mark*. 5th. London: Methuen.

Roberts, J. M., and Odd Arne Westad. 2013. *The History of the World*. Sixth. New York: Oxford University Press.

Roberts, Vaughn. 2004. *God's Big Picture: Tracing the Storyline of the Bible*. Lisle, IL: Intervarsity Press.

Ryle, J. C. 1995. *Expository Thoughts on Matthew*. Carlisle, PA: Banner of Truth.

—. 2000. *The Upper Room*. Carlisle, PA: Banner of Truth.

Schaff, Philip, and Henry Wace. 1887-1894. *A Select Library of the Nicene and Post-Nicene Fathers of the Christian Church*. Edited by Philip Schaff and Henry Wace. Vol. 2. 14 vols. Buffalo, NY: Christian Literature.

Schreiner, Thomas R. 2017. *Covenant and God's Purposes for the World*. Wheaton, IL: Crossway.

—. 2008. *New Testament Theology: Magnifying God in Christ*. Grand Rapids, MI: BakerAcademic.

—. 2023. *Revelation: Baker Exegetical Commentary on the New Testament*. Grand Rapids, MI: Baker Academic.

—. 2013. *The King In His Beauty: A Biblical Theology of the Old and New Testament*. Grand Rapids, MI: BakerAcademic.

Stephens, Alexander H. 1861. "Doc. 48-Speech of A. H. Stephens." In *The Rebellion Record: A Diary of American Events*, edited by Frank Moore, 46. New York: Putnam.

Survey, Jesus and the Gospels: An Introduction and. 2009. *Craig L. Blomberg*. Nashville, TN: B&H Academic.

Syrian, Ephrem the. 1947. "Commentary on Genesis." *Fathers of the Church: A New Translation*. Washington, D.C.: Catholic University of American Press.

Vatican.va. 2005. *Compendium of the Catechism of the Catholic Church*. Accessed May 14, 2024. https://www.vatican.va/archive/compendium_ccc/documents/archive_2005_compendium-ccc_en.html#The%20Sacraments%20of%20Healing.

Waltke, Bruce K., and Charles Yu. 2007. *An Old Testament Theology: An Exegetical, Canonical, and Thematic Approach.* Grand Rapids, MI: Zondervan.

Walton, John. 1994. *Covenant: God's Purpose, God's Plan.* Grand Rapids, MI: ZondervanPublishingHouse.

Walton, John H. 2018. *Ancient Near Eastern Thought and the Old Testament: Introducing the Conceptual World of the Hebrew Bible.* 2nd. Grand Rapids, MI: BakerAcademic.

Waterfield, Robin. 2018. *Creators, Conquerors, and Citizens: A History of Ancient Greece.* New York: Oxford University Press.

Weinfield, M. 1970. "The Covenant of Grant in the Old Testament and in the Ancient Near East." *Journal of the American Oriental Soceity* (90): 185.

Wellum, Stephen J., and Brent E. Parker. 2016. *Progressive Covenantalism: Charting a Course between Covenant and Dispensational Theologies.* Nashville, TN: B&H Academic.

Wenham, G. J. 1986. "Sanctuary Symbolism in the Garden of Eden Story." *Proceedings of the World Congress of Jewish Studies* (9): 19.

Williamson, Paul R. 2007. *Sealed with an Oath: Covenant in God's Unfolding Purposes.* Downers Grove, IL: InterVarsity Press.

Woods, Robert. 2007. "Ancient and Early Modern Mortality: Experience and Understanding." *The Economic History Review* vol. 60 (no. 2): 373-399. Accessed 02 16, 2024. www.jstor.org/stable/4502068.

Wright, Christopher J. H. 2018. *The Mission of God: Unlocking the Bible's Grand Narrative.* Downer's Grove, IL: IVP Academic.

Xenophon. 1972. *The Persian Expedition.* Translated by Rex Warner. London: Penguin Books.

www.ingramcontent.com/pod-product-compliance
Lightning Source LLC
Chambersburg PA
CBHW030335240426
43661CB00052B/1637